Serene Urbanism

Serenity is becoming alarmingly absent from our daily existence, especially within the urban context. Time is dense and space is tumultuous. The idea of the serene has gained currency in postmodern discussions, and when combined with urbanism conjures questions, even contradictions, as the two ideas seem improbable yet their correspondence seems so inherently desirable. Integrated, these two constructs present design challenges as they manifest in differing ways across the rural–urban transect.

In response, Part I of this book establishes the theoretical framework through different contemporary perspectives, and concludes with a clear explanation of a theory of serene urbanism. The positive characteristics of urbanism and beneficial qualities of the serene are explored and related to sustainability, biophilia, placemaking and environmental design. Both principles and examples are presented as compelling portraits for the proposal of these new urban landscapes. Part II of the work is an in-depth exploration and analysis of serene urban ideas related to the intentional community being created outside of Atlanta, Georgia, USA. "Serenbe" is the name given to this place to commemorate the value and nuance between the serene and urban.

Phillip James Tabb is Professor of Architecture and Liz and Nelson Mitchell Professor of Residential Design at Texas A&M University. He completed a PhD dissertation, "The Solar Village Archetype: A Study of English Village Form Applicable to Energy-integrated Planning Principles for Satellite Settlements in Temperate Climates" in 1990. Among his publications are *Solar Energy Planning* (McGraw-Hill, 1984), *The Greening of Architecture: A Critical History and Survey of Contemporary Sustainable Architecture and Urban Design* (Ashgate, 2014), and *Architecture, Culture, and Spirituality* (co-edited with Thomas Barrie and Julio Bermudez, Ashgate, 2015). He received his BS in Architecture from the University of Cincinnati, Master of Architecture from the University of Colorado, and PhD in the Energy and Environment Programme from the Architectural Association in London. He teaches studio design, sustainable architecture, and the theory of placemaking, and is a practicing urban designer and licensed architect.

Serene Urbanism

A biophilic theory and practice
of sustainable placemaking

Phillip James Tabb

Routledge
Taylor & Francis Group

LONDON AND NEW YORK

First published 2017
by Routledge
2 Park Square, Milton Park, Abingdon, Oxon OX14 4RN

and by Routledge
711 Third Avenue, New York, NY 10017

Routledge is an imprint of the Taylor & Francis Group, an informa business

British Library Cataloguing in Publication Data
A catalogue record for this book is available from the British Library

Library of Congress Cataloguing in Publication Data
The LOC data has been applied for.

ISBN: 978-1-4724-6137-7 (hbk)
ISBN: 978-1-3156-0843-3 (ebk)

Typeset in Sabon
by Out of House Publishing

This work is dedicated to overcoming placelessness, unsustainability, profaneness, and environmental degradation, by recovery of perennial design patterns of the serene and most vital and healthy qualities of urbanism. It is in gratitude to my students, the residents, and developers of Serenbe Community that this work is mainly dedicated.

Contents

List of figures

List of tables

About the author

Phillip James Tabb is Professor of Architecture and Liz and Nelson Mitchell Professor of Residential Design at Texas A&M University, USA. He served as head of the department from 2001–5, and was director of the School of Architecture and Construction Management at Washington State University from 1998–2001. He completed a PhD dissertation, "The Solar Village Archetype: A Study of English Village Form Applicable to Energy-integrated Planning Principles for Satellite Settlements in Temperate Climates" in 1990. Among his publications are *Solar Energy Planning* (McGraw-Hill, 1984), *The Greening of Architecture: A Critical History and Survey of Contemporary Sustainable Architecture and Urban Design* (Ashgate, 2014), and *Architecture, Culture and Spirituality* (co-edited with Thomas Barrie and Julio Bermudez, Ashgate, 2015). In the late 1960s he worked for Walter Netsch at Skidmore, Owings & Merrill (SOM) in Chicago and was exposed to his field theory method of design. He worked with Keith Critchlow and taught sacred drawing in the Kairos School of Sacred Architecture (1986–7), at Dar al Islam in Abiquiu, New Mexico (1988–9), and at Naropa Institute, Boulder, Colorado (1996).

Since 2001 he has been the master plan architect for Serenbe Community, an award-winning sustainable community being realized near Atlanta, Georgia, and he was a planning consultant for Babcock Ranch Community in Florida, the Millican Reserve project in Texas, the Summit Series Community in Utah, and the Howell Mountain Conservation Community in Angwin, California. He has lectured internationally on the concept of placemaking as a viable sustainable strategy. He received six solar energy research and demonstrations awards from the American Institute of Architects/Research Corporation, US Department of Housing and Urban Development, and US Department of Energy, and was a consultant to the Solar Energy Research Institute. He is a founding fellow of the Sustainable Urbanism Certificate Program at Texas A&M University. He received his BS in Architecture from the University of Cincinnati, MS in Architecture from the University of Colorado, and PhD in the Energy and Environment Programme from the Architectural Association in London. He teaches studio design, sustainable architecture, and the theory of placemaking, and is a practicing urban designer and licensed architect. He has been a long-time member of the American Institute of Architects, and holds a National Council of Architectural Registration Boards (NCARB) Certificate.

Foreword

Thomas Barrie and Julio Bermudez

The desire to reclaim and recreate our essential relationship with the world through architecture and the built environment has been a consistent theme in Western culture. In *De Natura Deorum*, Cicero describes our impetus to build as the desire for a second, presumably improved, nature:

> We enjoy the fruits of the plains and of the mountains, the rivers and the lakes are ours, we sow corn, we plant trees, we fertilize the soil by irrigation, we confine the rivers and straighten or divert their courses. In fine, by means of our hands we essay to create as it were a second world within the world of nature.[1]

For Cicero, humans "came into existence" to both contemplate and imitate "the world."[2] Roman country villas often aspired to embody these themes, and country retreats such as Pliny the Younger's Laurentian villa were celebrated as cultivated places of retreat from the affairs of the world, as well as settings for individual development, contemplation, and study.[3] Palladio wrote:

> The ancient sages used to retire to such places where being oftentimes visited virtuous friends and relations, having houses, gardens, and suchlike pleasant places, and above all their virtues, they could easily attain to as much happiness as could be attained here below.[4]

The Roman patrician estates served, at least in part, as models for English exurban country houses, which were similarly positioned as settings of retreat from the city and as a reclamation of what were deemed the most valuable components of lives well lived – cultural and spiritual pursuits, and closeness to nature. Early English and North American suburbs reflected the ideals of their aristocratic predecessors by the creation of places that paired shared-values communities with the autonomy promised by their naturalistic surroundings. The desire for the comfort of human society and the transcendence promised by the natural world are long-standing. At its core is the desire for connections: with others, the natural world, and ourselves. In a talk in 1963, Aldo van Eyck stated: "The job of the planner is to provide built homecoming for all, to sustain a feeling of belonging. I would go so far to say that architecture is built homecoming."[5]

What we have lost has been often cited as what we must now gain. Much ink has been spilled regarding the environmental, social, and economic impacts of contemporary Western, and increasingly global, settlement patterns. This much is clear: we simply cannot continue to build in the manner that we have been doing – but what are dependable alternatives? Many have addressed this question, resulting in a plethora of urbanisms, from everyday urbanism to post-urbanism. The author of this volume points out that serene urbanism is not a new paradigm, but one that synthesizes and interprets a number of established approaches. Its core argument is that the skillful and diverse pairing of urbanism and nature – vibrant social interaction and contemplative spiritual reflection – is the most dependable means to secure a more hopeful and meaningful future.

At the core of this book is the development of the theory of serene urbanism and demonstration project of Serenbe, a planned community near Atlanta, Georgia. It is where the author demonstrates the interrelationship of *episteme* and *praxis*: a mature knowledge base applied to ethical practice. In this context, the major contributions of this book are not its argumentation, theoretical constructs, or precedent analyses, nor its heartfelt aspirations for a soulful, ethical, healthy, and "serene" urbanism. However illuminating and valuable these points may be, they are clearly in support of the placemaking principles and built form of Serenbe. After all, propositions of new urban models abound, but it is quite rare to find actual examples that test such speculations – and this is exactly what Phillip James Tabb offers us here. As the master plan architect of Serenbe, he cogently describes the process of creating an American urban arcadia. As a result, the reader is presented with a seasoned and realistic (in the best sense of the term) set of tested urban strategies, elements, concepts, and organizations.

Equally remarkable are the intentions of this placemaking and community-building experiment to go beyond delivering a "sustainable," "functional," and "livable" built environment. Indeed, the ultimate goal of Serenbe is nothing less than materializing the spiritual dimensions of community and nature. On the one hand, it is truly refreshing and timely to see an urban designer and community recognize and respond to the transcendental needs of human dwelling – something that is hardly discussed, much less pursued, in the scholarly and professional work in architecture and urban planning.[6] On the other hand, many will point at the extraordinary difficulty in succeeding at this, while others will question the right of a designer and even a small community to represent the needs of a contemporary multiethnic, multireligious, and diverse society.[7]

The validity of the author's claims are evidenced by Serenbe itself, and having been there, we can attest to the impossible-to-define *genius loci* that is embedded in its natural surroundings, and its authenticity of community that is hard to come by in present-day exurban developments. That said, this book provides what a visit cannot: the rationale and models utilized that promise more broad-based applications. No one will claim that Serenbe is the cure for all our ills, or "the" solution to the unprecedented urban growth of humanity that must be undertaken in the following decades. Yet Serenbe does offer a compelling model of how to respond sensibly to the challenges of twenty-first-century civilization, and thus is worthy of our attention and consideration. This book offers us an invaluable resource to do just that.

Notes

1 Cicero, *De Natura Deorum, II, 152*, in *Cicero: De Natura Deorum, Academica*, trans. Harris Rackham, Harvard University Press, Cambridge, MA, 1951, p. 271.
2 Ibid., p. 159.

3 Archer, John, *Architecture and Suburbia: From English Villa to American Dream House, 1690–2000*, University of Minnesota Press, Minneapolis, MN, 2005, pp. 35–6.
4 Fishman, Robert, *Bourgeois Utopias: The Rise and Fall of Suburbia*, Basic Books, New York, 1987, p. 46.
5 van Eyck, Aldo, "How to Humanize Vast Plurality," in Ligtelijin, Vincent and Strauven, Francis (eds) *Aldo van Eyck: Collected Articles and Other Writings, 1947–1998*, Sun Publishers, Amsterdam, 2008, p. 442.
6 Crosbie, Michael J., "The Sacred Becomes Profane," in Barrie, Thomas, Bermudez, Julio and Tabb, Phillip (eds) *Architecture, Culture, and Spirituality*, Ashgate, London, 2015, pp. 59–69.
7 Britton, Karla, *Constructing the Ineffable: Contemporary Sacred Architecture*, Yale University, New Haven, CT, 2011.

Acknowledgments

My thanks go to Valerie Rose, who initially was the editor at Ashgate working on this project, and who gave great encouragement and enthusiasm for the work, to Sadé Lee with Routledge, Sarah Green with Out of House Publishing, and others involved in the editing and production of the book. They all gave valuable feedback throughout the entire process. Steve and Marie Nygren, developers of Serenbe Community, provided a context for the case study discussed in this book. Their dedicated hard work has made Serenbe the wonderful place that it is today. Thanks to the community members and friends who live in Serenbe and help make the dream a reality. Special gratitude goes to Thomas Barrie and Julio Bermudez who gave great encouragement, reviewed the manuscript, and wrote the foreword to this book.

College of Architecture Dean Jorge Vanegas and Department Head Ward Wells were very supportive of this project from its inception, and encouraged the inaugural study-away program at Serenbe in the fall of 2015. The Liz and Nelson Professorship at Texas A&M University provided funding for many of the expenses for the preparation of the final manuscript. I am extremely indebted to all of the students at Texas A&M University, especially Nessrine Mansour, and the students who participated in the Serenbe Rural Studio in the fall of 2015: Kevin Clapp, Jordan Cox, Mirely Cordova, Jocelyn Zuniga, and Yiming Guan.

Very special thanks go to my family, especially Michael, David, Shea, Kristin, Emrys and Caius Tabb, my sister Janice, brother-in-law Richard and niece Jing Nourse, and to all friends, and all of us now living in the world and future generations for whom this work is ultimately intended. Finally, very special thoughts go to the memory of my parents, Frank and Tryphosa Tabb who, I am sure, would be proud of this book.

Part I

Theoretical framework for serene urbanism

1   Introduction

On the sidewalks everyone holding either a giant coffee or a cell phone, as though a law had been declared against public displays of empty-handedness.[1]

Serenity is becoming alarmingly absent from our daily existence, especially within the urban context. Time is dense and space is tumultuous. The modern world that surrounds us is complicated, contradictory and bewildering. It is complex in its overwhelming response to a world population of more than 7 billion people, the complicated infrastructures, political and economic systems, religious differences and conflicts, and inheritance of a built environment largely constructed and maintained by climate-changing, fossil-fuel energy sources. It is contradictory because many of the built works and technologies no longer support the solutions to the housing of a contemporary culture; rather, they are the cause of many of the problems that are a consequence of it. It is perplexing because of the enormity of the problems, and the time and resources necessary to actually overcome them.

The contemporary environment has evolved to sustain and better the human condition, yet it has come with unintended consequences. We continue to use our renewable resources at an unprecedented rate, global population is ever-increasing, the natural environment is shrinking and suffers from deforestation, neglect, species extinction, and the effects of global warming, and we continue to remain vulnerable to disease. In response, the concept of serene urbanism is designed to provide an alternative approach for future urban designs that is applicable to both new and existing contexts, and large and small settings. For certain, there is a need for more reflective, engaging, and insightful approaches to creating and sustaining habitation.

The contemporary condition

Contemporary culture is a complex global phenomenon that has left in its wake a trace in both time and space, and while not necessarily unique to our time, arguably it is one that defines it. Temporal density is a modern human condition where experiences, data, inputs, and information are processed within a shorter and increasingly compressed interval of time.[2] In other words, time becomes dense, filled with a throng of thoughts, emotions, considerations, and multitasking activities. Contemporary lifestyles, particularly within urban areas, demand a great deal of attention from which to navigate everyday functions that seem to accumulate more and more undertakings to think about and do. Over-attention to these complexities tends to create greater separation from direct experience and quality of presence in the places that we inhabit.

Sometimes we can become so preoccupied that we walk from one room to another forgetting why we did so, or daydreaming while waiting at a stoplight. These are a consequence of temporal density. According to Walter Benjamin in his essay, "On Some Motifs in Baudelaire":

> Shock serves as a figure of hyper or over-stimulation, where a high degree of stimulation results in the shock defense cutting in, protecting by desensitizing and thereby impoverishing perception.[3]

Spatial tumultuousness is a by-product of rapidly changing urban growth, incessant geographic migration, and the need to respond to the evolving complexities of contemporary life. It is characterized by great disorder, commotion, turbulence, and agitation. It also can be accompanied by its opposite tendencies, with an environment of vapid spatiality, monotony, wearisome sameness, and soullessness. Found in locations dominated by the automobile, extant public utilities and infrastructure networks, and derelict districts abandoned to suburban migration, these territories display an inhuman and placeless character.

The consequences of these dimensions affect our vision and ability to meet future needs. They reach every area of the urban-to-rural transect, in which appropriate levels of the blend of serene natural spaces are integrated to varying kinds of urban places. Addressing critical issues such as world population and growth, placelessness, climate change, unsustainability, overreliance on technology, and profaneness are central to a truly livable future – and one with healthy, sustainable, and numinous qualities.

Population and growth

Is our survival dependent on maximizing population growth, or should we be more strategic, looking at other more controlled and balanced models? World population was under 1 billion people until the 1800s; in 1930 it doubled, and 30 years later it reached 3 billion. By the millennium, the world population reached 6 billion, and by 2015 it was more than 7 billion people.[4] The growth rate peaked in the 1960s at around 2 percent and presently is in slow decline, but continues to increase in overall numbers. The "Blue Marble" was a NASA photograph taken on December 7, 1972 by the crew of the Apollo 17 spacecraft: a vivid expression of the wholeness as well as finite nature of our world. It gave us a perspective that previously had been only imagined. Realization of these events has led to the understanding of planetary carrying capacity: a concept positing that there is a finite amount of resources, including potable water, fresh air, food, and energy, that are necessary to manage and sustain human habitation now and in the future.

According to the United Nations Commission on Population and Development, global life expectancy increased from age 65 in 1994 to 70 in 2014.[5] There is a planetary shift in population distribution from rural to urban areas. The developed world became mostly urban around 2009, and developing regions, including Africa and Asia, which are still mostly rural today, are projected to have more people living in urban than rural areas by 2030. Cities are focal points of economic growth, innovation, cultural functions, and paid employment. Rural areas provide agriculture, recreation, species habitation, and preservation of natural reserves. Yet, this bifurcation is cause for many challenges, and has a tremendous impact on the forms of habitation appropriate for these differing environments. Modernity's legacy manifests innumerable benefits as well as devastating assaults. We are a global culture: connected, mobile, and interdependent with improved living standards, health, life expectancy, production efficiency, agricultural practices, and tremendous advancements in technology. Yet the unintended consequences of many of these achievements threaten our contemporary ways of life, as evidenced by the increasing effects of climate change and species extinction. Growth by gross addition might be better achieved through intelligent multiplication of populations in sync with the carrying capacities of our local ecological regions.

> You encounter a new event – a severe flood, a storm that floods the city, a fracking corporation rumbling into your neighborhood, an oil pipeline projected for your area, water bubbling up from storm pipes onto streets, a devastating hurricane that breaks through flimsy bulwarks built for another era. Now you become ready to rethink and connect.[6]

Placelessness

Placelessness pervades the contemporary built environment with its soulless qualities that anesthetize the senses. It is characterized by monolithic concrete surfaces, spatial incongruity, lack of human scale, devoid of any redeeming meaning, falling into disrepair, and absent of living things. According to geographer Edward Relph, it is a less authentic attitude that is the "casual eradication of distinctive places and the making of standardized landscapes that results from insensitivity to the significance of place."[7] Placelessness manifests in different ways within the varying territories: urban, suburban, exurban, and the interstitial network environments connecting them all.

Placelessness is one of the negative by-products of urbanism. It can occur everywhere but most often is found in urban areas, particularly those in decline or neglect. Placelessness is pervasive there, as previously functioning parts fall into disrepair and decrepitude, caused by changing population and urban migration patterns, zoning and political redistricting, restructuring, such as highway insertions through discrete neighborhoods, political disenfranchisement, unemployment, and high rates of crime. Often caused by external events, the aftereffect in economic changes and then social conditions result in decay, blight and dereliction. According to phenomenologist Christian Norberg-Schulz, it becomes "flatscape," lacking in authenticity and intentional depth with mediocre experiences.[8] Characteristics of placelessness include inauthenticity, monotony, uniformity, scalelessness, soullessness, and lacking diversity and the presence of nature.

Placelessness is a geographic territory devoid of four important ingredients necessary for healthy human habitation: diversity, authenticity, meaning, and nature. According to Relph, placelessness is not only confined to urban areas, but also to new industrial and commercial developments, instant new towns, and suburbs where mass culture is informed by mass consumerism and mass media, displaying standardization and impersonal uniformity. Further, they are superficial expressions where "they not only look alike but feel alike and offer the same bland possibilities for experience."[9] The topographical, ecological, geographical, historical, and cosmological conditions of architecture and urban environments are very much part of the present atmospheric that gives a place its meaning. When these reference points are missing, place seems to mutate into a vapid and purid spatiality of nothingness – and this is where the lifeless nature of placelessness sets in, devoid of any redeeming qualities. In his book *Home from Nowhere*, James Howard Kunstler suggest that suburbia is an abstract notion of place lacking particularity. He goes on to say that the modern environment has few redeeming characteristics, and is one that continues to be dominated by a car-centered culture. At center stage is our sedentary autocentric lifestyle and the settlement pattern it requires:

> Americans log two trillion miles a year behind the wheel. Growth in vehicle miles traveled (VMT) far exceeds the growth of population or jobs in the United States.[10]

Climate change

Climate change and environmental degradation are other consequences of our contemporary condition, and recently have come into public awareness. Politicians are only now acknowledging that climate change is actually real; however, they do not agree on the source of this change. The global scientific community explains that the causes are made from human activity, created by trapped solar radiation due to rising anthropogenic greenhouse gases, through the burning of fossil fuels within the building, power, and transportation sectors of our culture. Earth's warmest year since 1880 was 2014, according to two separate analyses by National Aeronautics and Space Administration (NASA) and National Oceanic and Atmospheric Administration (NOAA) scientists. Indicators of this phenomenon include shrinking ice sheets, warmer ocean temperatures, global air temperature rise, global sea level rise, ocean acidification, glacial retreat, declining Arctic sea ice, decreasing snow cover, and extreme weather events. Natural disasters such as the Indian Ocean tsunami (2004), Hurricane Katrina (2005), the Kashmir earthquake (2005), Cyclone Nargis (2008), the Haiti earthquake (2010), the Tohoku earthquake and tsunami (2011), Superstorm Sandy (2012), and Mount Everest avalanche (2014), all contributed to greater awareness and recurring dangers of our relationship with the natural environment.[11] Some predictions concerning climate change suggest that the incremental shifts eventually may become more abrupt and even irreversible, which could lead to massive disruption. Accompanying global warming is global cooling in winter and an increasing number of storms and weather anomalies. Climate scientists are reporting that these changes are affecting urban areas in significant ways. Included are six different factors:

1. sea-level rise including coastal region increase of hurricanes;
2. extreme precipitation, including heavy downpours with flooding;
3. extreme drought;
4. "urban island" effect;
5. average temperature changes; and
6. after-precipitation changes.

As For The Left states:

> The current warming trend is of particular significance because most of it is very likely human induced and proceeding at a rate that is unprecedented in the past 1,300 years.[12]

Unsustainability

Where most of our apparent concerns and efforts to improve the built environment have been directed toward sustainability, they have in fact focused on correcting what John Ehrenfeld called "unsustainability": that is, unsustainable technologies, buildings, design practices, and continued consumer-oriented lifestyles.[13] An unsustainable culture displays certain characteristics according to Ehrenfeld, including the following: reductionist determinacy, anthropocentrism, techno-optimism, and denial. Conversely, a sustainable culture supports wholeness, interconnectedness, biocentrism, technoskepticism, and avowal (public affirmation). The Porsche Design Tower in Miami, Florida is a case in point, as the "sustainable building design" supports an "unsustainable program" with multimillion dollar condominiums that come complete with a special elevator for resident cars, which can be seen in two or four-car garages adjacent to individual living rooms throughout the 60 stories. A majority of the 132 units have been purchased by foreign investors and are used as second and third homes.

Unsustainability is a contemporary phenomenon that occurs most dramatically in and between these inextricably linked territories. As defined by Ehrenfeld, the term "unsustainability" also refers to mainstream values and consumption patterns that continue to dominate the production, use, and disposal of goods, and are the proximate cause of damage to the environment.[14] Unsustainable cultural characteristics support a rational science and technology optimism and myopic determinacy. Further, they follow fragmented measures rather than interconnected ones, anthropocentric measures rather than ecocentric ones, and mechanistic measures rather than natural systemic approaches.

The consequences of unsustainable cultural structures and activities include climate change, renewable resource depletion, and environmental degradation. Scientists agree unequivocally that the climate is changing. Political debate continues to question the root cause and whether or not it is the result of a natural cycle or function of human activity. If it is human activity, then this is a clear mandate to rethink and correct the unsustainable structures responsible for its cause. If caused by natural cycles and processes of nature, then does it absolve us from continuing unsustainable consumption and practices, or do we continue to seek increasingly effective sustainability? As John Ehrenfeld states:

> Unsustainability springs from the cultural structure of modernity … Unsustainability is an unintended consequence of the addictive patterns of modern life.[15]

Technopoly

The belief that technology is the solution to the problems of climate change, unsustainability, placelessness, and the profane is overrated. Americans, for example, tend to withdraw inward, spending 87 percent of their time indoors, escaping into cyberspace, electronic media, and other entertainment distractions, as technology further separates us from the direct experience of the outside world.[16] Culture seeks authorization in technology and, according to Neil Postman, technopoly is a "totalitarian technocracy" that demands the submission of all forms of cultural life to the sovereignty of technique and technology. It is characterized by a surplus of information generated by technology, and the reduction of meaning to machines.[17] The original meaning of technology was taken from the Greek *technê* meaning the art, skill, and sleight of hand. It is no longer this. Technology is the prowess of computers, devices, and machines. Like a giant Ponzi scheme, technology seduces users into greater dependence on ever-newer technologies.

In Plato's *Phaedrus* is a story that Socrates tells his friend Phaedrus about King Thamus Ammon while entertaining the god Theuth, who presented to him many of his inventions of that time, including numbers, calculation, geometry, astronomy, and writing, for Thamus to inquire into and approve.[18] These were in fact inventions that later formed the basis of the Seven Liberal Arts. The story goes on to describe King Thamus's inquiry into the introduction of writing as an established new technology. Theuth argued that writing would improve the wisdom and memory of all Egyptians. King Thamus countered that memory would not be improved, but lost; and that writing was a recipe only for recollection. He further argued that wisdom would be acquired, but not gained, through proper instruction and direct experience, and ultimately that this false wisdom, gained through the "drug of forgetfulness," would become a burden to society. The Judgment of Thamus is a reminder that the introduction of new technologies has consequences, and that these consequences can generate unforeseen detriment and repercussions, as well as great benefits and blessings. As Neil Postman states:

> Thamus, speaking from superior understanding and possessing the final word, claims that writing hinders both memory and wisdom: memory is a purely internal process, so writing, an external entity ... Thamus accepts Theuth's connection of memory and wisdom, he disputes the claim that writing enhances them both.[19]

In 1976, regional planner Marcia Echenique observed the inextricable relationship among the type and abundance of the source of energy, the kind of transport system, and the nature of settlement form.[20] If energy is cheap and the prevailing transport method the automobile then, according to Echenique's formula, this naturally translates into a dispersed, low-density settlement form.[21] Alternatively, mass transport and pedestrian movement suggest a more concentrated and dense form, configuring two very different cultural styles of living. In *Technopoly: The Surrender of Culture to Technology*, Neil Postman challenges that technological progress is the instrument by which our most profound dilemmas may be solved.[22] The question arises: is technological invention an ever-ending process of substituting one temporary fix with another? It is clear that cultural behavior is driven by the introduction of new technologies, such as the automobile, elevator, telephone, airplane, computer, Internet, drones, cell phone, and nanotechnology, and that they have altered our cultural structure, which is constantly evolving. What are the repercussions for an increasing global middle class and their insatiable consuming needs? Has technology become self-replicating and purblind? As Ann Casement and David Tacey state:

> New technologies alter the structure of our interests: the things we think about. They alter the character of our symbols: the things we think with. And they alter the nature of community: the arena in which thoughts develop.[23]

In 1993, Postman claimed that we are "amusing ourselves to death" through our interactions and even obsession with media. Today the situation is compounded with the ubiquitous nature of the Internet, social media, personal computers, tablets, the proliferation of mobile devices, and access to a plethora of programs, games, movies, and music. In an instant we have access to an immense number of entertainment and communications venues. Where the Internet renders the world a smaller place, it also distances us from the direct experience of that same place.

Profaneness

The lack of sacrality and numinous experiences within the places we inhabit has become progressively pervasive. The numinous (from the Latin, *numen* for "divine will") now refers to the emotional content found in the presence of the sacred. The numinous found in the natural world is regarded as an encounter with the divine present in all things. The numinous in architecture and urbanism have visual impacts and a quality of luminosity. They provide a trigger or threshold through which to experience something extraordinary, where time stands still and these environments reflect a certain presence. This is an integral quality found in nature and serene urban places. According to Casement and Tacey, the numinous is not restricted to religious spaces, but also occurs in everyday and secular places:

> Along with the concept of spirituality, which also exist outside formal religion, the numinous has been transformed, and is included in humanist, secular [architecture and urbanism] and scientific views.[24]

We live in an age of corporality, where profane and material functions of maintaining everyday life dominate both contemporary culture and the urban environment that is a result of it. Contravening this pattern were ancient cultures that did not separate corporal or everyday activities from a spiritual understanding of the world. The Aboriginal Peoples of Australia, the Hopi Native Americans of southwest United States, and the Druidic and Celtic cultures of Western Europe seemed to share a more integrated worldview, where nature and elemental processes were sanctified in everyday existence. According to architect David Saile, the Pueblo Native Americans viewed their dwellings as not only a place of living, but also a "place of potential communication with the spirit world."[25] Each house was situated so that it could form "a 'break' or a channel through which a connection could be formed between the three levels of the Pueblo world." Spirit was seen as an integral part of everything.

In time, certain sites were the location for great cities of religious, holy, or spiritual significance. Examples include Jerusalem and Bethlehem, Israel, Vatican City, Italy, Varanasi and Pushkar, India, Mecca and Medina, Saudi Arabia, Kyoto, Japan, and Lhasa, Tibet. These are places where world religions were born and still flourish today. Seats of learning were often outposts of the major religious centers in monastic settings, where spiritual practices were blended with everyday secular activities. In the eleventh and twelfth centuries in Western Europe, education shifted to focus on science and the liberal arts in urban centers such as Bologna and Padua, Italy and Paris, France.

Creation stories are symbolic narratives and sacred accounts that provide profound explanations – whether mythical, spiritual, or scientific in nature – of the beginning of the world. Philosopher Edward Casey suggests that understanding the first place is a problematic posit, and that this first place of creation derives from "no-place" or utter void.[26] According to Marie-Louise Von Franz, "they [creation myths] represent unconscious and pre-conscious processes which describe not the origin of our cosmos, but *the origin of man's conscious awareness of the world*."[27] Creation myths help explain concepts, such as something from nothing, horizontal versus vertical, descent and ascent, the meaning of the cosmos, conjugation of opposites, the elements, and earthen materiality – all of which are in service of place creation.

Paradise Lost is the biblical story of the temptation of Adam and Eve by the fallen angel Satan in the guise of a snake, and their expulsion from the Garden of Eden for eating fruit from the Tree of the Knowledge of Good and Evil.[28] This narrative describes the transition of human existence from innocent obedience to a state of guilt and disobedience. The event was known as the "original sin," bringing corruption to the entire natural world. This narrative might explain two important contradictions: "anthropocentrism," our continued dominance over and disrespect for the natural environment; and "ecocentrism," our insatiable attraction to nature, which in some ways might suggest our need to experience or reenact the paradise that was lost. The fall from paradise seems to be a reminder of a lost tranquillity and beauty that resides at the core of our desire for the serene. Our relationship to nature often reenacts a sense of our lost paradise, with the creation of parks, gardens, lawns, greenhouses, and even flower arrangements within the home. Similarly, proponents of biophilia suggest that this same nostalgia of landscape is seeded in the human origins in the African savannah, which also is home to some of the world's most exotic wildlife – lions, cheetahs, tigers, leopards, elephants, buffaloes, giraffes, rhinos, gazelles, antelopes, hippopotamus, crocodiles, and other wild animals. As the first lines from John Milton's epic poem *Paradise Lost* (Figures 1.1a and 1.1b) state:

> Of MANS First Disobedience, and the Fruit Of that Forbidden Tree, Whose mortal hast Brought Death into the World, and all our woe, With loss of Eden, till one greater Man Restore us, and regain the blissful Seat.[29]

Lost in the mire of modernity, visions of paradise have all but been blurred as the throng of everyday contemporary life moves on, with the advent of more highways, suburbs and tall buildings, and our infatuation with technology and electronic media. Yet there are glimpses of paradise possibly still extant in this life. Growth of the travel, hospitality, and tourism industries may explain an increase in the desire to experience new, beautiful, and serene places, from Italian hilltowns, the Greek islands and coastal villages near Bodrum, Turkey to cruises up the Rhine River, Alaska or the Caribbean Islands. Agrotourism, too, is a growing interest where natural and real-life experiences concurrently occur, especially in wine-producing locations such as the Napa Valley, Tuscany, Italy or the south of France. Common activities include farm tours for families and schoolchildren, day camps, hands-on chores, self-harvesting of produce, hay or sleigh rides, and overnight stays in a bed and breakfast. According to James Howard Kunstler, only 2 percent of the American population is engaged in farming often done through large monocultures, which exacerbate further our separation from nature, but also our connection to the critical food resources necessary to sustain us. The good news is the renaissance in agricultural urbanism that is re-situating food production with habitation.[30]

Figure 1.1 Paradise Lost: a) Fall from Paradise, by John Milton
Source: © lian_2011/Shutterstock
b) Contemporary urbanism
Source: Photograph by Phillip Tabb

Explanations of the future seem to project dystopian visions with vast destruction, ugliness, bleakness, scarcity, and anarchy. Even Pope Francis exclaimed that the Earth is our home and is beginning to look more like "an immense pile of filth" in part due to our heedless worship of technology, addiction to fossil fuels, and compulsive consumerism.[31] *Koyaanisqatsi* in the Hopi language, meaning "things out of balance," suggests that our present life is characterized by an imbalance among nature, humans, and the built environment.[32] Current solutions vacillate among vapid conformity, corporeality, and self-absorbed, heroic designs. With the enormity of our planetary problems, from climate change, resource depletion, habitat destruction, and environmental degradation to poverty, disease, cultural, religious and political strife and ineptness, are we to believe that it is science and technology or prophetic media fiction that are leading the way into our future, or could it be something completely different and more noetic – something which may inform other reflective and effective approaches to sustaining our existence?

Inculcation of the serene

The idea of the serene has gained currency in postmodern discussions. When combined with urbanism it conjures questions, even contradictions, as the two ideas seem improbable, and so unlikely as a combinatory admixture. The contemporary human-made environment is no longer composed of simple functional zones separated by preference and utility. Rather, it has evolved into a dispersed and relational network urbanity, and according to Tom Mayne, has formed a "constellation of poly-nucleated attractors."[33] While acknowledging that the new innovative territory has liquefied into a more spontaneous, non-linear, and unpredictable process reflecting a fickle contemporary culture, it seems to place little value in stillness, solitude and reflection. As Mayne states:

> Combinatory urbanism offers an alternative method of urban production that designs flexible frameworks of relational systems within which activities, events, and programs can organically play themselves out.[34]

Other postmodern theories and manifestos on urbanism include Nan Ellin's *Integral Urbanism* (2006),[35] which attempts to reverse fragmentation with approaches that are proactive in enhancing a better habitat for human activity through five qualities of integral urbanism: hybridity and connectivity, porosity, authenticity and vulnerability. David Grahame Shane supports a recombinant urbanism[36] characterized by urban morphology, scaling, and experience modeled by ever-changing ordering systems subject to constant feedback. The physical characteristics of green urbanism follow Michel Foucault's systems of organization, as they function as both place and network architectures, sharing complicit roles in creating an interconnected and seamless urbanism focused on stasis as well as flow.[37] Janine de la Salle and Mark Holland posit an agricultural urbanism centered on food production as a catalyst for community-formation.[38] These are approaches that reject simple functional zoning schemes, nostalgias of stylized urbanism, and escapist expressions of hypermodernity.

In the light of these propositions, serene urbanism is not a new paradigm, but one that extends these contemporary principles with the added intention of raising the integrity, inclusiveness, and quality of experience appropriate to each environmental territory by integrating serene qualities with desirable urban patterns. For the experience of serenity, the urban environment integrates everyday access to outdoor places, elemental forces, and natural environments, and contains spaces of contemplation, solitude, and beauty. For the urban experience, the natural environment houses a diversity of commercial and institutional functions, cultural activities, stimulating public gathering spaces and pedestrian systems of engagement and circulation. Taken together, they are in service not only to create natural, environmentally sensitive, and contemplative places, but also are conjoined with rich, spirited, stimulating, diverse, and enriched architecture and urban design. Serene urbanism is an intersection that seeks to combine the best qualities of these extremes. It is not a blend, but rather a coexistence, of the beneficial qualities of each.

This work is organized in two parts that explore the concept and application of serene urbanism. Part I establishes the theoretical framework through different contemporary perspectives, and concludes with a clear explanation of a theory of serene urbanism. The positive characteristics of urbanism and beneficial qualities of the serene are explored and related to sustainability, biophilia, placemaking, and environmental design. Both principles and examples are presented as compelling portraits for the proposal of these new urban landscapes. Part II is an in-depth exploration and analysis of serene urban ideas related to the intentional community being created outside of Atlanta, Georgia. "Serenbe" is the name given to this place to commemorate the value and nuance between the serene and urban. This part concludes with an analysis of the dimensions of serene urbanism and placemaking patterns associated with the community.

Serenbe Community provides an interesting case study and model, as it is an experiential laboratory for the working principles of serene urbanism. Its location, land, programming, planning, design, and realization represent a self-evolving and intentional development process that encourages resident participation with agriculture and the integral natural environment. Further, it provides a context for the formation of a community supported by a broad range of cultural activities. Serenbe is both a serene and urban environment with a numinous quality of place. It is neither a model within a dense urban center, such as downtown Atlanta, nor is it suburban. Rather, it is a living example of the interacting principles that can be applied to any habitable context along the urban–rural transect. Consequently, Part II is an attempt to relay in detail the story of its creation.

The name "Serenbe" relates directly to serenity and the serene. So embedded in the very name is an affirmational or intentional quality that has guided the development process and created this unique community. Serenbe received the Inaugural Sustainability Award from the Urban Land Institute of Atlanta in 2008, and is considered an exemplar of land preservation, with creative mixes of use, density, agrarian urbanism, connectivity and "walkability," wellness and active living, green architecture, and construction practice, as well as associations to the numinous. According to an early Serenbe resident, John Graham in 2006:

> Serenbe is marked by an extraordinary sense of community. What has contributed to this remains something of a mystery: the founder's vision, the inculcation to the sacred, and the commitment to the principles of sacred geometry in physical design, have resulted in a strong sense of place that attracts residents sharing a commitment to the land, the environment, and to each other.[39]

According to C.C. Kraemer, a large segment of America wants the bigger homes, larger yards, better schools, and relative safety that is typically found in the suburbs.[40] The combination of the serene and urbanism offers a compelling alternative to typical suburban planning practice, where homes are large, separated, grouped without other nearby amenities, and totally dependent on the automobile for access to everything. Serene and urbanism are not antithetical; rather, they are complementary, and intended to balance these two sides of human nature and the environments that reflect them. Somewhere between the neo-traditional seaside, site of *The Truman Show*, and the hypermodern *Blade Runner*, is an antidote to urban design that is far more effective as an ultimately integrated urbanity. This new urban portrait is not focused on a single urban territory, but can be applied to the varying transect of habitation lying more seamlessly between the most extreme city centers and natural rural edge.

Figures 1.2a and 1.2b shows two pen and ink drawings by the author that illustrate the visible contradistinction between the serene landscape of Monte Miata framed by Cyprus trees and viewed from one of the high walls in Pienza, Italy, and the urban character of Via dei Servi terminated by the Duomo in Florence, Italy. It is fusion of these seemingly opposites that serene urbanism posits to unite. Both images evoke positive and extraordinary feelings especially when present in these two places. The picturesque Tuscan landscape is soothing, even breathtaking, and is terminated

Figure 1.2 The serene and the urban: a) Monte Amiata, Pienza, Italy b) Via dei Servi and *duomo*, Florence, Italy

Note: The two drawings were sketched in situ in Pienza and Florence, then enhanced with Micron pens in a studio in Castiglion Fiorentino, Italy. The drawings represent the beauty of the Italian countryside in contrast with the excitement of a street scene in Florence, with its active street and high building walls.

Source: Drawings by Phillip Tabb

with Monte Amiata, Tuscany's largest mountain in the distance. While the Via dei Servi connects Florence's healing district with the *duomo* of the Cattedrale di Santa Maria del Fiore, it has a strong urban character, commercial activity and pedestrian circulation.

Notes

1 Pyper, Andrew, *The Damned: A Novel*, Simon & Schuster, New York, 2011, p. 188.
2 Steele, John, *Geomancy, Consciousness and Sacred Sites*, Trigon Communications Inc., New York, 1985.
3 Benjamin, Walter, "On Some Motifs in Baudelaire," in *Illuminations: Essays and Reflections*, trans. Harry Zohn, ed. Hannah Arendt, Schocken, New York, 1968, p. 163.

4 United Nations Department of Economic and Social Affairs, "World Population Prospects: Key Findings and Advanced Tabled". Available online at http://esa.un.org/unpd/wpp/Publications/Files/ (accessed June 12, 2016).

5 Klein, Naomi, *This Changes Everything: Capitalism vs. the Climate*, Simon & Schuster, New York, 2014; Berger, Michelle, "The Weather.com Climate Disruption Index," *The Weather Channel*, 2016. Available online at http://stories.weather.com/disruptionindex (accessed July 2015).

6 Klein, Naomi, "The Contemporary Condition," in *This Changes Everything*. Available online at http://contemporarycondition.blogspot.com/2015/03/naomi-klein-in-the-eye-of-anthropocene.html?m=1 (accessed June 14, 2016), p. 1.

7 Ibid, p. 2 (preface).

8 Norberg-Schultz, Christian, *Genius Loci: Towards a Phenomenology of Architecture*, Rizzoli International Press, New York, 1979.

9 Relph, Edward, *Place and Placelessness (Research in Planning & Design)*, Pion Ltd., London, 1984, p. 132.

10 Kunstler, James Howard, *Home from Nowhere: Remaking Our Everyday World for the 21st Century*, Simon & Schuster, New York, 1996, p. 67.

11 NASA, "Climate Change: How Do We Know?" Available online at http://climate.nasa.gov/evidence/ (accessed March 2015); Berger, "The Weather.com Climate Disruption Index."

12 For The Left, "Here's What to Tell Stupid Climate Change Deniers, NASA: Climate Change: How Do We Know?" Available online at http://fortheleft.blogspot.com/2013/10/hereswhat-to-tell-stupid-climate.html?m=1 (accessed June 14, 2016).

13 Ehrenfeld, John R., *Sustainability by Design: A Subversive Strategy for Transforming Our Consumer Culture*, Yale University Press, New Haven, CT, 2008, pp. 175 and 178.

14 Ibid.

15 Ehrenfeld, *Sustainability by Design*, p. 7.

16 Postman, Neil, *Technopoly: The Surrender of Culture to Technology*, Vintage Books, New York, 1993.

17 Ibid.

18 Plato, *Phaedrus*, Cambridge University Press, Cambridge, 2011.

19 Postman, *Technopoly*, p. 12.

20 Echenique, Marcia H., "Function and Form of the City Region," in Hancock, Tom (ed.) *Growth and Change in the Future City Region*, Leonard Hill, London, 1976.

21 Ibid.

22 Postman, *Technopoly*.

23 Casement, Ann and Tacey, David (eds), *The Idea of the Numinous*, Routledge, London, 2006, pp. xvi–xvii.

24 Ibid.

25 Saile, David G., "Making a House: Building Rituals and Spatial Concepts in the Pueblo Indian World," *Architectural Association Quarterly* 9(2–3), 1977, pp. 72–81, p. 76.

26 Casey, Edward S., *The Fate of Place: A Philosophical History*, University of California Press, Berkeley, CA, 1997.

27 Von Franz, Marie-Louise, *Creation Myths*, Spring Publications, Dallas, TX, 1972, p. 8; emphasis in original.

28 Milton, John, *Paradise Lost*, The Franklin Library, Franklin Center, Pennsylvania, PA, 1979, (orig. pub. 1667), p. 7.

29 Ibid.

30 Kunstler, James Howard, *The Geography of Nowhere: The Rise and Decline of America's Man-made Landscape*, Free Press, New York, 1994.

31 Pope Francis, "Pope Francis Addresses the Environment." Available online at www.wptz.com/politics/urgent-pope-francis-addresses-the-environment/35458694 (accessed September 2015).

32 *Koyaanisqatsi* (dir. Godfrey Reggio, 1982), music by Philip Glass.

33 Mayne, Tom (Morphosis Architects), *Combinatory Urbanism: The Complex Behavior of Collective Form*, Stray Dog Café, Culver City, CA, 2011, p. 27.

34 Ibid.

35 Ellin, Nan, *Integral Urbanism*, Routledge, New York, 2006.

36 Shane, David Grahame, *Recombinant Urbanism*, Wiley Academy, Chichester, 2005.

37 Foucault, Michel, *The Order of Things: An Archaeology of the Human Sciences*, reissued edition, Vintage, New York, 1994.

38 de la Salle, Janine and Holland, Mark, *Agricultural Urbanism: A Handbook for Building Sustainable Food and Agricultural Systems in 21st Century Cities*, Green Frigate Books, Winnipeg, 2010.

39 Email communication from John Graham to the author, July 15, 2006.

40 C.C. Kraemer, "Beware New Urbanism," *Foundation for Economic Education*, October 1, 2001. Available online at http://fee.org/freeman/detail/beware-new-urbanism (accessed July 2015).

2 Serene perspectives

There is a serene and settled majesty to woodland scenery that enters into the soul and delights and elevates it, and fills it with noble inclinations.[1]

Spirituality is understood to be a broad construct that includes many dimensions including serenity. The concept of serenity and its relationships to spirituality, health and well-being first appeared in the nursing literature in the mid-1960s. Serenity has been defined as a spiritual state that decreases stress and promotes optimal health,[2] a sustained state of inner peace,[3] and a universal health experience related to quality of life.[4] Boyd-Wilson et al. describe serenity as a spiritual quality that involves inner peace despite vicissitudes and even feeling, thus a person can feel grief, yet be serene.[5] According to Roberts and Aspy,[6] certain factors have been associated with the serene including inner haven, acceptance, belonging, trust, perspective, contentment, present centeredness, beneficence, and cognitive restructuring.

Serenity found in urban contexts is increasingly rare. According to James Howard Kunstler in his 2006 TED talk,[7] in the United States there are some 38,000 placeless urban spaces. This is probably an underestimation. However, certain environments seem to appear as moments of sanity that possess many of the scales of enchantment-creating serenity. The combination of serenity along with urban experiences is becoming an increasingly desirable admixture. In this regard, it is important to understand the importance of and role that serenity plays in habitation, and the ways in which it manifests, especially in the design of urban form.

Serenity has roots in Greek third-century BC stoic philosophy, and later in the stoic school, with Roman emperor Marcus Aurelius (AD 161). Epictetus' stoic philosophy was basically that the goal of life is to live in harmony with nature.[8] This means to live a good life, we must both live in accord with our human nature – as essentially rational, reflective, and thoughtful beings – and conform our actions to the actual conditions of the natural world. This suggests a kind of empowerment that derives from living simply, appropriately, and living in accordance with nature – both human and universal. According to philosopher Keith Seddon, the notion of spiritual path – taken to mean way of life, outlook on life, personal growth, and personal healing – is in fact the very essence of stoicism.[9] Of course, this brings up the question of how this balanced relationship with the natural world might occur within the context of contemporary culture.

Serene environments

Associated with contemporary times has been the evolution of increased complexity and pluralism served by advancing technology. Together they have contributed to what archeologist John Steele calls "temporal density," where any given interval of time is filled and saturated with a myriad of events, processes, information, and thoughts.[10] Time is dense, requiring great mental and emotional attention, and affords little escape or solitude.

Coupled with temporal density is spatial density, which is an outward expression of the same characteristics in physical terms. It is space with the diversity, complexity, number, and proximity of things within it. The positive consequences of this phenomenon include social accessibility, access to amenities, and the economic benefits of clustering and market concentration, along with a host of sustainable strategies. The negative effects of density produce congestion, pollution, tumultuousness, reduced privacy, increased crime, egregious social attitudes, and undesirable behaviors. Serene philosophy applied to this context requires targeted and accessible interventions in order to restore balance with nature and spatial nontumultuousness.

Tranquillity and peacefulness

A design objective for serene environments is to create a context that is peaceful and tranquil. This is true for any territory found within the urban–rural transect, yet it naturally occurs in differing ways appropriate to each context. Tranquillity is a state of calmness and reflection, which is restorative compared with the stressful effects of sustained attention in day-to-day life. All the external place-pollution sources, exemplified by cars, buses, planes, sirens, and construction, combined with the overscheduling and "too much information" of our information age, are the main contributors and distractions. Stress and anxiety reduction, access to the present, and recharging well-being are all obvious positive manifestations of peacefulness and tranquillity.

Places that are clear and quiet contribute to a serene experience. Clarity allows for an expression that is understood, meaningful, and remembered. Quiet places contribute as a gateway to tranquillity, healing and restoration. For many of the positive benefits of serene places to occur, environments need to be safe and untroubled. Safe places can be defined as free from danger, harm, or hurt, both emotionally or physically. Contributing factors to feeling safe include familiarity of people, place and objects, suspension of defensive barriers, and allowing for vulnerability. In the context of this work, this includes participating in environments that are essentially serene instead of chaotic and tumultuous.

The picturesque, meaning "in the manner of a picture," was an aesthetic movement first introduced in France as *pittoresque*, in Italy as *pittoresco*, and in the eighteenth century in England, and was understood through the ideals of beauty and the sublime. Picturesque arose as a mediator between these two, showing the possibilities that existed in-between the rationally idealized states. Rather than classic proportions and symmetry, the picturesque tended toward accidental irregularity and contrast, sensuous pastoral scenography, and ruinous or rustic qualities of materiality. William Gilpin described it as being a combination of smoothness, regularity, and order contrasted with magnitude, vastness, and intimations of power.[11] It is a whole with a variety of parts. The picturesque differs from the serene in a major way. Serene environments

Figure 2.1 Picturesque serenity: a) Selborne, Hampshire, UK b) Winter scene, Stowe, Vermont, USA
Source: Alamy Stock Photo

tend to be bucolic and contain natural features, meaning that they possess pastoral elements or references to beautiful natural landscapes. The primary function of a serene environment is to help facilitate personal transformation or a transformative experience. The picturesque tends to separate the viewer from the scene, where the serene directly engages the participant within the environment. While there are numerous examples of picturesque places, Selborne in Hampshire, UK is a good example of a nestled English village along the Wellhead stream (Figure 2.1a). The town of Stowe is an idyllic winter haven and postcard picture place in the Mount Mansfield State Forest of Vermont (Figure 2.1b).

Serene environments are transformative. This suggests that experience of these places becomes a trigger of, or threshold into, an elevated state of being and enhanced presence. Two kinds of experiences are possible. The first is the personal experience where transformation occurs internally, initially as a felt sense. This is often accompanied by feelings of euphoria. The second is an epistemically transformative experience, which provides knowledge that is normally inaccessible to the participant until he or she interacts with place. This experience is highly place-bound and derives meaning, certainty, and cognitive concepts directly from the local environment.

Hypernatural is an approach to contemporary culture and technology that works directly with natural forces and processes. Nature plays a key role in these emergent approaches to technology, where it is no longer separate; instead, it is an extension possessing qualities of nature's dynamic processes. The positive effects of nature on sustainability are well known, particularly in processes that harness natural on-site resources: earth, wind, water, light, solar energy, and the thermal benefits of day-to-night cycles.

Relations to nature

While nature has infinite manifestation on all levels, from galaxies and star systems to atoms and quarks (macro to micro), earthbound nature or terrestrial nature can be generally experienced on three different scales:

1. extraordinary large-scale environments, such as the Grand Canyon, mountain ranges, or the ocean's edge;
2. medium-scale, such as views of valleys, forests, lakes, or ponds; and
3. more intimate scales such as landscapes, meadows, springs, gardens, or even a flower.

The serene can exist on any of these scales; however, natural experiences that are accessible, self-transcending, quiescent, and tranquil, possess qualities of the serene. Thoreau remarked on where he lived and what he lived for:

> I went to the woods because I wished to live deliberately, to front only the essential facts of life, and see if I could not learn what it had to teach, and not, when I came to die.[12]

It goes without saying that not all natural experiences are positive. Many are negative, dangerous, and even destructive. Natural disasters such as earthquakes, avalanches, floods, volcanic eruptions, tsunamis, hurricanes, and tornados cause countless deaths worldwide. Droughts and consecutive famines are also responsible for human casualties. It is estimated that nearly 250,000 lives are claimed globally by natural disasters every year. According to the *Annual Disaster Statistical Review*, nearly 400 natural disasters occur annually. Viruses, bacterial infections, and other microbes are sources of other negative consequences of nature. Bacteria, viruses, and parasites cause around 2 million cases of cancer in the world each year. According to the Centers for Disease Control and Prevention,[13] approximately half of all deaths caused by infectious diseases each year can be attributed to just three: tuberculosis, malaria, and Acquired Immune Deficiency Syndrome (AIDS). As can be seen, the quest for survival for any living organism can be violent and destructive – the antithesis to serenity.

Therefore, for serene environments to function effectively, it is important that the nature experience is positive, safe, and beneficial to health rather than destructive. The restorative benefits of nature can occur in several ways. Time in the open air and being outside increases capacity for creativity and enhances problem-solving skills. Another benefit occurs for people who have been suffering from stress, sickness, or a trauma if they can spend quiet contemplative time in gardens, or be taken to the mountains or woods to heal. Research by the UK mental health organization Mind, published by the University of Essex, found that taking a walk in nature reduced depression scores in 71 percent of participants.[14] Even viewing scenes of nature reduces anger, fear, and stress, and increases pleasant feelings. Other studies have shown that reconnecting with nature can help improve energy and boost overall well-being, including physical health, cognitive performance, and psychological well-being. According to an article by Ryan and colleagues in the June 2010 issue of *Journal of Environmental Psychology*, being outside promotes higher levels of activity with increased vitality.[15] Securing stable supplies of drinking water and creating air filtration of pollutants with access to appropriate levels of oxygen, are also healthful. A benefit of sunlight is its ability to boost the body's vitamin D supply; most cases of vitamin D deficiency are due to lack of outdoor sun exposure. A final benefit – and an obvious one – is the production of, and access to, food necessary for human survival.

Celestial nature represents our relationship to the heavens, including annual changes of the seasons and diurnal changes. Special moments such as solstices, equinoxes,

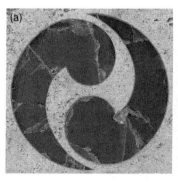  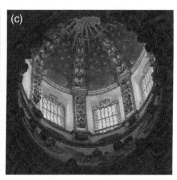

Figure 2.2 Celestial expressions: a) Museo Galileo, Florence, Italy b) The Pantheon, Rome, Italy c) Siena Cathedral, Italy
Source: Photographs by Phillip Tabb

comets, the Aurora Borealis, lunar and solar eclipses, and the myriad of stars and constellations sparkling in the night sky have inspired us since the beginning of time. Not only have these phenomena served calendrical purposes, but they also possess spiritual qualities informing myths, philosophies, and religious celebrations. Meridians within many Renaissance churches mark the seasonal movement of the sun, such as the one embedded in the sidewalk outside the Museo Galileo in Florence, Italy (Figure 2.2a). The Pantheon in Rome, Italy (AD 118–128) is an extraordinary example of the sun and rain's interaction with architecture enabled by its open-air oculus (Figure 2.2b). More recent is the work of artist James Turrell, whose architectural constructions are featured with roof-opening skylights, such as the Dallas Skyspace at the Nasher Sculpture Center, Texas, the Twilight Epiphany Skyspace at Rice University, and Live Oaks Friends' Meeting House, both in Houston, Texas. The interior of Siena Cathedral is adorned with a host of celestial images (Figure 2.2c). A consequence of our experience of the night sky is twofold: the incredible wonder of its vastness, and the immense wholeness of nature. Over time and across cultures, the night sky has been a symbol of unity, both in time and space.

The elemental qualities of nature contribute to transformative experiences. Water, fire, earth, and air have been symbols, and embody qualities, of the physical world. Ether, a fifth element, corresponds to the realm of the unseen. In some traditions these elements correspond to human attributes of will (fire), emotions (water), mind (air), body (earth), and spirit (ether). In nature they express in mesmeric ways that are highly engaging.[16] They reflect the qualities of Robert Lawlor's dynamic and living seven-fold cycle:

1. pre-forming;
2. in-forming;
3. per-forming;
4. de-forming;
5. re-forming;
6. trans-forming; and
7. re-performing.

Biodiversity is a measure of the variety of organisms present in different ecosystems. One of the reasons that biodiversity is important is because it helps to keep the environment in natural balance, and is more resilient and adaptable. According to Pamela Collins, a biologically diverse environment is usually very beautiful, and endlessly fascinating.[17] Natural environments that are accessible allow for greater interaction and immersion. When coupled within a residential community, they allow for greater proximity to, and reinforcement of, everyday interactions. While natural places can be more rugged and less predictable, they must maintain a relatively safe environment in order for benefits to occur. Biodiversity, instincts for feeling safe, proximity, accessibility, and the sensual qualities of presence are important in creating beneficial terrestrial nature experiences. It is important to recognize the living qualities of nature and the unfolding processes that they represent.

> I recall as a young boy in my teens a time on one of our typical family vacations to Island Park in northeast Idaho. We stayed in a cabin along the Buffalo River, which was a pristine river that eventually fed the Henry's Fork dam. Early one summer's morning I was alone in the middle of the river in my waders, fishing for trout. Standing still, I became aware of all the nearby sounds, but particularly the gentle sound of the rushing water. As I slowly moved downstream, I realized the sounds changed with the local composition of rock outcrops and fallen trees. The water was so clear, the rocks on the bottom seemed to amplify. Then suddenly about 30 feet away, a female moose came out of the brush for a drink at the river's edge. She barely noticed me, maybe because I had become so attuned into the serenity of the place.[18]

Nature spirits might describe an unseen quality of nature. They were instrumental in the formation of Findhorn community, guiding the co-creation of their garden there. The communications, according to one of the co-founders, Dorothy Maclean, came in the form of an indwelling presence and deva consciousness. An interesting communication was received that, within a human-made landscape or garden, places be kept wild and uninhabited by our presence for the dwelling of certain devas who do not want to interact with us, or were not ready to do so.[19] Today, Findhorn is the single intentional community in the UK and functions at half the UK average for an ecological footprint.

The presence of nature is found everywhere, and for most people its experience has been present but limited. For those living in cities, perhaps it is the park, or tree-lined streets, and summer vacations in the woods. For those living in rural areas, nature is an everyday occurrence. Figure 2.3 shows a few examples of nature within: a poppy and honey bee (Figure 2.3a); a night photograph of the Northern Lights (Figure 2.3b); a play in the woods (Figure 2.3c); the Highline Park in New York City (Figures 2.3d and 2.3e), and the Bloomingdale Trail in Chicago, Illinois (Figure 2.3f). With the preponderance of placeless urban environments and the fragmented spaces in-between them, it is often difficult to see the presence of nature or to see that nature is not something from the outside that presents periodic appearances, but rather that we all are a part of the web of nature. To this end, the serene and urban form an important partnership across the transect of human habitation. Nature manifests in many diverse and varied ways, from light reflecting off a crystal to the enormity of the night sky.

Figure 2.3 Nature within: a) Poppy and honey bee
Source: Photograph courtesy of Robert Armon
b) Celestial serenity and the Northern Lights c) Play in the woods d) Highline Park, New York, before e) Highline Park, New York, after f) Bloomingdale Trail, Chicago, Illinois, USA
Source: Alamy Stock Photo

Deep ecology, a term coined by the Norwegian philosopher Arne Næss in 1973, argued that the natural world is a subtle balance of complex interrelationships in which the existence of one organism is dependent on the existence of others within ecosystems.[20] Deep ecology's core principle is the belief that the living environment as a whole should be respected: this is sympathetic to the intentions of serene urbanism, where human habitation coexists with nature and is part of the same whole. Deep ecology, along with landscape urbanism and landform architecture, advocates wilderness preservation, agricultural land preservation, and more conscious living with nature.

Atmospheric qualities

Numinous qualities give serene environments mysterious and transformative dimensions. These qualities are not limited to serene environments, but are associated with spiritual and religious buildings, as well as experiences with extraordinary architecture. The religious historian Mircea Eliade explained that we become aware of the sacred because it manifests as something wholly different from the profane.[21] The numinous experience has a personal quality, in that the person feels to be in communion with a "wholly other." The numinous experience can lead in different cases to belief in deities, the supernatural, the sacred, the holy, and/or transcendent. A numinous place is filled with, or characterized by, a sense of wonder, with a supernatural and elevated presence. The term "numinosity" derives from the Latin *numen*, meaning a divine power or spirit inhabiting a place. Benefits to the numinous experience include:

- momentary healing;
- renewal;
- stress release and anxiety reduction;
- emotional cleansing; and
- inspiration leading to positive affirmations.[22]

The numinous supports various unknown elements that are thought to make up existing forms of matter, or a substance seen as an elemental or pure form of something else. According to the theologian Rudolf Otto, the numinous expresses in two paradoxical ways:

1. *tremendum* – the numinous has elements of the awful, overpowering, and urgency. This manifests as a quality of overwhelming awe and excites the instinctual, both of which enhance the experience of presence. Experiences include overwhelm, trembling, eeriness, humility, urgency, bewilderment, mental agitation, and haunting, daunting, monstrous feelings. The fascinating mystery creates a trembling awe;
2. *mysterium* – the numinous has elements of fascination and the "wholly other." This manifests as a quality of overwhelming mystery and transcendence, which can involve an invisible presence that causes a peculiar alteration of consciousness. Experiences include sublimity, awe, excitement, bliss, rapture, exaltation, entrancement, fascination, attraction, allure, moments of illumination, and what Otto called an "impelling motive power."[23]

The numinous associated with the serene manifests through more nuanced and attuned relationships to nature. It is not as paradoxical, as the tremendum in serenity is less overpowering but does excite the senses, enhances perception, and awakens natural instincts. This opens up the way to mysterium and the experience of serenity. One experiences overwhelm and awe, yet remains safe. This process tends to follow a sequence, moving from the forgetting of everyday worries and considerations to a remembering that facilitates an opening or threshold into transcendent experiences. In remembering the felt sense, experience of presence, and the feelings of innate behavior stimulated by the trigger of being in nature and uncontrollable environments, one of the objectives of this process is to experience more intense levels of presence.

The archeologist John Steele explained that sacred transcendences cross from one realm to another and back, and that our experiences between these differing states of consciousness are likened to amphibious transformations.[24] Often, we experience a kind of geomantic amnesia, and we forget the experiences of one place from the other, much like the disappearing and reappearing surf or a vivid dream that fades after waking. However, it is important to remember or carry over insights from one realm to the other, much as an amphibian is able to breathe in both air and water environments. This phenomenon is linked to the philosopher Michel Foucault's concept of heterotopic space, which has more layers of meaning or relationships to other places than is immediately apparent.[25] Along similar lines, Reverend Mark D. Roberts wrote about the Celtic tradition and the concept of "thin places," where the boundary between heaven and earth is especially close.[26] It is posited here that serene environments can become thin places, where the threshold and divide between secular and sacred begin to dissolve, and the divine can be more readily sensed or accessed. According to Ann Casement and David Tacey, the currency of the numinous is no longer exclusive of religious experience:

> Along with the concept of spirituality, which also exists outside formal religion, the numinous has been transformed, and is now included in humanist, secular and scientific views of the world.[27]

Given the nuanced conditions required for our awareness of the spirit of place, what, then, is the nature of the transcendent experience within a serene environment? We know transcendence when we hear certain music or taste extraordinary food. Going beyond the limits of ordinary experience, in a wonderful environment, the feeling or quality of being takes over. The sense of a separate self is abandoned, and in its place is the unity experience; according to the philosopher Johann Friedrich Herbart, crossing the limen of consciousness becomes a "transcendental apperception."[28] The new experience becomes assimilated and transformation ensues. As the psychiatrist Lionel Corbett states:

> The [numinous] experience is mysterious, tremendous, and fascinating. The important factor is the affective quality of the experience rather than its specific content. In its grip, we feel we are facing something quite outside our usual experience, something awesome, uncanny.[29]

The luminescent quality of photosynthesis is another reminder of the numinous in everyday experience (Figure 2.4a). A good example of a numinous experience is with a bonfire: gazing into it is mesmerizing, as the flickering flames seem to dance and the scintilla of sparks disappear into the night sky, transforming into wonder, fascination, and the sublime (Figure 2.4b). The mysterious Yerebatan Cistern in Istanbul is one of the largest ancient underground cisterns, constructed in a marvel of orange color, luminescent light, and incredible reflections (Figure 2.4c). Filled with a forest of classical marble columns of mainly Iconic and Corinthian capitals, the cavern contains a huge capacity of water, nearly 3 million cubic feet (80,000 cubic meters). The

Figure 2.4 Numinous experiences: a) Luminescent photosynthesis b) Flickering bonfire c) Yerebatan Cistern, Istanbul, Turkey
Source: Shutterstock

experience is truly mysterious and transformative, especially walking through it with the sound of classical music.

Biophilic perspectives

According to Blane Brownell and Marc Swackhamer, technology need not be anti-nature, but rather there is a positive capacity of technology, as evidenced in the increasing interest in the fields of sustainability, biophilia, biomimicry, and landscape urbanism.[30] In many ways, biophilia is more a theory rather than practice, and posits that there is an instinctive bond and affiliation between human beings and other living systems. According to Terrapin Bright Green, there are 14 biophilic patterns in design, which include:

- visual and non-visual connections with nature;
- sensory stimuli;
- thermal and airflow variability;
- the presence of water;
- direct and diffused light;
- material interfaces possessing complexity and mystery, and having a certain level of risk or peril.[31]

Translating to architecture, this would support adaptive designs that enhance access to resources, food, views, and direct exposure to nature.

Biomimicry, on the other hand, is inspired by elements, structures, materials, and models of natural systems in order to solve complex problems. In architecture and planning it does not seek to copy nature, but to understand and utilize the inherent principles that govern it. Michael Pawlyn explains that biomimicry contains sustainable principles and initiating inspirations, such as super-efficient structures, high-strength biodegradable composites, self-cleaning surfaces, low energy and waste systems, and water retention methods.[32] Principle design features include:

- proportional geometry;
- harmonious fields;
- physiognomics;
- skeletal structures and shapes;
- organic plasticity;
- morphological growth patterns; and
- biological forms.

Biological forms have influenced projects such as the Sagrada Familia and Frank Gehry's *Peix* (fish) sculpture in Barcelona, Spain, the TWA Terminal Building at JFK International Airport, New York, Sydney Opera House, and Herb Greene's Prairie House in Norman, Oklahoma. The Metropol Parasol (2011) is a remarkable serene urban redevelopment project within the dense medieval inner-city fabric of Seville, Spain, designed by Jurgen Mayer-Hermann. The work was a compelling result of an international competition in which this project came in first place. The serene organic form and waffle parasol structure is made of bonded timber construction with a polyurethane coating, and reported to be the world's largest wooden structure. Its

Figure 2.5 Biophilic serenity: a) Metropol Parasol, Spain b) Yellow Treehouse Restaurant, Auckland, New Zealand
Source: Alamy Stock Photo

interlocking forms are sensuous and provide a soothing unity within the Plaza del la Encarnacion (Figure 2.5a). Another example is the Yellow Treehouse Restaurant near Auckland, New Zealand (2008), which was designed by architects Pacific Environments (Figure 2.5b). Like a delicate cocoon attached to a tree 30 feet (10 meters) in the air, it presents beautiful views of the surrounding forest while creating a serene sense of place. Both of these examples display sensual, rhythmic, and serene qualities of form.

The conflation of landscape and built structure was investigated within a larger context with theories of landscape urbanism. The principal posits are that urban themes are designed to achieved urban effects through interdisciplinarity, systemic ecology of place, adaptable territories, fluidity and spontaneous feedback of morphological development, and most importantly, through horizontal fields of urbanism (agrophilia). Another spin-off of landscape urbanism is landform architecture, which draws its inspiration from the geology, topography, and geography of the land, and as architectural reconstructions of nature, it sequesters their qualities of more fluid, adaptable, and responsive forms. The term "hypernatural" might be overzealous, especially within the context of concepts of serene urbanism, yet it emphasizes the importance of rethinking the relationship between human culture and nature.

Less remarkable, yet equally important, are qualities of serene environments that include safety and authenticity. If a place is not safe or authentic, it discourages or decreases the possibility of transcendent experiences. Being safe (from the French, *sauf*) can be defined as free from hurt, and the conditions of being protected against physical, social, cultural, emotional, and psychological harm. So, feeling safe means that one does not anticipate wounding, suffering, or pain, emotionally or physically. Natural landscapes are not always thought of as places of peace and safety. "Barren," "desolate," "oppressive," "brooding," "dark," and "untamed" are often applied to descriptions of wilderness or wild places. Generally, they are not significantly disturbed, modified, or humanized.

Authenticity is a living, real, and genuine experience of nature. It suggests that there is truth and integrity in expression contributing to existing ecological processes within which the natural landscape may exist. An authentic sense of place celebrates the individual and unique characteristics of a particular place or landscape, including topographic, cosmologic, ecologic, and inherent or embodied cultural conditions. Integrity within a serene environment is maintained with continuation and maintenance of the original natural fabric, rather than the need for kitsch or scenographic modifications.

Restoration of the serene combines celestial and terrestrial experiences, tranquillity and beauty, living qualities of the picturesque, and the new directions of biophilia, biomimicry, and landscape urbanism in architecture and planning. From this discussion, it is clear that serenity is a function of nature and human-made environments, and that they are not really separate, but part of an important, sympathetic continuum. In a letter to the World Jewish Congress in 1950, Albert Einstein wrote the following:

> A human being is a part of the whole called by us universe, a part limited in time and space. He experiences himself, his thoughts and feeling as something separated from the rest, a kind of optical delusion of his consciousness. This delusion is a kind of prison for us, restricting us to our personal desires and to affection for a few persons nearest to us. Our task must be to free ourselves from this prison by widening our circle of compassion to embrace all living creatures and the whole of nature in its beauty. Nobody is able to achieve this completely, but the striving for such achievement is in itself a part of the liberation and a foundation for inner security.[33]

Characteristics of serene environments

The serene has been traditionally associated with healing environments and places of exceptional beauty. Serene qualities find expression in these varying places in ways that are applicable to a larger range of place types, especially with residential development. The attributes can be present either in single spaces, infrastructure or within an entire urban environment. Following are 12 primary characteristics associated with a serene environment.

1. *Safe and untroubled* – it must have relative certainty and be calm, stress-reducing, trusting, ordered versus chaotic, comfortable, nonthreatening, and safe from harm.
2. *Authentic* – it must be original and with essential features, honesty, integrity, and truth in expression, that is profoundly real.
3. *Coherent and identifiable* – it must have a lucid atmosphere of serenity with healthy boundaries, an oasis of peacefulness, detached from external interference, clear, and intelligible.
4. *Human scale* – it must be relatable, with measures correspondent to human size and physical capabilities; anthropomorphic dimensions that are well fitted.
5. *Harmonious and balanced* – it must be harmonious, allowing us to revel in the evanescence of all things toward optimum health.
6. *Connectedness with nature* – it has *Wa* (balance with nature), must be aligned with nature, develop a positive relationship with all living things, have experience of the four elements, visible life, and be imbued with vitality.

7. *Mysterious and fascinating* – it has feelings of apprehension, all-powerfulness, wonderment, the sublime, and a sense of the secret.
8. *Enhanced perception and experience of the senses* – it has instinctual aliveness, hearing every sound, seeing broadly and with clarity, detecting smells, touch and materiality, energy detection, along with heightened awareness.
9. *Increase presence* – it has a slow-speed scale, being in the moment, centeredness, experience of reverence, and experience of well-being.
10. *Transformative healing* – it has reduced temporal density, stress reduction, wellness, sanctification, and experience of the numinous.
11. *Existence of grace and beauty* – it has beneficence, material quality, is elegant, subjective, and illusive experience of spirit in form.
12. *Possessing the spirit of place* – it has an intrinsic power, enchantment, cherished qualities of a place, and the presence of something "other."

A serene environment must be safe and untroubled, and this is true for both everyday secular functions as well as for more personal, transcendent purposes. According to the numinous concepts of tremendum and mysterium, this environment can present a certain level of wildness and mystery. This suggests that emergence from a safe urban environment that is known, understood and untroubled into a natural environment is met with certain apprehension, which manifests a certain aliveness.

The place must be authentic, understandable, and easily read, which contributes to a more easily transformative experience. This also aids in the feeling of safety. According to the sociologist Ning Wang, with accelerating globalization under postmodern conditions, it is increasingly difficult for the authenticity of the original, such as the marginal ethnic culture or a natural landscape, to remain immutable.[34] For Turner and Manning,

> authenticity is only possible once the taken-for-granted world and the security it offers are called into question. This is dependent on a specific mood anxiety, which, in subjecting everydayness to questioning, reveals the groundlessness of human existence.[35]

Authenticity can occur on many levels, from overall place form and material selections to actual use and changing functions. The experience of authenticity can be seen as being present, real, and easily perceived in logical, systematic, and practical ways. It also can be felt qualitatively in emotional and experiential terms. Is there an emotional connection, and is the feeling real?

Both authenticity and sense of place can exist in social, geographical, physical, and spiritual ways. One can feel a sense of place within a family, community, or even associated with a nation. A geographic sense of place can relate to identity to a particular region, city, or neighborhood. A physical sense of place can relate to a more intimate landscape or urban setting, even the human body. In this regard, as Kent Rydon explains, "a sense of place results gradually and unconsciously from inhabiting a landscape over time, becoming familiar with its physical properties, accruing history within its confines."[36] A sense of place spiritually is more difficult to define, as it can combine the other ways as well as being something wholly Other. A place identified in these ways has certain characteristics, and as a scene it can be comprehended through experience of momentary connections to them.

A serene environment is coherent and identifiable. It can be read and absorbed, as its boundaries are clear and its form is perceived. This is important in the experience of a physical sense of place.

While many natural environments are awesome and extraordinary in scale, serene environments tend to be more intimate and respond to human scale. This is not to suggest that an expansive view of undulating sand dunes, a snow-filled mountain pass, soft valley fog, ocean view sunset, or even the stillness of a night sky are not serene – they possess a grand or monumental serenity. Human-scale serenity suggests that the place possesses both qualities and characteristics relating to human beings: their size, movements, measures, and speed or timescales. In the habitable environment this refers to the scale of streets, alleys, walking distances, building heights, presence of sidewalks and landscaping elements, material textures, and other spatial complexities and qualities. In the natural environment human scale is found with similar characteristics: paths and the ground cover on which someone walks, clearings, overhanging branches or the height of trees or rock outcrops, plant life, mushrooms, other familiar life forms, even the sounds.

Healing and well-being are positive manifestations made possible by interactions with nature and serene environments. According to Rachel Naomi Remen, MD, it is a healing that is rooted in mystery, and these manifestations are not necessarily cures, but can contribute to positive results.[37] There have been many different outcome measures for research into the benefits of nature and well-being. These include:

- observable clinical signs or medical measures – hormones, blood pressure, and intake of pain-relieving drugs;
- subjective measures such as reported satisfaction, mood, or pain level and developmental observations;
- estimated measures, which may include crime rate changes in part due to natural areas, preventative and general wellness benefits by being in nature; and
- economic measures such as rehabilitation or staff costs due to turnover.

Key to a positive nature experience is an affinity for being outdoors and connected with nature, sensing patterns in nature, and being aware of subtle changes in the outdoor environment. According to Edith Cobb, having a sense of place is important to a child's evolving imagination and personality, as well as to adult creativity.[38]

To be in accord creates harmony, yet opposites and diversity create balance. Taken together in a natural environment, they contribute to the healing and well-being process. Connectedness with nature is important, and there needs to be a balance between stimulation and repose. This paradox results in experiences that are complementary: both invigorating and enlivening, along with stillness and calm. This kind of immersion enhances perception of and activates the senses, so the participant is collected and centered. This in turn can lead to the presence of grace and beauty, involving a deeper transformative experience. As in contemplation, a tranquil beauty occurs – clarity within and quietness without.

In the Zoroastrian tradition, *Spenta Armaita* means progressive serenity: the presence of grace and beauty. According to philosopher Alain de Botton:

> Architecture does possess moral messages; it simply has no power to enforce them. It offers suggestions instead of making laws. It invites, rather than orders us to emulate its spirit, and cannot prevent its own abuse. When we call a chair

or a house beautiful, really what we're saying is that we like the way of life it is suggesting to us.[39]

Grace, deriving from the Latin *gratus* or lucid beauty, is further defined as the seemingly effortless beauty and charm of movement, landscape, form, balance, or proportion, and is considered a state of divine influence. In the Chinese I-Ching or Book of Changes, grace is described in hexagram 22, where the essential nature or function and outer appearance cannot be separated, and success is accomplished in small matters.[40] This is apt because it presupposes the profound experience of beauty with modesty, humility, gratitude, and embodied kindness. Although the word "beauty" is often used and generally understood, it remains difficult to actually define. It is associated with the perceptual experience of giving satisfaction, pleasure, and well-being. Related to a serene environment, it is the positive emotional effect of the serene qualities of the setting on the observer or participant. Both beauty and grace are important characteristics for the healing and calming qualities of place.

It is difficult to discuss numinous environments without addressing spirit of place. From a variety of traditions, such as the Chinese Feng Shui, India's *Vastu Shastra*, Western geomancy, Aboriginal dream places, and the Native American spirit world, the spirit of place is recognized and possesses numerous qualities. The use of *Feng Shui* (literally meaning "wind–water") was a system of auspicious placement of buildings relative to a site's physical and energetic features, such as bodies of water, hills or mountains, slope of the land, orientation to compass points or geomagnetic currents in the ground called "dragon lines." *Feng Shui* was certainly not a new concept, as it had been practiced as early as 4000 BC. The principal goal of *Feng Shui* was to enhance the *chi*, or life force, of a place, thereby improving the health and safety of its inhabitants. As for the Greek myth of Pegasus (see Figure 2.6a), Gail Thomas explains:

> Pegasus springs from duende. From this deadly and potent earth force he soars, and it is when his hoof hits the ground that a well springs forth and the Muses come to dance and sing.[41]

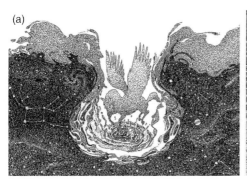

Figure 2.6 Spirit of place: a) Pegasus the divine stallion
Source: Drawing by Phillip Tabb
b) Glastonbury Pool, UK
Source: Photograph by Phillip Tabb

Located near the bottom of the sacred mound and tor, the vertical place-marker at Glastonbury, UK is the chalybeate Chalice Well, also known as the "Blood Well" because of its reddish color due to iron deposits in the water. Flowing downhill from the well is the pool in the shape of a Vesica Pisces (vessel of a fish), an ancient Greek example of sacred geometry (Figure 2.6b). The Vesica Pisces is the seed for the progression of polygonal geometry.

Examples of serene environments are numerous, and most exist undisturbed in nature. Stereotypically, the serene is associated with green rolling hills, sandy curving beaches, beautiful landscape gardens, serpentine ski slopes, tranquil meadows, gentle springs, streams and rivers, and still waters. These places have certain quiescent qualities in common. An obvious natural example is with the oasis that is typically nestled among sensuous sand forms and surrounded by palm trees, giving it a protected sense of place. In the center sits a pristine pool of water.

The example of Portmeirion, North Wales, built between 1925 and 1975, shows a gentle blending of both landscape and architecture (Figure 2.7a). Portmeirion village center was designed by Welsh architect Sir Clough Williams-Ellis in the early twentieth century: he imported fragments from demolished buildings and reconstructed them along the estuary of the River Dwyryd. Portmeirion's architectural bricolage and deliberately fanciful nostalgia have been noted as an influence on the development of postmodernism in architecture. Portmeirion was the setting for the cult television show, *The Prisoner* (ITV, 1967–8) and *Doctor Who* (BBC, 1976 season). The serene qualities are evident in the close relationship between landscape and other human-made elements of the design. The central garden space provides a focus and organization to the entire place. To Lewis Mumford, the architecture was "both romantic and picturesque in Baroque form, 'with tongue in cheek'."[42]

Another example is with Gouverneur Beach on the southern side of Saint Barthélemy Island with its beautiful perspective, gentle shallow waters, privacy, and white sandy beach (Figure 2.7b). The serene is obvious, with the sensuous curving beach, forested hill-defined sense of place, and the changing quality of the surf – seawater and sand beach. There is always something mesmerizing about the ebb and flow of the mutable surf against the sensuous sand.

The Shire, featured in the epic film trilogy *Lord of the Rings* (dir. Peter Jackson, 2001–3), is depicted as a serene community of Hobbiton set apart from the terror and fighting occurring throughout most of Middle Earth. The Shire is depicted as a small but beautiful and fruitful land, beloved by its Hobbit inhabitants. There are green, rolling hills, fertile and freshly tilled earth, ponds and streams, along with gardens and gentle landscaping. The buildings are mostly earth-sheltered and well fitted into the undulating landscape along gently curving trails. The serene qualities permeate the environment and constellation of earth-sheltered cottages, small hamlets and hobbit-scaled villages of the Shire (Figure 2.7c).

Serene environments are present in small doses throughout the built world. Theologian Reinhold Niebuhr's familiar "Serenity Prayer" (adapted by Alcoholics Anonymous) is thoroughly Stoic:

> God, grant me the serenity to accept the things I cannot change;
> The courage to change the things I can,
> And the wisdom to know the difference.[43]

Figure 2.7 Serene environments: a) Portmeirion, Wales, UK
Source: Alamy Stock Photo
b) Gouverneur Beach, Saint Barthélemy Island
c) Tolkien's Shire near Matamata, New Zealand
Source: Shutterstock

Santa Clara Pueblo resident Rina Swentzell concluded a presentation of "Being in Place":

> We all seek significance in our lives,
> It is the way that we go about it is the sacred.[44]

According to Henry David Thoreau:

> Nature will bear the closest inspection. She invites us to lay our eye level with her smallest leaf, and take an insect view of its plain.[45]

Notes

1 Seddon, Keith, *Stoic Serenity: A Practical Course on Finding Inner Peace*, 2007. Available online at www.lulu.com/shop/keith-seddon/stoic-serenity-a-practical-course-on-finding-inner-peace/ebook/product-17560006.html, p. 19.
2 Roberts, Kay and Cunningham, George, "Serenity Concept Analysis and Measurement," *Educational Gerontology* 16(6), 1990, pp. 577–89.

3 Gerber, William, *Serenity: Living with Equanimity, Zest, and Fulfillment by Applying the Wisdom of the World's Greatest Thinkers*, University Press of America, New York, 1986.
4 Ibid.
5 Boyd-Wilson, B.M., Walkey, F.H. and McClure, J., "Serenity, Much More than Just Feeling Calm," *Advances in Psychological Research*, 29, 2004, pp. 35–55.
6 Roberts, Kay T. and Aspy, Cheryl B., "Development of the Serenity Scale," *Journal of Nursing Measurement*, 1, 1993, pp. 145–64.
7 Kunstler, James Howard, "The Ghastly Tragedy of the Suburbs," *TED Talks*, February 2004. Available online at www.ted.com/talks/james_howard_kunstler_dissects_suburbia?language=en (accessed October 2015).
8 Inwood, Brad (ed.), *The Cambridge Companion to The Stoics*, Cambridge University Press, Cambridge, 2003.
9 Seddon, *Stoic Serenity.*
10 Steele, John, *Geomancy: Consciousness and Sacred Sites*, Trigon Communications, New York, 1985.
11 Gilpin, William, *Three Essays: On Picturesque Beauty; On Picturesque Travel; and On Sketching Landscapes; to Which is Added a Poem on Landscape Painting*, London Publishers, London, 1792.
12 Thoreau, Henry David, *Walden: Or, Life in the Woods*, Shambhala Books, Boston, MA, 1992 (orig. pub. 1854), p. 73.
13 Centers for Disease Control and Prevention, "Preparing for and Responding to Extreme Heat and Cold Events." Available online at www.cdc.gov/nceh/hsb/disaster/heatandcold.htm (accessed November 2015). Guha-Sapir, Debarati, Hoyois, Philippe and Below, Regina, Annual Disaster Statistical Review 2012, Centre for Research on the Epidemiology of Disasters, Brussels, 2013.
14 Mind, "Ecotherapy – The Green Agenda for Mental Health," University of Essex. Available online at www.mind.org.uk/media/273470/ecotherapy.pdf (accessed June 9, 2016).
15 Ryan, Richard M., Weinstein, Netta, Bernstein, Jessey, Brown, Kirk Warren, Mistretta, Louis, and Gagne, Marylene, "Vitalizing Effects of Being Outdoors and in Nature," *Journal of Environmental Psychology*, 30, 2010, pp. 159–68.
16 Lawlor, Robert, *Sacred Geometry: Philosophy and Practice*, Thames and Hudson, London, 1982.
17 Collins, Pamela, "Biodiversity: Its Benefits to People and the Environment," November 12, 2012. Available online at www.scsoft.de/et/et2.nsf//C6C22D110A22560A05256885004D1 DD9?OpenDocument&gt (accessed October 2015).
18 Phillip Tabb, testimonial of a serene experience in Island Park, Idaho, 1960.
19 The Findhorn Community, *The Findhorn Garden: Pioneering a New Vision of Man and Nature in Cooperation*, Harper & Row, New York, 1975; "The Findhorn Ecovillage." Available online at www.findhorn.org/aboutus/ecovillage/ecovillage-at-findhorn/ (accessed December 10, 2015).
20 Devall, Bill, *Deep Ecology: Living as if Nature Mattered*, Gibbs Smith, Layton, UT, 2001.
21 Eliade, Mircea, *The Sacred and the Profane: The Nature of Religion: The Significance of Religious Myth, Symbolism, and Ritual within Life and Culture*, trans. William R. Trask, Harcourt Brace & Company, San Diego, CA, 1961, p. 11.
22 Otto, Rudolf, *The Idea of the Holy*, Oxford University Press, Oxford, 1958.
23 Ibid.
24 Steele, *Geomancy.*
25 Foucault, Michel, *The Order of Things*, New York: Vintage Books, 1971.
26 Roberts, Mark D., "Thin Places: A Biblical Investigation," 2012. Available online at www.patheos.com/blogs/markdroberts/series/thin-places/ (accessed June 2015).
27 Casement, Ann and Tacey, David (eds), *The Idea of the Numinous*, Routledge, London, 2006.
28 "Johann Friedrich Herbart," *Stanford Encyclopedia of Philosophy*. Available online at http://plato.stanford.edu/entries/johann-herbart/ (accessed June 6, 2016).
29 Corbett, Lionel, "Varieties of Numinous Experiences: The Experience of the Sacred in the Therapeutic Process," in Casement and Tacey (eds) *The Idea of the Numinous*, p. 54.

30 Brownell, Blaine and Swackhamer, Marc, *Hyper-natural: Architecture's New Relationship with Nature*, Princeton Architectural Press, New York, 2015.

31 Browning, William, Ryan, Catherine and Clancy, Joseph, *14 Patterns of Biophilic Design: Improving Health and Well-being in the Built Environment*, Terrapin Bright Green, LLC, New York, 2014.

32 Pawlyn, Michael, *Biomimicry in Architecture*, RIBA Publishing, London, 2011.

33 Einstein, Albert, "Quotes on Compassion." Available online at http://hubpages.com/education/Albert-Einsteins-Quote-on-Compassion (accessed October 2015). Calaprice, Alice, *The New Quotable Einstein*, Princeton University Press, Princeton, NJ, 2005, p. 206.

34 Wang, Ning, "Rethinking Authenticity in Tourism Experience," *Annals of Tourism Research* 26(2), 1999, p. 349–70, p. 358.

35 Turner, Charles and Manning, Phil, "Placing Authenticity – On Being a Tourist: A Reply to Pearce and Moscardo," *Journal of Sociology* 24(1), 1988, pp. 136–9.

36 Kent Rydon, in Christy, Larry, "A Sense of Place," 2011. Available online at www.fishdecoys.net/pages/SenseofPlace.htm (accessed November 2015).

37 Remen, Rachel Naomi, *Recovery of the Sacred: Some Thoughts on Medical Reform*, Context Institute, Langley, WA, 1997, p. 1.

38 Cobb, Edith, *The Ecology Imagination in Childhood*, Spring Publishing, Washington, DC, 1988.

39 de Botton, Alain, *The Architecture of Happiness*, McClelland & Stewart, Toronto, 2006, p. 7.

40 Wilhelm, Richard, *I-Ching: The Book of Changes*, Bollingen Series XIX, Princeton University Press, Princeton, NJ, 1950.

41 *The Muses*, ed. Gail Thomas, Dallas Institute Publications, Dallas, TX, 1994, p. 7.

42 Mumford, Lewis, "From Crochet Castle to Arthur's Seat," in *The Highway and the City*, New American Library, New York, 1964 (orig. pub. 1962), n.p.

43 "The Serenity Prayer" by Reinhold Niebuhr, 1943.

44 Rina Swentzell is a Native American resident of New Mexico, and gave a keynote address at the symposium for Architecture, Culture, and Spirituality at Ghost Ranch, New Mexico in June 2015.

45 Henry David Thoreau, diary entry, October 22, 1839, in *The Heart of Thoreau's Journals*, ed. Odell Shepard, Dover Publications, Mineola, NY, 2003, p. 9.

3   Urban perspectives

A city is a place where a small boy, as he walks through it, may see something that will tell him what he wants to do his whole life.[1]

The process of urbanism is integral to human habitation and existence, and an investigation of the history of settlement form-making reveals some common placemaking threads that are even present in contemporary urbanism. Placement adjacent to transportation corridors, natural resources, and land free from the effects of natural hazards such as flood plains, volcanoes and earthquakes, is common. Nucleation, specialization, and immediate connections to agriculture have been an integral part of urbanization. Also, there are differences in which some characteristics and locations are beneficial, while others are more detrimental. However, with modern city-making has come the challenge of increasing populations, growth, larger buildings, more complex transportation networks, and further separation of functional uses.

Contemporary urbanism

Modern, postmodern, and hypermodern approaches to urbanism vary, both in philosophical approaches and in form and character. The values that drive these movements also differ. The idealistic values afforded by the enlightenment of the nineteenth century were left in favor of modernism with its values placed on technology and market liberalism, and in architecture on pure idealistic, functionalist, and homogenous forms. According to the French philosopher Gilles Lipovetsky, modernism was linked to autonomy of the individual and the breakaway from tradition, and it possessed two values: freedom and equality.[2] Postmodern urbanism displayed a shift from expert-driven planning designs toward participatory processes; from a planning view assuming superiority of new, "modern" forms toward a view appreciative of the historic nature of settlement design; and from a planning focus on functionalism and efficiency toward a focus on human-scale, urbane, and site-derivative forms.[3] Postmodern values included pluralism, diversity, and participatory engagement. Hypermodern urbanism, which also has been referred to as "post-postmodernism" or "metamodernism," promotes advanced technology with its ability to overcome detrimental natural phenomena and repudiation of the past. Hypermodernity is hyperpower, hyperconsumptive and hypernarcissistic.

Urban territories are a function of location, zoning, density, transport technology, economic opportunities, and function. If energy was cheap and the prevailing transport method was the automobile, then, according to Echenique's formula, this naturally translates into a dispersed, low-density settlement form.[4] Alternatively, mass transport and pedestrian movement suggest a more concentrated and dense fabric – suggesting two very different cultural styles of living and settlement form. This suggests that the different territories common to urban areas will have different relationships among these three contributing factors.

These differences can be generally traced using an urban transect, which articulates these varying forms from urban to rural environments. A transect is essentially a geographical cross-section between the most urban part of a settlement center or core, to the most rural area at the edge. A transect articulates the agglomeration of people, buildings, roads, other urban elements, and natural features of the place in a hierarchical spatial fashion. The term "transect" was borrowed from ecology, which describes changes in habitat and plant distribution over an ecological gradient or zone, usually defined by two edges from the ridge of a wooded hill through a meadow to a water source below. Biologists and ecologists use transects to study the many symbiotic elements that contribute to habitats where certain plants and animals thrive. In the urban context, the transect delineates the sectional transition from the more focused, dense, diverse, and intense parts of the urban fabric, gradually decreasing in incremental stages to the most open, tranquil, and natural land uses beyond the settlement. Andrew Thorburn and Leon Krier[5] articulated the urban–rural transect. The town planner Andres Duany created a six-zone classification as follows:

1. urban core;
2. urban center;
3. general urban;
4. suburban;
5. rural; and
6. natural.

According to Duany, all possible urban kinds of development fall into this model. In other words, human habitation can be modeled into this hierarchal spatial system and locational organization, offering coding and urban design guidelines for each of the zones.[6] The urban-to-rural transect offers the possibility for all kinds of urban development. Human habitation can be placed within a hierarchal spatial system of varying densities, as well as varying degrees of connection to nature and urban activities.[7]

Figures 3.1a and 3.1b shows a seven-zone transect that progresses from hinterland to urban core, and a typical urban house found in Charleston with side entry, porch and garden.

A healthy urban environment will embody diversity, authenticity, and meaning. These are features that support the functional and symbolic experiences of a particular place. They are active and engaging through the efforts of the insiders, those living and committed to participating and sustaining the place. There is humanness in the scale that contributes to creating an enhanced cultural setting, community formation, and greater depth of meaning. It is a place of human life, of personal involvement. According to architect Louis I. Kahn, who hints that there is something less profane: "A street is a room by agreement,"[8] meaning that human participation is needed for community.

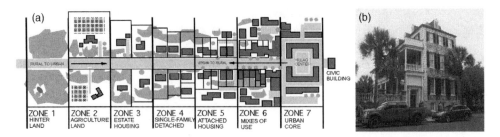

Figure 3.1 Urbanism: a) Rural-to-urban transect b) Charleston house, South Carolina, USA
Note: The plan diagram of a seven-zone transect was adapted by the author from earlier rural–urban transects by Thorburn (1971), Krier (1985) and Duany (1999).
Source: Drawing and photograph by Phillip Tabb

The rural environment encompasses fertile ground for agriculture, open space for ecological processes, forest land, geological sites, recreational areas, and land of natural beauty, and is punctuated with small settlement areas of low population and density. Rural territory is geographic area considered to be outside of cities (urban areas and clusters). Quantitative definitions use population size as a determinant, where rural areas comprise open country and settlements with fewer than 2,500 residents and densities as high as 999 per square mile, or as low as one person per square mile. Qualitative definitions apply diversity of mixed uses, agglomerations contributing to community formation, and the feeling that it is an urban place.

The in-between environments, which include suburbs, interstitial infrastructural space, and exurban enclaves, occupy the territory between discrete inner cities and natural hinterlands or rural areas economically tied to the urban catchment of large cities or mega-agglomerations. Often fragmented, these areas are characterized by commuting connections to the host city, functional or single-use zoning, and lower in density. Suburbs have grown more rapidly than city centers since 1920 in the United States; however, 2010 marked a shift back to urban areas because of quality-of-life factors including improved safety, lower commuting distances, and access to cultural amenities.

There are three general urban territories in which to direct sustainable planning and design approaches. They are the urban center, suburban areas, and exurban environments (counter-urban). For city centers, strategies should focus on:

- improved transportation modes;
- upgrading to more efficient energy technologies;
- in-fill, mixed-use development;
- provision of more housing and schools;
- introduction of urban agriculture;
- creation of coherent pedestrian and bicycle networks; and
- provision for more life-support functions.

For the suburban areas, they require restructuring to provide:

- greater mixes of use;
- densification;

- less dependence on the automobile;
- attention to pedestrian zones that are safe and accessible; and
- the introduction of suburban agriculture.

Finally, for the exurban areas, there could be greater nucleation, and the creation of more self-sufficient settlement forms. This would include provision of:

- appropriate mixes of use;
- density and urban amenities in the nucleated centers; and
- connection to nearby agriculture.

Each zone should develop a set of sustainable measures appropriate to its context, and it should be recognized that greater levels of sustainability can be achieved by interdependence with the other adjacent territories and urban enclaves.

Between-place transportation, cross-programming, and area connections are equally critical. While migration patterns have moved generally from the country to the city, this trend is changing. A study by the Carsey Institute at the University of New Hampshire in 2006 reported that much of the twentieth-century urban areas experienced growth, but that migration direction changed in the 1970s to nonmetropolitan areas.[9] With 75 percent of inhabitants living in urban areas, they have settled on only 2 percent of the land in the United States, and growth is naturally redirecting. According to geographer Brian Berry, counter-urbanization is a demographic process whereby people move from urbanized areas to rural areas, as a reaction to overcrowding and inner-city deprivation.[10]

With advances in digital technology, new employment opportunities, and the increase of urban decay and associated problems, people are moving to the suburbs and beyond. In some instances there have been better preschool, elementary, and middle school educational opportunities as new communities have formed. In addition, there is a retirement migration to rural regions. According to the urban planner Timothy Beatley, sprawl is caused by many factors, including economic and cultural factors.[11] At the center of this urban flight and drift outward is a desire to return to the sanity of a more rural life and the values that it has afforded. Many are settling further away from urban concentrations to avoid the chaos, complexity, and lack of health and safety associated with urban modernity. Growth is inevitable, as is decay; but the problem is that the demand for dynamic change and expansion is feeding rapid uncontrolled growth, or sprawl – particularly evident at the edge of urban development. Piecemeal and counter-urban growth patterns have emerged to accommodate this change.

At the heart of this pattern are our lifestyle choices, our dependency on certain life-support systems, and the resulting disorder, dysfunction, and fragmentation, giving rise to a contemporary placelessness. Moreover, the current discourse and applications in response to growth seem to continue to be dominated by vapid suburban sprawl or formalist approaches, creating conservative nostalgia and offering short-term solutions rather than addressing long-term sustainable issues. Moreover, in some instances there is what the urban planner Nan Ellin calls "razzmatazz," or a hypermodernity born from a cynical and even desperate urbanism. The great recession of 2007–9 slowed development down, which was somewhat disempowering, but at the same time it gave reason to rethink the way we may want to proceed with urban development.[12]

This may be a blessing in disguise. Designing for serene and livable settlements requires that architecture, planning, and design decisions be based on assumptions different from those of reductionist, prescriptive, heroic, utopian, formalist, and wasteful planning approaches:

- *vapid suburbanism* – sprawl, uncontrolled growth, single-use development, low urbanism and low density, automobile dependent, and large land area usage;
- *nostalgic formalism* – prescriptive, controlling, neo-traditional, formulaic, focused on compositional elements, and postmodern new urban forms;
- *utopian design* – idealistic, unrealistic, sociopolitical, unyielding perfection, noble, nuanced visionary urbanism, climax community,[13] and quixotical;
- *hypermodernity* – self-indulgent, ahistorical, high-technology-driven, narcissistic, controlling, heroic urbanism, and preoccupied with hypercontemporary culture;
- *dystopian visions* – media-driven images of future urban designs with high-density, high-rise architecture, advanced technology, science-fiction modes of travel, and often accompanied by destructive forces.

In research conducted at the Centre for Configurational Studies in 1985, the architect Peter Rickaby analyzed six different regional growth patterns and found that there were substantial variations in fuel consumption between the scenarios.[14] Two growth configurations showed fuel savings along with increased transport benefits. First was the pattern called "urban containment," where growth occurred within existing cities, and second was "dispersed nucleated villages." The village model contained about 1,000 people and a mix of nonresidential functions supporting reduced automobile use. This research showed that sustainably responsible development could be achieved at both the center and the edge of metropolitan areas. Developed by the German geographer Walter Christaller, central place theory suggests that a settlement functions as a set of services surrounded by a residential community, which is the process of nucleation; and as a settlement increases in size, the greater the range and number of goods and services.[15] In 1985, architect Leon Krier suggested that a community should reach an optimum size, then grow through a process of multiplication rather than continuing expansion through gross addition.[16] The size of a nucleated place is of consequence in determining serene urbanism.

Although systemic constellation theory was applied originally to family dynamics, it suggests that independent yet interconnected parts of a system create a combination of actions affecting the collective whole. This means that interrelated communities, and the individual sustainable practices that they employ, can support an even greater constellation and synergy of sustainability. Taken together, these concepts and theories form a basis for a way of looking at the anatomy of sustainable urbanism from a placemaking viewpoint. The assertion here is that the more a development becomes a place, the greater the opportunities for sustainability. The included benefits are long-term positive health, community, and livability effects. Further, place provides a nurturing context for the possibilities of serene and numinous experiences, both urban and rural.

A view of existing villages and hamlets provides examples of evolving settlement patterns that usually represent rich and human places, notwithstanding their embodied sustainable characteristics. Also, the combination of golf courses and residential

Figure 3.2 Aerial view of Castiglion Fiorentino, Italy
Source: Photograph by Phillip Tabb

communities suggests the idea that an amenity can be a means to attract community life. Many sustainable communities of the past several decades have demonstrated residential-scale renewable technologies and the constraints that render them more efficient.

The New Urbanism and its neo-traditional approach to urbanism have certainly provided interesting discourse and steps toward more dense, coherent suburb-making. Sustainable urbanism, as well as the emerging agricultural urbanism, are taking a more holistic and integrated approach to residential development. Although not common, spiritual communities demonstrate a highly place-bound settlement model where care and stewardship of the place are highly valued. Traditional settlements embody many urban characteristics that can be clearly seen. Figure 3.2 is an aerial view of the Tuscan town of Castiglion Fiorentino, with its perimeter surrounded by agricultural land, the medieval bounding wall, dense urban block fabric, pedestrian streets, and central cathedral with public plaza.

Placemaking is an approach where nature, health, sustainability, and community are all vital ingredients for a next generation of urbanism. Informing studies and examples include:

- *traditional village form* – thousands of English villages demonstrate a close relationship to the land, pedestrian scale, and an evolved layering of nonresidential land uses organically woven into the village fabric;
- *amenity-driven development* – projects that integrate magnet functions to attract, complement, and enhance residential development;

- *sustainable communities* – the introduction of sustainable technologies and green building practices into community planning and design;
- *New Urbanism* – the development of traditional settlement forms and urban components promoting walkable neighborhoods, density, and smart growth;
- *sustainable urbanism* – the development of sound principles of sustainability and urbanism focused on settlement form, transportation and building practices;
- *agrarian urbanism* – the introduction of organic agriculture as an integrated complement to residential development ("farm-to-table");
- *constellating urbanism* – where discrete individual and walkable settlements are formulated into a greater, interconnected whole; and
- *spiritual communities* – the infusion of sensitivity, stewardship, health and fellowship with the land, community, and evolving manifestation process.

Alternative urban perspectives

The spatial territories defined from the intensity of an urban center through to the edge and natural environment beyond was one defining dimension. Most think of urban as being large geographical areas of continuously built-up density, cities composed of tall buildings, street canyons, and networks, and large populations of people. Suburbs and adjacent townships are counter-urban strategies common to most large urban complexes. They tend to follow re-nucleated settlement patterns with centers located adjacent to highways. Another way to view urbanization is in the smaller-scale interactions between individual elements. For example, in the UK, two residences sited adjacent to one another and separated by a distance of 164 yards (150 meters) or more are at a sufficient distance from one another that they do not relate, and therefore are not considered urban. However, closer distances offer opportunities for certain relationships or "urban" amenities, such as a shared driveway, alley, utility service, or green space.

Modern urbanism

Modern urbanism grew largely from emerging industrial cultures, progressive social transformations, and rapid population growth. It was characterized by rejection of the designs of the past, which were replaced by new forms, technologies, equipment, and materials. It represented a socially progressive trend of thought that affirmed the power of human beings to create, improve, and reshape their environment. Power production, transportation, and building technology were all changing, enabling the relatively rapid creation of our modern cities worldwide. For example, suburban shopping centers and the evolution of the high-rise building type occurred because of this confluence and many technological innovations, including steel and concrete construction, curtain wall facades, the elevator, mechanical air conditioning; least considered was the telephone, which allowed for communication to the outside world from within these towers (Figure 3.3a). Not only did growth project skyward; correspondingly, it spread outward horizontally. Single-use functional zoning created a patchwork of disconnected land use functions between city centers and the surrounding suburbs. Functional zoning is another consequence of modern planning where human activity is divided into an organization of separate uses: residential, commercial, religious, recreational, and office park, all connected by automobile networks. Automobile highways

Figure 3.3 Modern urbanism: a) Chicago city center, Illinois, USA
Source: Alamy Stock Photo
b) Shopping center development
Source: Shutterstock

and large expanses of parking adjacent to fragmented commercial developments prolif-
erated this in-between urban landscape (Figure 3.3b). Finally, the uncontrolled process
of growth by addition and outward expansion created residential districts that con-
sumed agricultural land, and were oversized and lacking in pedestrian connections to
critical, nonresidential land uses such as schools, shopping, and health care.

As the complexity of urban planning has increased, so have the length of time and
costs required to complete the process. The time-intensive nature and high costs of
planning are two of the biggest criticisms. Proposed schemes may be obsolete before
they are fully implemented. Most contemporary urban design continues along lines of
automobile-intensive planning, single-use development, top-down urban design practices, and realized through global rather than local economies.

Postmodern urbanism

Collective postmodern measures such as the New Urbanism movement were largely
influenced by the postmodern agenda, and reacted to the rampant suburban sprawl,
functional zoning laws, and low density, promoting more compact, mixed-use, and
neo-traditional settlement designs. New Urban developments were influenced by central place theory[17] with intensive optimum markets in settlement centers. Places such
as Poundbury in Dorset, UK (Leon Krier), Seaside, Florida (Duany Plater-Zyberk), and
the transit-oriented developments in California (Calthorpe Associates) were among
the notable examples of this new movement.

There were two initial schools of thought in the early stages of New Urbanism in
the United States. The first was the development of new satellite communities, commonly located in the east and southeast that were based on traditional town planning
practices. These included organizational planning devices such as orthogonal grids,
city blocks, hierarchy of roads, tree-lined streets, village centers, walkable scale, and
varying lot sizes and housing typologies. The second was planning and design reforms
to conventional large-scale housing development practices, most often located on the

Figure 3.4 Postmodern urbanism: a) Poundbury, Dorset, UK (Leon Krier)
Source: Alamy Stock Photo
b) Seaside, Florida, USA (DPZ)
Source: Photograph by Phillip Tabb

West Coast, which generally included use and density mixes, transportation nodes and modal changes, formal geometry, and usually with larger-scale and relatively functional zoning schemes.

According to Ruth Durack, the New Urbanism models were, by necessity, fully planned and regulated environments, fiercely resistant to change and any deviation from the rigid encyclopedic rules that govern their form and function.[18] While they incorporated some sustainable planning strategies, such as densification, mixed-use, pedestrian orientation, and varying transportation modes, they were far from being truly "green." Their architecture was largely nostalgic, referential and spurious, as opposed to authentic, climate, resource, and energy-responsive. For example, criticisms of Laguna West, California, were aimed at the extreme automobile dependency and the conforming singularity-of-style architecture (many of the more recent homes incorporated four-car garages). However, its improved density of seven dwelling units per acre (17 units per hectare) and the transit service were considered a success (Figure 3.4a and 3.4b illustrate Poundbury, Dorset, UK and Seaside, Florida, USA).

Utopian designs

Utopian designs are not a new approach to planning, as they seek to express ideal and model qualities. Throughout history and until recently, many utopian projects have been a research laboratory for both urban planners and theorists. The term *utopia* in Greek means "not-place," suggesting that utopian designs were ideal and unrealistic in physical manifestation.[19] They are near-perfect concepts for social order, human habitation, and relations between nature and the built environment.

New Harmony, Indiana, USA is an intentional community that was established in 1814 as a utopian experiment to advance education, scientific research, and governance models. Originally, the German immigrant George Rapp led the New Harmony Society. In 1825, the town was purchased by Scottish industrialist Robert Owen, but soon became unsustainable due to several factors, including the lack of individual sovereignty and private property ownership. Socialist programs quickly transformed into

Figure 3.5 Utopian propositions: a) New Harmony, Indiana, USA b) Brasilia, capital city
    of Brazil
Source: Wikimedia Commons

individualism by 1828.[20] Today, New Harmony has nearly 800 residents (2010 census), and is considered a historic town that is viewed as a vacationers' and researchers' dream place (Figure 3.5a).

The design for Atlantis in Adeje, Tenerife was designed by architect Leon Krier and, while using a mythical Greek in name, it more resembled a composition of Italian and Egyptian buildings and monument forms. It was designed as a completely pedestrian environment cascading down to the coast of the Atlantic Ocean. The town was created for art and culture and was conceived as an urban academy covering 12 acres (5 hectares). Its program called for a host of exhibitions, meetings, performances, and activities connected with the life of an artists' colony. It was seen as a gathering of scientists, thinkers, patrons and students living together, working, debating and taking part in the revitalization of ecological, cultural and aesthetic values.[21]

Other utopian experiments were Octagon City near Humbolt, Kansas (1856) that was considered a vegetarian utopia, Ebenezer Howard's Garden City (1902) was a diagram with a nucleated center, concentric urban zones, radial circulation connections and parks, agriculture and green spaces, Ville Radieuse (1924) designed by Le Corbusier was considered a machine utopia, Broadacre City (1932) was designed by Frank Lloyd Wright and expressed large open spaces, low density, locally produced goods and services, and rural character, Richard Buckminster Fuller's geodesic dome designs applied to the urban scale (1971), and Black Rock City, which is a tribute to Burning Man, and an annual week-long Labor Day pilgrimage with nearly 70,000 people leaving no trace (1990). The utopian design for Brasilia was founded in 1960 (Figure 3.5b). These and many other utopian schemes were forward thinking and to some extent influenced planning practice of today.

Hypermodernism

Hypermodernity in architecture refers to designs that are self-referential, outright repudiations of the past, and which champion extremes in form, materials, and new technologies. Hypermodernity differs from modernity in that it has even more commitment to reason and to an ability to improve individual choice and freedom.

Gilles Lipovetsky argues that we have entered a new phase of hypermodernity, characterized by hyperconsumption and hypermodern individualism, and that hypermodernity is furthered by environments that encourage individuals to consume for their own personal pleasure, rather than to enhance their social status.[22] It reflects a deepening or intensification of modernity. Typically this is manifested in a forward-looking commitment to science and knowledge: it posits a particular regard to the convergence of technology and biology, and a diminution or outright rejection of forms of the past. According to Michael Weinstock, discussing the hypernatural:

> Culture evolves; it is a system of descent with modifications, in which social and ecological forces determined which cultural variants are transmitted through time.[23]

Hyper-urbanism describes city-making that is extremely, even deeply, modern and futuristic, with a forward-looking commitment to science and knowledge. It is the adoration of the emergent as physically productive, and the rise of the new economically prosperous. Cities such as Shanghai, China, Abu Dhabi, United Arab Emirates, Songdo, South Korea, and Dholera, India are among a host of shiny new cities displaying hypermodern tendencies (Figure 3.6a). References to magic, and an underlying flexible self-identity often coupled with a strong irony of statement, categorize this antithetical approach. Even the capricious and complex designs that might be considered hyper-postmodern are present, such as the Gas Natural building in Barcelona, Spain by architect Enric Miralles Moya (Figure 3.6b). These expressions represent the idea that in this age, anything is possible regardless of its appropriateness. At this scale the so-called "American Dream" transformed and shifted to national and cultural survival objectives, with access to vast amounts of global resources in order to build and sustain a future world; and it reflected what Fareed Zakaria refers to as: "the rise of the rest."[24]

Figure 3.6 Hyper-urbanism: a) Dubai cityscape b) Gas Natural building, Barcelona, Spain (Enric Miralles Moya)
Source: Alamy Stock Photo

Dystopian urban fiction

Visions of future urbanism are led by progressive new developments and, to some extent, science-fiction media depictions. Even the discovery of the Higgs Boson has been question by theoretical physicists such as Stephen Hawking, as leading to a vacuum decay and doomsday scenario. In the film *Terminator* (dir. James Cameron, 1984), technology was characterized as "the machines," which became a self-aware synthetic intelligence on Judgment Day in 1991. In the interest of self-preservation, they waged war on the entire human race to fulfill mandates of their original programming. The future was depicted as a dystopian, mechanized world in a dark, post-apocalyptic landscape. The world is seen as a soulless, lifeless environment, the architecture industrial and mechanical in nature. *The Matrix* (dir. Wachowski Brothers, 1999) presented a world created by sentient machines to subdue the human population. The present is characterized much as it is today; however, the future in the twenty-first century is bleak, where machines harvest humans for bioelectricity. A resistance exists in a subterranean environment, out of reach of the machines. The vision is of dense habitation devoid of natural sunlight and other lifeforms.

Avatar (dir. James Cameron, 2009) takes place on the uninhabitable moon Pandora, where humans in search of a valuable mineral, unobtanium, are in conflict with the local population of inhabitants.[25] The indigenous Na'vi possess a biological neural network connection with the life force and mother goddess, Eywa. The Na'vi practice a reverent way of living in harmony with this incredibly beautiful and extraordinary environment. The film contrasts the anthro-technological prowess, disrespectful, and concurring nature of humans versus the interconnected, sensitive, and respectful ways of the local inhabitants. Contrast is amplified between the magical and vital local environment with the controlled and high-tech human environment. *Elysium* (dir. Neill Blomkamp, 2013) is a science-fiction action film that presents two diametrically opposed settings in 2154: a ravaged, over-populated, and polluted Earth, and a utopian, luxurious, and technically advanced and terra-formed space habitat. The film brings to light themes that are present today, such as overpopulation, poverty, exploitation, immigration, health care, and injustice. Elysium is shown as a sterilized, clean, spacious, ultramodern, and suburban space habitat.

The *Divergent* series (dir. Neil Burger, 2014) is set in the isolated and post-apocalyptic ruins of Chicago, Illinois, where the social structure is organized into five distinct groups: the selfless, peaceful, honest, brave, and intelligent. Designed with these specific roles to maintain social stability within society, human nature and individual will are suppressed. The urbanism is functionally zoned, with adaptive reuse of the ruinous Chicago environment. *The Giver* (dir. Phillip Noyce, 2014) is a social science-fiction film that depicts humanity with a strict social system designed to preserve and order daily life. Weather is controlled, the past is forgotten, with the exception of one member called a "receiver," emotions are repressed, and individuation is discouraged. Inhabitants live on top of a flat, mesa-like landform, with repetitive communities and identical dwellings that are all positioned in a highly structured, geometric-mandalic pattern.

Dozens of other films, such as *Back to the Future* (dir. Robert Zemeckis, 1985), *Total Recall* (dir. Paul Verhoeven, 1990), *The Stand* (dir. Mick Garris, 1994), *The Postman* (dir. Kevin Costner, 1997), *The Day After Tomorrow* (dir. Roland Emmerich, 2004), *The Hunger Games* (dir. Gary Ross, Francis Lawrence, 2012–14), *District 9* (dir. Neill Blomkamp, 2009), *The Book of Eli* (dir. Albert and Allen Hughes, 2010), *Inception* (dir.

Christopher Nolan, 2010), and *Tomorrowland* (dir. Brad Bird, 2015) all portray the future with grim imagery filled with violence, mass destruction, resource depletion, environmental degradation, social disorder, insatiable desire for power, or obsessive struggles for survival (Figures 3.7a–c). The settings for these fictions often display disorder, chaos, destruction of nature, and advanced technology. The cityscapes are seen either as places of destitution and destruction, or visions of ultramodern, high-rise or sculptured architecture as foundations for fictional worlds. Thankfully, these visions incorporate some moments of sanity and glimmers of hope. There is concern about the role that these images play in becoming affirmations and prophetic visions for actual city-making and present-day urban design. As the urban environment changes to meet the evolving future, new paradigms may be required to inform more resilient and appropriate places to inhabit. Hopefully, these evolving places will retain some degree of humanness and respect for nature.

While these projections depict a rather bleak future, today there is development that echoes them. In China, urbanization is much more lucrative than conserving agricultural land, so the municipalities are eager to build. As a result, many new cities called "ghost cities" were constructed, devoid of inhabitants (Figure 3.7c).[26] Overzealous urbanization has raised speculation that the list of ghost towns will continue to grow, as the central government reins in speculative buying and property prices. Places such as Zhengdong (planned for 5 million people), Kangbashi (planned for 1 million people), Ganzhou (planned for 500,000 residents), Wenzhou, Changzhou, and Sanya are dense ghost cities, with vacant 20-story apartment buildings and lifeless streets. Most of the housing that has been built in these empty districts are luxury condominiums and villas. This gives new meaning to the concept of "heaven on earth." While these are dramatic images for future urbanization, more earthly and humane solutions are needed. However, in the face of current global economic interests and hypermodern tendencies, it will take a powerful turnabout to change this popular direction. Perhaps the best consequence of these dystopian visions is the move toward greater density, but they still need more attention to human scale and integrated nature:

> When you drive the new expressway to the airport in the Chinese city of Luliang, you are as likely to come across a stray dog as another vehicle. When I recently drove it, a farmer was riding in a three-wheel flatbed truck and heading in the wrong direction. But it didn't matter. There was no oncoming traffic.[27]

Beneficial characteristics of urbanism

While problems continue to accompany city-dwelling, there are also numerous benefits – especially given the fact that half of the world's population lives in urban environments at this time. According to the United Nations, today 54 percent of the world's population live in urban areas, a proportion that is expected to increase to 66 percent by 2050, and this includes 28 mega-cities worldwide with populations of more than 10 million people in 2014. July of 2007 marked the first time that the population balance shifted to urban areas. According to Melinda Beck, for many urban dwellers, the country conjures up images of clean air, fresh food and physical activities.[28] However, in the United States, people residing in major cities live longer, healthier lives overall than their country cousins – a reversal from decades past. Major benefits of urban living include public transportation and walkability, proximity of attractions, amenities and entertainment, diversity of restaurants, shopping and other retail commerce,

Figure 3.7 Dystopian fiction: a) Futuristic *Tomorrowland*

Source: Image courtesy of Atlaspix/Alamy

Note: The urban images presented in *Tomorrowland* were not too dissimilar to many that already exist today. These images are dominated by vertical high-rise buildings, the spaghetti of roadways and infrastructure, density of form and the nonexistence of nature.

b) Dystopian *District 9*

Source: Alamy Stock Photo

c) China's "ghost cities"

Source: Shutterstock

possibilities of social engagement and networking, access to medical care and services, and to all levels of education from preschool through continuing education for adults. With earlier and smaller cities, access to employment was fairly convenient, but unfortunately, with the horizontal expansion of larger cities and their associated suburbs, this commuting distance has increased. Among the benefits to urban living are the following:

- more robust commerce and economic activity;
- employment opportunities and work specializations;
- access to urban amenities, including large community venues;
- access to diversity of goods and services;
- access to municipal services (fire, police, utilities);
- places for spontaneous social interaction and networking;
- concentrations allowing for cultural and institutional functions;
- ability to support larger social, entertainment, and sport venues;
- access to a diversity of health facilities;
- attraction of more multicultural and diverse populations;
- place-marking and identity-making;
- sustainable measures are enabled in more dense environments;
- varying transportation modes: plane, train, mass transit, pedestrian;
- greater land preservation;
- infrastructure efficiency.

One of the major advantages to urbanism is the occurrence of exciting, stimulating, diverse and complex urban spaces and amenities, such as those shown with Burano, Italy and the Pearl Street Mall in Boulder, Colorado (Figures 3.8a and 3.8b). Both of these urban places are colorful, festive, human in scale, and possess qualities of nature. They are inviting and support social engagement with shops, restaurants, and cafes within well-defined urban outdoor spaces. Figure 3.8c shows the interesting urbanism of Oia, Santorini with its complex, almost random, cascading and iconic architectural forms. At the top is a meandering narrow street filled with shops and restaurants.

Another of the advantages to urbanism is the benefit afforded by close proximity to commercial and economic development. The urban context places people closer to one another and in more direct contact with goods and services. The economic effects suggest that the cost of living should be more affordable due to proximity, convenience, and reduced travel cost. The design of the commercial–residential interaction is also a factor in potential economic benefits. According to John Mathews, urban layout and density have a significant effect on the magnitude and reach of the travel and straight-line effects on price.[29] As urban layout becomes more integrated, the positive price effect of proximity increases. Both are a positive consequence of urbanization. It should be noted that the larger the population base, the greater the quantity and diversity of commerce. However, even small agglomerations of residences can support a certain level of nonresidential or commercial activity.

Access to greater employment opportunities is another enormous economic benefit. In areas of higher density and population, greater levels of specialization can occur. This is particularly important for a contemporary culture that emphasizes professional specialization. High-paying employment opportunities occur in urban areas for highly skilled and trained candidates. Most scientists, business executives, engineers, and other professionals work at laboratories or firms in metropolitan areas. Urban

Figure 3.8 Urban environments: a) Burano, Italy b) Pearl Street Mall, Boulder, Colorado, USA
c) Oia, Santorini, Greece
Source: Photographs by Phillip Tabb

centers need service industry workers as well as knowledge-based professionals, so there is usually a large pool of jobs.

The larger the market, generally there is opportunity to develop a wide variety of amenities, including health, education, fire and police protection, religious preferences, and organized recreation. This also includes those functions that contribute to sustainable living and cultural opportunities. Sustainable functions include energy, water, food, sewerage, transportation, and communications. Having hospitals, medical centers, dentists, pharmacies, and other medical specialists in close proximity provides both convenience and critical access. It is important to be near healthy grocery stores and markets, which provide a context for social interaction but also present indirect connections to nature through the produce and goods typically found in these markets.

While migration to urban centers continues to increase worldwide, there is evidence of a counter-movement from urbanized areas back to more rural environments. This "un-urban" trend seeks to create habitation in less dense areas, with more open space, access to nature, and supporting a lifestyle that is less hectic. While the context of these places is within a rural area, they are still designed with urban characteristics and within fairly close connections to more dense urban centers.

Traditional urban settlement forms offer many principles and strategies relevant to this counter-urban migration pattern. Titchfield village, located in the south of the UK, is a good example (Figure 3.9a). Titchfield is an existing village located in the south of Hampshire, about a mile from the Solent, opposite the Isle of Wight. It is between the larger cities of Portsmouth and Southampton. The name comes from *ticcefelda*, which is thought to mean "open land where goats were pastured." The population of Titchfield is around 2,500 people living in 891 households within a 124-acre site (50 hectares), all contained within a 1 kilometer circle. This yields a gross density of seven dwelling units per acre (approximately three units per hectare). Residents living in dwellings located at the perimeter experience no more than a 12-minute walk to the village center. The furthest house is 2,850 feet (877 meters) away.[30] There is an intricate pedestrian path system throughout the village and along streets. Titchfield was founded and sited by the Romans in the first century, and as a result nearly all the streets are oriented along cardinal directions, which give good solar access to the village's buildings and streets, especially residences.

There are more than 60 nonresidential land uses in Titchfield, many of which have occupied a place in the village center for centuries. Nonresidential functions include five public houses, two food stores, two hotels, two banks, two hair salons, two motor garages, several restaurants, a butcher, baker, pharmacy, doctor's office, post office, parish church, cemetery, and undertaker. Also, the village has two primary schools – one is public and the other is private. Titchfield has an evolved complement of housing typologies, from single-family detached homes to semi-detached homes and senior apartments.

The serene qualities of Titchfield occur with the natural fingers that interface with the urbanized areas of the village that are between double-loaded building placement along the tessellating roads (see the figure–ground drawings in Figures 3.9b and 3.9c). They provide immediate access from a majority of residences within the village. In addition, the terraced settlement forms gentle steps to the River Meon and its picturesque landscape. Major automobile traffic is channeled around the perimeter of the village, thereby reducing congestion and noise. As mentioned previously, the village is extremely walkable, with the furthest residences within a 12-minute walk. This reduces automobile use and noise, and provides opportunities to interact with nature and the urban amenities of the place. Surrounding Titchfield is agricultural land that provides produce supporting the greengrocers and market within the village. Titchfield village center is the place that gives it identity and community focus. Originally, it was a pedestrian market place, and today it is used for parking and seasonal ceremonies that take place there.

Masdar City was designed as an emerging global hub for renewable energy and clean technologies in the Middle East, with the target of Leadership in Energy and Environmental Design (LEED) Platinum Certification, in which energy will be entirely derived from renewable sources. It was designed by the British architectural firm Foster and Partners, and construction began in 2008. It is intended to use 80 percent less energy than conventional development, and to be carbon neutral. Its regionally derived urban design for 50,000 residents incorporates integrated mixes of use, traditional narrow streets, window shading, courtyards and wind towers. The architecture is made with terracotta walls of high mass rather than high-tech, thereby having the ability to reduce temperatures substantially below those of the surrounding desert. Rather than the more heroic high-rise building typology that is typical in the Middle East, Masdar City was designed with compact medium-density, interconnected streets and blocks, "thick-walled" buildings within a "clean-tech" automobile-free environment. Masdar City will be the latest of a small number of highly planned, specialized, research and technology-intensive municipalities that incorporate a living environment. Unlike many of the more spectacular green projects of this time, Masdar City is modest in design, and climate and culturally appropriate for its geographical location (Figure 3.10). The serene qualities of Masdar City include the mitigation of hot daytime sun with narrow streets and shading devices, and the wonderful desert nighttime sky. Its urban qualities are evident with its density, close-packed urban design and diverse mixes of use.

Masdar City Center was designed by the Laboratory for Visionary Architecture (LAVA), and began construction in 2014. The Center design was referred to as "the oasis of the future." The project had three prime goals: to create an architectural environment that was modern and iconic; to utilize renewable energy; and to serve as a hub for dynamic social activity. The large open-air plaza features a forest of dynamic shading devices called "Pedals from Heaven," designed to provide shade during the hot days and open at night to release heat. The project was certified at the LEED Platinum level.

While these two examples are very different from one another – a 2,000-year-old traditional English village located in a temperate humid climate, and a new, contemporary urban development constructed in this millennium, located in a hot-arid desert – they do have some important similarities. First, they both have well-defined urban edges surrounded by open space. They are coherent and understandable. Second, they both are organized with nucleated centers, which act as cultural and economic incubators of activities. Third, both are walkable, supporting pedestrian movement and outdoor activities and events. Fourth, they are medium density, with no monumental or high-rise buildings: this makes for relatively close proximity to the commercial, cultural, and religious functions of the place. Fifth, nature is allowed to flow in and become an integral part of the settlements' design. Finally, both are safe, authentic and human scale. Their urban characteristics are visibly apparent and support land preservation, social engagement, spontaneous interaction and support, and they are safe and stimulating places to be.

Established in the first century AD, Titchfield was a completely sustainable community for centuries where all goods and services were provided from within the nearby territory (woodlands and farms). The built form of the village is presently contained within less than a 1-mile diameter circle (1 kilometer). Today, with the advent of modernity – with a growing dependence on imported technologies and the introduction of large-scale retail (big box) located outside of the village – Titchfield is suffering from the loss of many of these essential, nonresidential uses, rendering between-place automobile connections necessary. For example, in 1990 there were four greengrocers in the village, the number of which was cut in half by 2000. Despite these losses, Titchfield maintains more than 60 nonresidential uses, which is quite good for a community of only 2,500 residents (Figures 3.9a–c). Unfortunately other villages and hamlets around Titchfield are suffering from the same phenomenon, where commercial districts are located outside of residential settlements. This forces the use of the automobile to access these goods and services.

Masdar City is a completely new place: it is sparkling, full of vitality and promise, yet it has not existed long enough to create a history and soulful quality (Figures 3.10a–c).

Figure 3.9 Urban perspectives: a) Titchfield, UK b) Titchfield, UK figure c) Titchfield, UK ground
Source: Photograph and drawings by Phillip Tabb

Figure 3.10 a) Masdar City, Abu Dhabi, United Arab Emirates b) Masdar City center, day
              c) Masdar City center, night
Source: Images courtesy of Laboratory for Visionary Architecture (originally published in Sergi
Costa Duran and Julio Fajardo Herrero, *The Sourcebook of Contemporary Green Architecture*,
Collins Design and Loft Publications, New York, 2010).

However, it does have a vibrant center that is used both day and night. Both of these examples offer principles of agglomeration, density, nucleating and mixes of use that support contemporary culture, as it exists today. They exist in completely different climatic and cultural contexts as well. Serene urbanism can borrow from the best that these places have to offer.

Residential developments and utopian ideas have affected our towns and cities profoundly and in varying ways. While many have been relatively small demonstrations or ideal designs, they tend to project certain desirable qualities, regardless of size.[31] The ills of modernism and hypermodernism are in part due to developing of many uses and forms that are out of proportion to these ideals, because they grew out of gross addition. The rural-to-urban transect provides a spatial system where density, mixes of use, transportation modes, and other sustainable strategies are articulated. Modern and hypermodern urbanism seem to focus on the extremes of this transect, where high-rise buildings frame city centers, and low-density, single-family suburbs are located far away from these centers. What seems to be largely missing is attention to the middle of this transect, with more dense housing types, commercial, retail, and cultural uses. In the context of serene urbanism, nature and natural process can be fully integrated, helping create a more seamless flow of urbanism from the greatest density at the center to the edge, where nature and agriculture can abound.

Notes

1 Wurman, Richard Saul (ed.), *What Will Be Has Always Been: The Words of Louis I. Kahn*, Rizzoli International Press, New York, 1986, p. 164.
2 Lipovetsky, Gilles, *Hypermodern Times*, Polity Press, Cambridge, 2005.
3 Tachieva, Galina, *Sprawl Repair Manual*, Island Press, Washington, DC, 2010.
4 Echenique, Marcia H., "Function and Form of the City Region," in Hancock, Tom (ed.) *Growth and Change in the Future City Region*, Leonard Hill, London, 1976; Tabb, Phillip, "The Solar Village Archetype: A Study of English Village Form Applicable to Energy-integrated Planning Principles for Temperate Climates," PhD dissertation, Architectural Association, London, 1990.
5 Andrew Thorburn, "Planning Villages," Estates Gazette Limited, London, 1971; Krier, Leon, *Houses, Palaces, Cities*, Architectural AD Editions, London, 1984, pp. 32–3.
6 Duany, Andres, Sorlien, Sandy and Wright, William, "The Smart Code," *Town Paper*, 2003.
7 Duany Plater-Zyberk & Company, "The Urban Transect." Available online at www.dpz.com/Initiatives/Transect (accessed June 20, 2016).
8 Louis I. Kahn quotation from http://arkistudentscorner.blogspot.com/2011/05/louis-kahn-quotes.html (accessed August 2015).
9 Johnson, Kenneth, *Demographic Trends in Rural and Small Town America*, Carsey Institute, University of New Hampshire, Durham, NH, 2006.
10 Berry, Brian, "Suburbanization, Urbanization," in Miller, Fredric P., Vandome, Agnes F. and McBrewster, John (eds) *Counter Urbanization: Demographics, Social, Urban area, Rural area, Overpopulation, Human Population*, Alphascript Publishing, Beau Bassin, Mauritius, 2010, p. 1.
11 Beatley, Timothy, *Biophilic Cities: Integrating Nature into Urban Design and Planning*, Island Press, Washington, DC, 2010.
12 Ellin, Nan, *Integral Urbanism*, Routledge, London, 2006.
13 "Climax community" is an ecological term contrasted to pioneering communities (ecological). Climax has an energetic balance among all the living parts. A pioneering community is new and required a great deal of energy to create.
14 Peter Rickaby is an architect who studied the energy aspects of urban planning. His PhD dissertation focused on differing urban land use configurations for a theoretical site in the UK: "Towards a Spatial Energy Model," Open University and Centre for Configurational Studies, Milton Keynes, 1986.
15 Christaller, Walter, *Die zentralen Orte in Süddeutschland [Central Places in Southern Germany]*. Gustav Fischer, Jena, 1933.
16 Krier, Leon, *Leon Krier: Houses, Palaces, Cities*.
17 Christaller, *Die zentralen Orte*.
18 In this essay Ruth Durack suggests that the adopted village model of the New Urbanist and sustainability are contradictory concepts. Further, she proposes a far more indeterminate urbanism that is more open, adaptive to change, and responsive to inconsistencies. Durack, Ruth, "Village Vices: The Contradiction of New Urbanism and Sustainability," *Places* 14, 2001. Available online at https://placesjournal.org/article/village-vices-the-contradiction-of-new-urbanism-and-sustainability/ (accessed June 16, 2016).
19 "Utopia," *Concise Oxford Dictionary*, Clarendon Press, Oxford, 1982, p. 1183.
20 Carmony, Donald, "New Harmony, Indiana: Robert Owen's Seedbed for Utopia," *Indiana Magazine for History*, 76(3), 1999, pp. 161–261.
21 Krier, Leon, *Atlantis*, Les Archives d'Architecture Moderne, Brussels, 1988, pp. 27–30.
22 Lipovetsky, *Hypermodern Times*, pp. 29–70.
23 In Brownell, Blaine and Swackhamer, Marc, *Hyper-natural: Architecture's New Relationship with Nature*, Princeton Architectural Press, New York, 2015, p. 17.
24 Zakaria, Fareed, "The Rise of the Rest," May 12, 2008. Available online at http://fareedzakaria.com/2008/05/the-rise-of-the-rest/ (accessed June 16, 2016).
25 The epic science-fiction film *Avatar* was a future depiction of human need in the twenty-second century for colonizing foreign planets for resources, at the expense of the indigenous population of Pandora.
26 SBS Dateline, *Ghost Cities*, documentary, March 24, 2011. Available online at www.youtube.com/watch?v=rPILhiTJv7E (accessed December 2015).

27 Langfitt, Frank, "China's White Elephants: Ghost Cities, Lonely Airports, Desolate Factories," October 15, 2015. Available online at www.npr.org/sections/parallels/2015/10/15/446297838/chinas-white-elephants-ghost-cities-lonely-airports-desolate-factories (accessed January 2016).
28 Beck, Melinda, "City vs. Country: Who Is the Healthier? Urban Areas Clean Up, Residents Live Longer, Stay Fitter; But Stress Is Less in Rural Regions," *Wall Street Journal*, July 12, 2011, p. 1.
29 Matthews, John William, "The Effect of Proximity to Commercial uses on Residential Prices," PhD dissertation, Georgia State University, 2006.
30 Tabb, "The Solar Village Archetype."
31 Newitz, Annalee and Stamm, Emily, *10 Failed Utopian Cities That Influenced the Future*, 2014. Available online at http://io9.gizmodo.com/10-failed-utopian-cities-that-influenced-the-future-1511695279 (accessed December 2015).

4 Placemaking

Of all the memberships we identify ourselves by (racial, ethnic, sexual, national, class, age, religious, occupational) the one that is most forgotten and that has the greatest potential for healing is "place".[1]

Placemaking is important in the discussions about serene urbanism, as it becomes the context and structure within which values and qualities of the serene and urban are expressed. We have experienced place since time immemorial, and according to John Donat, "places occur at all levels of identity: my place, your place, street, community, town, city, regions, country and continent, but places never conform to tidy hierarchies of classification."[2] Complexity and variety of scale are inherent qualities of the experience of place, which are important when considering urban applications. Questions arise as to what characteristics make a place, and more specifically, a serene place. Additionally, what makes an urban place, and how does it differ from serene places?

Place creation myths

Our origins and their relationship to place have long been expressed by cultures worldwide. One quality that all of them share is an inextricable connection to the context or place within which they occur. Place myths, as they are often called, describe and explain the creation of the world and our place within it. Two generalized myths prevail: those that posit that the world has existed forever and is part of a never-ending continuum; and those that suggest that the world was created and had a beginning. According to Edward Casey, "just as there is no place without a world for, and of, places, so there is no world without places, without definite loci in which things and events can appear; every world is a place-world."[3]

Yi-Fu Tuan makes a distinction between space and place, as they are fundamentally existent within the world in which we live: "What begins as undifferentiated space becomes place as we get to know it better and endow it with value."[4] Space is abstract, and place is endowed with definition and meaning. In this regard, space is amorphous, intangible, or pragmatic; whereas place embodies location, diverse meaning, personal involvement, and reflection. Edward Relph explains that:

the relationship between community and place is indeed a very powerful one in which each reinforce the identity of the other, and in which the landscape is very much an expression of community held beliefs and values and of interpersonal involvements.[5]

According to Christian Norberg-Schultz:

> What, then do we mean by "place?" Obviously we mean something more than abstract location. We mean a totality made up of concrete things having material substance, shape, texture, and colour. Together these things determine an "environmental character."[6]

In a 1985 series of works by the architect and architectural educator Michael Brill and his students at State University of New York at Buffalo, a set of archetypal patterns were identified as being present with sacred sites.[7] They believed that a "charged" site might contain a common set of fundamental characteristics by which placemaking can be supported, and its special nature revealed. These patterns followed a sequence that seemed to echo the very process of place creation. They emanated from the center, moved outward to the edge, reached containment at the boundary, evolved through morphology of form, included nature, materials and light and, finally, were given qualities that reached a consummatory completion and eventual use. Common to most creation myths is the phenomenon of creation from the void into the first place. In this sense, both the creation of our physical world and the creation of place are inextricably linked – they coexist. Several creation myths are summarized as follows.

- *Genesis* – in the beginning was diffusely regionalized place, made evermore determinant by several stages of creation, beginning with the dark-deep place without body, going from light to human beings in seven days.
- *Hesiod* – the "Theogony" model begins with no preexisting matter, but has a gap whose action brings about places of many sorts. The gap is filled with Eros, Kronos and Zeus. Eros is the god of equal attraction.
- *Navaho* – the fateful horizon of cusps of heaven and earth and an underworld of mist arise out of chaos. Place is of emergence.
- *Hopi* – begins with endless space within which neither regions nor actions are possible, followed by an act of gap-filling with gods, mainly *Taiowa* (the sun).
- *Buddhist* – creation occurs repeatedly throughout time. At the beginning of each cycle, land forms in darkness, on the surface of the water. Spiritual beings who populated the universe are reborn; one of them takes the form of a man and starts the human race. Unhappiness and misery reigns. Eventually, the universe dissolves; all living creatures return to the soul life, and the cycle repeats.
- *Hindu* – a cosmology where from an ocean of nothingness came an original beginning or place of creation: that is, a continuum made of alternatives, an eternal plenitude, and sequence of cycles.
- *Babylonian* – a co-mixturing in water between salt and sweet, as represented by *Apsu* and *Tiamat*, who are the first bitter and sweet waters that comingled form and substance creation.
- *Taoist* – in the beginning was the cosmic egg filled with chaos. In the chaos was *P'an* and *Ku*, the divine and undeveloped embryo. Light poured out to build the sky and the heavy dimness formed the earth; thus the yin (+) and yang (–).

- *Platonic* – regions occupy the "receptacle," which is pre-elemental and character-less, yet made of primal zones through sympathetic resonance, as qualities gather into the primal regions and become a locality matrix for things. They are comprehended not through the senses, but by understanding.
- *Big Bang* – modern scientific accounts of the origin state that the universe began as a small singularity that was in a very high density state, then expanded and began to cool off, forming sub-atomic particles and atoms, and eventually creating stars and galaxies over the past 13.8 billion years.

What can be gleaned from creation myths are concepts that derive from empty space or nothingness, and that explain the unknown origin of nature and human existence, which gathers in matter, substance, and form. Relative to place, they suggest the form-making process that is potentially characteristic to the creation of any place and progress of consciousness. The myth of the twin brothers, Romulus and Remus, and the founding of Rome is an interesting example of sacred placemaking. After being saved and suckled by the Shewolf (Figure 4.1a), one account of this foundation myth indicates that when grown, the brothers wanted to create a sacred city near the River Tiber, where earlier they had been left to die. Romulus wanted a higher protection wall around the Palatine Hill, the site of the new city, but Remus made fun of the wall and was so bold as to jump over it in jest. Romulus took this as an act that desacralized the space, deflating the sacred space that had been previously created; they quarreled, and Remus was killed. Another account has the quarrel over the location: either the Palatine Hill or the Aventine Hill.[8]

The Allegory of the Cave in the Seventh Book of Plato's *Republic* is a dialogue between Plato's brother Glaucon and his mentor Socrates.[9] While this allegory is not strictly a creation myth, it does express the notion of humanity's narrow and profane existence of illusions. In this allegory, humanity is seen as chained while dwelling deep in a cave, where shadows are projected onto a back wall of the cave that shows objects placed in front of a fire behind them. This was their apparent reality, and it is the philosopher who is able to break away, climb out, experience the world in full light and enter the world of real truth and beauty. No longer are there shadows and reflections, but rather the experience of real presence – the sky, sun, moon, mountains, and natural life (Figure 4.1b).

Figure 4.1 Place myths: a) The Shewolf of Rome b) The Allegory of the Cave
Source: Drawings by Phillip Tabb

Place myths are important, in that they create possible ways of understanding the significance and meaning of a particular place. They can give guidance and character to the evolution of the place. Finally, myths can explain the origins of the place, how it came to be; they can teach lessons and values, give identity to a place and, according to Joseph Campbell, evoke a sense of the mystery of existence, connecting to the larger cosmic context within which all places are situated.[10] Related specifically to serene urbanism, myths relay stories about the nature of the place and the function of its urban and rural counterpart. A place myth functions as a kind of "user's manual" populated with archetypes.[11] Myths address difficult questions with cultural significance.

Place archetypes

Where do principles come from? Some might observe that they come from the awareness of random acts of appearance – a chaotic context of revelation. Others may argue that principles are generated from rational participation in problem-solving, and that they are a logical product of a controlled process. Others still may even suggest that principles are divine and are derived through sacred processes or transmissions, such as clairvoyant activities or communication. It seems clear that ideas are born from somewhere and, more importantly, are the carriers of information and embodiment processes. Further, it seems as though the actual sources of ideas will certainly influence the kind of information and the nature of the informing processes. Therefore, it is important to understand the source of principles and the ways in which they transform our thinking and design methods – and ultimately, the process of placemaking.

An architectural source can derive from a theory, the context, environment, culture, patterns of behavior, artistic impulse, system of construction, emerging technology, an evolving language of form, or sacred intention. What makes it a source is the originating power, and the degree to which it can direct the development of a project into its concrete realization. The idea and current through which it passes are like a genetic code that guides the creative design process and methods of translating an architectural conception into a building language, and ultimate assemblage of tectonic parts.

In philosophy, the First Principles are a set of basic, foundational propositions or assumptions that cannot be deduced from any other proposition or assumption. The First Principles derive from a dynamic system that connects the purest of ideas to the most specific of concrete manifestations, particularly in architecture. Investigations of the First Principles, as they relate specifically to architecture, may provide an instrument of clarification, especially in a time of increasing temporal density, rapid technological change, and transparency, as well as in the emergence of more far-reaching global issues, of which architecture is inherently a part. This is not to dismiss an architecture for the sake of delight, but suggests that the principles from which architecture is born are holistic enough in content to encompass both the sacred and profane, the necessary and delightful, the science and art of making, the natural and human-made contexts, including the serene and urban.

However, First Principles are more than foundations from which something is created or built. They inform the foundations and precede them. In fact, the principles are the guiding intelligence informing the creative process. In architectural education, this practice is really at the seat of the creative design process. Design seeks to create forms that have inherent intelligence behind them. Within this context, design is the process that bridges the realm of ideas with the physical expression of form – plans, sections, elevation, models, and other depictions. The First Principles can be further explained through a progression of expressions that move from source to archetype, and then from ectype to type.

- *Source* – is the place of emanation: it is where something begins, where it springs into being. In architecture, it is the highest and most noble point of origin or inspiration.
- *Archetype* (from Latin, *archetypum*, or Greek *arkhetupos*, meaning original) – is the power activity which generates from the source. Some definitions of archetype view it as a model or pattern, but these are really ectypes. Archetypal energies can be understood through myths and other phenomenological examples or active ideas.
- *Ectype* – is a model or abstract representation of the informing archetype. It is a copy of an original energy that has previously existed, and an unmanifest guiding model for all in its type. In architecture, it is the conceptual plan or model describing the intent of the scheme.
- *Type* – is a concrete example of the ectypal model and archetypal energy: an example of something having common traits or characteristics that distinguishes it as a specific thing. It is existing, diverse, and variable. In architecture it is a specific building.

According to Robert Lawlor:

> [L]et us take an example of a tangible thing, such as the bridle of a horse. This bridle can have a number of forms, materials, sizes, colours, uses, all of which are bridles. The bridle considered in this way, is typal; it is existing, diverse and variable. But on another level there is the idea or form of the bridle, the guiding model of all bridles. This is an unmanifest, pure, formal idea and its level is ectypal. And above this is the archetypal level of the bridle, which is that of the principle or power-activity that is a process and essential purpose of the bridle, which the ectypal form and the typal example of the bridle only represent.[12]

Lawlor further explains that Platonic archetypes are part of a triad of concepts: *archetypal* energies, *ectypal* exemplifications and *typal* concrete examples. Archetypes represent the nature, intentions, and energetic qualities of a principle.[13] They are the action-force emanating from a spiritual or initiating source. Archetypes are an energetic form of a profound idea, spiritual concept, or principle: they are essentially non-physical, and represent the power-activity of these energetic processes. Related to place, archetypes represent the values and characteristics that render and give identity to a place, versus the abstract nature of pure space. Place archetypes are the fundamental elements that, when assigned meaning, give identity to a given place. Jung described archetypes as "active living dispositions," and according to Anthony Stephens, archetypes are living organisms endowed with a generative force, having the capacity to initiate and mediate, as well as transcend culture, "race" and time.[14]

Archetypes, then, are energies that come to be understood through a collective process that gains particular meanings, which are translated into sets of symbols or ectypes. The First Principles derive from a dynamic and a priori system – *from what*

Figure 4.2 Pseudo-Dionysian choir of angels: a) Seraph b) Archangel Michael
Source: Shutterstock

comes before and after – connecting origin with element. Ectypes are symbols mediating the archetypal energies into a process of manifestation.

The fourth-century pseudo-Dionysian accounts of the choir of angels explains a ninefold hierarchical system of angelic energies, that progress from light near the source to greater density as approaching angelic anthropomorphism (Figure 4.2a). The first choirs, Seraphim, Cherubim and Thrones, are attendants or guardians who provide access to God. They possess multiple wings, are light, and somewhat formless. The last several choirs provide the function of messages from God to humans (Figure 4.2b). They include principalities, archangels, and angels, and their forms are more dense and human-like. The source of faith is culturally determined from the Jewish and Christian God, the Islamic Allah, Buddha, the Hindu deities Shiva, Vishnu, and Shakti, or even Mother Nature. In the secular realm the source can be expressed with higher intentions, such as sustainability, sensitivity to the natural environment, health and wellness, and even serenity. The angelic choir model corresponds with the transformations that occur from source to typal examples in architecture and planning.

Ectypes are portrayals, models or patterns associated with archetypes. Similar to Joseph Campbell's *The Masks* [ectypes] *of God* [source of archetypes], ectypes are external depictions of the inner spiritual dimensions.[15] Types are physical and specific examples reflecting archetypal energy and ectypal model. Lawlor suggests that five principles (archetypes) from Plato's *Timaeus*[16] derive meanings related to the intrinsic significances embodied in the first numbers 1, 2, 3, 4, and 5.[17] According to Robin Waterfield in *The Theology of Arithmetic* (1988), numbers were seen as divine principles, and by extension, allegorical with inspirational powers.[18] Figures 4.3a and 4.3b show the Pythagorean Tetractys layered with four levels: source, archetypes, ectypes, and types, and Andrew Wedberg's exemplifications, perfect and imperfect.[19] In Wedberg's diagram, the source works through archetypes, ectypes and types in differing ways, from perfect and extraordinary expressions and secular everyday ways.

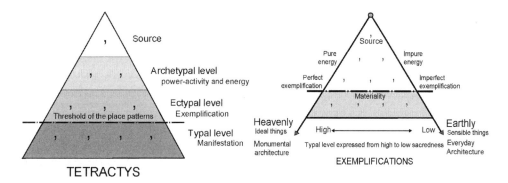

Figure 4.3 The Pythagorean Tetractys: a) Four levels b) Perfect–imperfect exemplifications
Source: Anders Wedberg, *Plato's Philosophy of Mathematics* (1977)

The number 1 relates the Unity Principle, and describes two alternating actions: the outward emergence and division of unity into harmonic parts, and the inward dissolving of parts into a comprehensible whole or atmospheric experience. The number 2 relates the Generative Principle, describing organic growth within a place, the organizational structure for its natural proliferation, and the power of urbanization. The number 3 relates the Formative Principle, describing varying ordering systems and geometric characteristics and structures of form – placemaking order. The number 4 relates the Corporeal Principle, which grounds placemaking into pragmatic, substantive, sustainable, and material realities. The number 5 relates the Regenerative Principle and describes the transformative, numinous, and mutable qualities of place:[20]

1. *Unity Principle* – wholeness, atmospheric presence, harmony, and proportional integration.
2. *Generative Principle* – duality, diversity, multiplication, proliferation, and urbanization.
3. *Formative Principle* – form, structure, order of space, and place formation.
4. *Corporeal Principle* – concrete volumetric, physical, sustainability, and material realities.
5. *Regenerative Principle* – transformation, numinous experiences, and qualities of renewal (Figure 4.4).

An archetype of the Unity Principle, for example, is wholeness experienced through circularity and singularity of focus, or the attracting energy of centeredness. It dissolves parts into an aggregate totality, which is both coherent and inclusive. In this instance, an ectype is described by the circle's shape, where its circumference is uniformly equidistant from the center point; that which is between the center and perimeter is contained or considered the domain experience of circularity. Taken together, they become a whole. Archetypes and ectypes are essentially nonphysical, where typal examples are physical and tangible actualizations with a specific nature and character, as the dome at the Pantheon in Rome, Italy is a unique expression of unity.

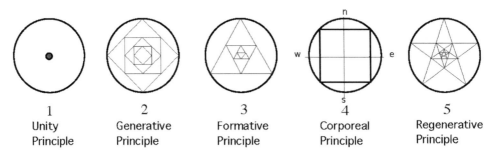

1	2	3	4	5
Unity Principle	Generative Principle	Formative Principle	Corporeal Principle	Regenerative Principle

Figure 4.4 First Principles expressed as geometric diagrams
Source: courtesy of Phillip Tabb

Unity Principle

The Unity Principle, or as it sometimes is referred to, the "creative principle," describes the relationship between the individual parts and the whole of a composition or place. It investigates the aspects of a given design that are necessary to tie the composition together, to give it a sense of wholeness, or to break it apart and give it a sense of connected accord and variety. The primary functions of this principle are to transform the place of fragments and pieces into the unity of oneness, which connects through the whole fabric of the place, and to emerge or divide intelligibly and harmoniously into multiplicity from wholeness. The unity patterns relate to the essential conception as a seed, and act as an impetus for the creative birth of the initial place schema. Centering is a process of determining the point of power and creativity, and to sustainability as it relates to central place theory. The patterns are attracted to and emerge from a center, moving and connecting outward, bounding or containing the territory in a porous way, then defining the domain or living area of the place. Constantinos Doxiadis called the area between a circle's center and circumference the "domain," the place of dwelling.[21] These patterns combine to form the embryo of a place and set its development into initial motion, growing outward and into greater levels of complexity. The Unity Principle also relates to the atmosphere of a place – a quality that creates a unified and common experience.

Generative Principle

The Generative Principle emerges from unity and gives further dimensionality to a place. This principle is the power of division of unity, where one becomes two, progressing into multiplicity; it also represents diversity and growth. The word "emanation" comes from the Latin *emanare*, "to flow forth". This principle is related to the metaphor of the root, which is the power from the germ to descend, involve, and transmute from below. Further, it can be related to the emergence of ecological communities that grow fast at first, using a great deal of energy, later evolving into climax communities that are in greater balance with the environment. The Generative Principle transforms through sequential intelligence, and can be related to urbanism or the process of urban growth. It embodies both the phenomenon of duality and proliferation or procreation. The patterns, in turn, find direction on the land, cohere with the ground, reach upward, and grow outward through multiplication into the world. Grounding is the first pattern in this group, as a place emerges from the ground in its initial cycle of growth.

Formative Principle

The Formative Principle is also known as the "mother of form." It is the formative power, giving rise to the polygonal world and orders for the measures of the Earth and time. It is related to the process of completion, where both shape and time are given form. The formative patterns define the design through accumulating ordering systems: geometric, structural, spatial, ecological, natural, and celestial patterns. Therefore, the defining characteristics of form are developed, shaped, and given specific properties. Geometry underlies all form. At the settlement scale, this means that geometry organizes the circulatory and spatial organization of the place. Nature and ecological flows can further determine urban form, especially in the context of serene urbanism.

Corporeal Principle

The Corporeal Principle is bodily and of the material world, and therefore is known as the "mother of substance." Since it is bodily and material, it relates to the volumetric world of objects, shapes, and forms, yet it is closely aligned with the substance and material construction of these three-dimensional forms. The dynamic aspect of this principle is the physical manifestation process. The corporeal patterns provide an anchoring into a pragmatic, physical, and tangible reality through attention to scale, function, economy, and the substantive characteristics of the material world. These are often referred to as the "real-world" determinants to a design: they are not theoretical or idealistic. Scale is a system of sizing indicating value or measurement. With a settlement, this is concerned with its size or area, walking distances, types and density of spaces, and the details of the built works. Urbanization is a function of the Generative Principle where a single building becomes several, multiplying to form urban spaces, and eventually towns and cities.

Regenerative Principle

The Regenerative or Transformative Principle is activated when growth has completed by addition. It relates to growth by addition and multiplication: a process that is integral to most natural and human systems. Multiplication is an accelerating form of addition, which displays a logically expanding transformation. The Transformative Principle is invested with a new and higher spiritual nature, which includes the experience of the numinous. The transformative patterns act as a catalytic opportunity for a higher experience through transitional passage from the mundane into the significant, the ineffable quality of light, to a place of wholeness and, finally, to consecration and ceremonial participation. There is a change from a lower to a higher state of being. Transformation generates cycles that initiate, grow, expand, and eventually regenerate.

Taken together, these principles and the patterns that they generate form a larger whole that, for the purpose of this work, focuses on serene urbanism and its various characteristics and dimensions:

- the Unity Principle is directly related to the serene and serene environments, and provides a language for an atmospheric perception of place;
- the Generative Principle is related to urbanism and urban processes of growth and expansion;
- the Formative Principle is related to placemaking and the forms and spatial structure that inform a place. It involves the building or settlement shape, and configuration and internal ordering structures;
- the Corporeal Principle relates to the pragmatic realities of manifestation and, more specifically with this work, focuses on sustainability as necessary and concrete building. Additionally, it relates to the material and substance of the place;
- the Regenerative Principle relates to the numinous and mysterious through engagement, participation, and transformative experiences.

Figure 4.5 is a photographic elevation of the Rotunda at the University of Virginia, designed in 1826 by Thomas Jefferson. It is a good example of how the five principles are clearly expressed and illustrated in its form.

The dome or rotunda is symbolic of the Unity Principle, as the sphere encompasses the entire structure. The Generative Principle derives from a progression of squares

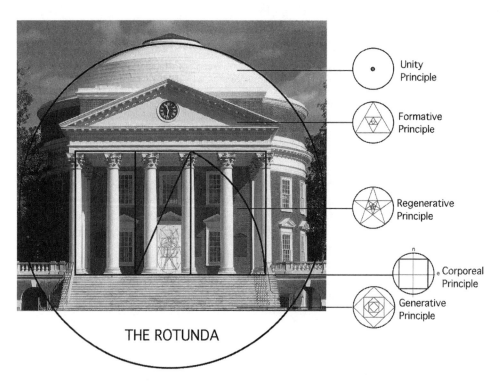

Figure 4.5 Jeffersonian Library, University of Virginia
Source: Photograph by Phillip Tabb

and the steps at the base, ascending to the main floor level. The Formative Principle of triangulation can be clearly seen at the pediment and over the major windows. The Corporeal Principle is found at the main ground floor, with cardinal orientations and the function of the building as the library. Finally, the Regenerative Principle is expressed with the golden mean proportions found on the entry façade.[22]

When residents become more placebound, they tend to spend more time in the places that they inhabit; they invest greater amounts of creative energy and resources in that place; and they grow with it and become familiar with it. Therefore, it is posited that the more a settlement becomes place-oriented, the greater the opportunities for an environmentally sustainable lifestyle and support for community. A sample of community-making patterns can be illustrated as follows:

- *centering* – exemplified by the island city of Mexcaltitán de Uribe, Mexico with its double-square center green and well;
- *bounding* – with an aerial view of the Castello di Gargonza, Italy with its medieval surrounding wall;
- *direction* – with Mesa Verde, Colorado, USA, that is tucked beneath the sandstone cave and oriented to the southern sun;
- *gravity* – with Park Guell, Barcelona, Spain, with its wonderful angled foundation and cave-like spaces;
- *reaching upward* – with a model photograph of the spiraling Crystal Island in Moscow, Russia by Foster and Partners;
- *nature within* – interior landscapes at Portmeirion, Wales;
- *celestial order* – inside the Chapelle Notre Dame du Haut at Ronchamp, France and its south-facing constellation wall;
- *light* – in a Hassan Fathy courtyard house in Shabrament, Egypt; and
- *ceremonial order* – at the Vidar Clinic in Järna, Sweden.

Much like chaos and complexity theory, these underlying patterns can help to understand the increasingly complex world of place.

The hierarchical levels expressing the archetypes, ectypes, and types can be further examined based on Anders Wedberg's diagrams. From source there are two paths. The first is toward "perfect exemplification" and "ideal objects". Here, the pure idea and pure form are given expression. This could equate to the creation of a special sacred building shared by the community for the purpose of prayer, healing, education, or government. From source, the other direction moves toward "imperfect exemplification" and "sensible things". This suggests that the sacred (source) is manifested, but not through perfect expression. This could relate to the design and building of more mundane or profane building types, such as dwellings, workplaces, commercial and ancillary structures, where worldly functions and considerations influence form.

- *Perfect exemplification* – is the progression from source to perfect expressions of archetypes, ectypes, and finally to materialized typal examples, usually found with highly spiritual, cultural, and significant buildings and urban designs that create extraordinary experiences.
- *Imperfect exemplifications* – is the progression from source to imperfect and more sensible expressions of archetypes, ectypes, and finally to materialized typal examples, usually found with more ordinary cultural and everyday buildings and urban designs that reflect some degree of sacredness.

The application of archetypes, and the principles they represent, has an interesting and deepening relationship to architecture and planning. In architecture they guide the intentions, function, form, structure, relation to the surrounding environment, materials, and use. Similarly, in planning and urban design, they inform the network, infrastructure, and place ordering systems, relations to nature, and ecology of place. There can be a powerful and inextricable relationship between a settlement's form and its ability to create place, which correspondingly affects its function, use, dwelling, and structure for patterns of behavior. Consequently, as a settlement becomes more place-oriented, its potential for livability, health, community, sustainability, and inculcation of the sacred increases. A finer-grained expression of the principles and archetypes can be found within the ectypal patterns that they inform.

Place ectypal patterns

A placemaking pattern is an ectypal model and a guide that embodies both principle ideas and the representational means by which to express those ideas. The patterns describe energetic qualities of different principles. According to Christopher Alexander, it is a "design language network" organized in a sequence from larger to smaller patterns – from niches and porches to neighborhoods and cities.[23] As mentioned previously, through a series of works, the architect and architectural educator Michael Brill and his students believed that a sacred or, in their words, "charged," site could contain a common set of fundamental characteristics by which the sacred was revealed.[24] In *Using the Place-creation Myth to Develop Design Guidelines for Sacred Space*, they identified 14 patterns that routinely accompanied sacred places. Research by the present author in 1990 focused on English villages, archetypes, and similar placemaking patterns at the small settlement scale.[25]

In *Chambers for a Memory Palace*, by Donlyn Lynden and Charles Moore, certain patterns such as "axes that reach," "gardens that civilize," "light that plays," 'shapes that remind," and "borders that control" were illustrated.[26] Similarly, Vitruvius in his *De Architectura* discussed patterns such as containment, direction, elemental and physical materiality, celestial references, and order and proportion, to name but a few.[27] Patterns utilized in the list that follows, derived from Vitruvius (15 BC), Relph (1976), Alexander (1977), Brill (1985), Tabb (1990), and Moore (1994),[28] and were primarily used to enhance the place-defining processes. For serene urbanism, the following patterns have been selected that form a set of useful and exemplary ectypal placemaking patterns. According to Brill:

> This is not a place for a specific ritual. Rather, the goal here [the charged place] is that the place itself be the myth in its physical form ... that is use and language of physical form rather than the language of the storyteller.[29]

The following list is a synthesis of the ectypal patterns extrapolated from this earlier research, while the order follows fairly closely Brill's investigations.

- centering, making location with a fixed point on the earth;
- orientation and direction with our bodies and the three axes;
- domain, internal order, and succession of spaces;
- celestial order and the heavenly canopy;

- visual symmetry (balance and order);
- differentiating the orientations (revealing their differences);
- reaching upward (levity and verticality);
- descent (triumph over the underworld and chaos);
- physical bounding (between place and formlessness);
- passage and thresholds (with a distinct place of pause);
- discriminating views (that do not break the charged experience);
- light (that provides time passage, orientation, and inspiration);
- physical materiality for making;
- nature within (beneficial, controlled, and ordered);
- consecration and finishing a place.

These ectypal patterns progress from a point, line, and boundary that form the context for place, to relations to nature, sky and light, and a finishing ritual of completion. There is a logical expansion and evolutionary connection among them, as they give form and qualities to a charged place.

Typal exemplifications

By relating these archetypal principles and ectypal patterns, a place can be analyzed and understood further. Mexcaltitán de Uribe, Mexico is an excellent demonstration of the expression of these place patterns (Figure 4.6a). It is a man-made island city off the coast in the municipality of Santiago Ixcuintla, in the Mexican state of Nayarit. Mexcaltitán was Aztlan (cradle of Mexico), the ancient home of the Aztecs. Mexcaltitán is also credited with the actual naming of the country Mexico. Currently it has a population of 1,300 residents.[30]

The island city has an identifiable center in the form of a public square and green, surrounded by larger, nonresidential buildings including a museum, hotel, restaurant, and the church (Figure 4.6b). The boundary can be seen with a serrated edge between

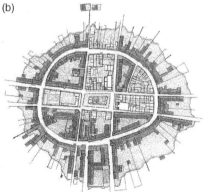

Figure 4.6 Mexcaltitán, Mexico: a) Aerial view
Source: Alamy Stock Photo
b) Plan
Source: Drawing by Phillip Tabb

the built space and the estuary of the mangrove swamps. Streets in a double-cross pattern and a circumferential road make the internal order. The curb of this road is more than a foot deep, allowing for water containment during the rainy season. Residents navigate using gondolas, hence Mexcatitán's reference as "Little Venice." Most of the buildings are attached and closely packed within the geometric sections left by the double-cross street pattern.

The center of the island is the high point, and it is there that the spire of the Church of Saints Peter and Paul towers upward, high above the city, and is significant as a placemarker. The island's surface slopes downward to the surrounding watery edges. The island is oriented with its slightly longer aspect along the north–south axis, giving both symbolic and good solar access to the city. Nature is found in the very center of the city in its double-square plaza, in courtyards brimming with tropical plants, and certainly around the perimeter at the water's edge. The streets and sidewalks are used to dry the shrimp, oysters, and fish caught in the estuary, and therefore perform a double-functional use. The overall shape of the urban fabric suggests a celestial diagram of the sun, which played a central role in Aztec beliefs. Festivals are numerous throughout the year.

Place typal examples indicate actual places that are unique and grounded in a specific location. It should be noted that both the list of guiding principles and corresponding place patterns within this chapter do not represent exclusive lists. Several defining characteristic establish varying place types. Location and purpose are important in giving places their form and function. Certain building types and development projects lend themselves to the demonstration of serene urban qualities, which include residential intentional communities that are oriented to amenities and mixes of use. Resorts and hospitality have intentional and powerful connections to nature. Agrotourism places feature hospitality with agriculture in interactive ways. Healing and wellness environments support important interactions with the natural world and processes. Contemplative and monastic environments include a diversity of activities and a strong participatory relationship to landscape.

Intentional communities

Place-oriented residential communities include neighborhoods, urban clusters, mixed-use suburbs, and remote nucleated hamlets and villages. They possess a combination of private residential functions and appropriate mixes of use and residential-scale amenities. A distinguishing feature is that they are planned and designed from the beginning and have a great deal of user or stakeholder involvement in the process, including site selection, determining dwelling types and community functions, and ways in which to deal with the automobile.

The Findhorn eco-community is a good example of this type of place. Findhorn was established in the early 1960s by Peter and Eileen Caddy and Dorothy Maclean, and it grew into a community because of a remarkable garden that they first created there.[31] They prepared the ground on the sandy barren soil of coastal Scotland, planted with care and phenomenal success, and became wonderful stewards of the place that evolved from a garden to an eco-community. Within a year of its planting, the garden grew to 65 different types of vegetables, 21 kinds of fruits and 42 different herbs, and was overflowing with life. Today the community is a constantly evolving demonstration of the spiritual, social, ecological and economic dimensions of life. Findhorn is the largest intentional community in the UK. The community also extends to individuals, businesses, and organizations within a 50-mile (80 kilometer) radius of the park, and to the islands of Iona and Erraid on the west coast of Scotland (Figure 4.7a).

Auroville is an experimental, transnational township in the state of Tamil Nadu, India. It was founded by the French teacher Mirra Alfassa in 1968, and designed by architect Roger Anger. The master plan was intended to foster unity and progressive harmony, conceived using the geometry of a spiral nebula with the *Matrimandir*, Sanskrit for "Temple of The Mother," at its center (Figure 4.7b). Auroville aspires to be a site of material and spiritual research for an actual living embodiment of human unity. The original plan for Auroville allowed for nature to correspond with the arms of the spiral toward the center.[32]

Yarrow Ecovillage is an intentional community located in British Columbia, Canada, consisting of 3,000 residents. It was founded in the late 1990s, and in 2014 the multi-generational co-housing part of the community was awarded the Sustainability Leadership Award. The village includes a 20-acre (8-hectare) organic farm that is part of a Community Supported Agriculture food program. The farm, a delicatessen, and multi-use commercial space make up the primary commercial entities.

Near Taos, New Mexico is an agglomeration of earthships designed by architect Michael Reynolds (Figure 4.7c). Intentional communities include collective households, cohousing communities, ecovillages, communes, survivalist retreats, kibbutzim, ashrams, housing cooperatives, and responsible developments.

The contributions of these examples to serene urbanism are fairly apparent, and include the following characteristics:

- typically accompanied by a mix of densities and housing types;
- a combination of residential and mixes of use, especially those supporting everyday living;
- agriculture is becoming an increasingly important amenity;
- mixed modes for transportation;
- contained within walking distances (1-mile diameter);
- diversity of demographics and housing choices;
- aggressive ways of dealing with the automobile;
- introduction of alternative technologies;
- climate-responsive urban design and architecture.

Figure 4.7 Intentional communities: a) Findhorn eco-community, UK
Source: Courtesy of the Findhorn Foundation
b) Auroville, India   *Source*: Shutterstock
c) Earthship Village, New Mexico   *Source*: Alamy Stock Photo

Resort and hospitality places

Typically, destination places are located near beautiful natural environments that include mountain, forest, vineyard, lake, river, and ocean sites. Often in remote locations, they feature highly interactive activities associated with the natural environment, are very serene, and generally are contained or isolated from the general public. These are places for restoration and recreation, and are not intended for permanent habitation.

Castello di Gargonza is a good example of an historic place reinvigorated into a resort and hospitality place (Figures 4.8a and 4.8b). About 15 miles (25 kilometers) west of Cortona as the crow flies, and a great deal further by car, is the little *borgo* of Gargonza, just outside of Monte San Savino. More of a castle whose walls contain a perfectly preserved thirteenth-century village, the Castello di Gargonza is sited with a great prospect of the Val di Chiana from the center of its own vast wooded estate. The village is surrounded with stone walls and cypress trees. Conte Roberto Guicciardini has presently turned all the tiny cell-like former peasants' houses into self-catering retreats. The 23 residences are simply furnished and efficiently run. The Castello di Gargonza is an excellent example of the application of the First Principles and the patterns which derive from them (including center, boundary, domain, grounding, reaching upward, and nature within). This is in part probably due to the fact that historically it was an outpost of Siena, and in need of protection and self-containment. Therefore, the basic physical characteristics of the place have remained pure and intact.

Today it serves as a bed and breakfast with residence vacation homes and corporate retreat. It also offers a swimming pool, restaurant, and meeting rooms, which have skillfully maintained the authentic character of the original antique village. Even today, the village homes maintain the names of the original inhabitants: Fattore, Niccolina the seamstress and Celso the gamekeeper. The La Torre di Gargonza Restaurant is the crown jewel of Castello di Gargonza, open for guests of the bed and breakfast and the Castello's vacation apartments, as well as external clients. The restaurant is located just outside the Gargonza city walls, near the swimming pool, where one can enjoy the views of Gargonza's woods and Val di Chiana. Its design is comprehensible with

Figure 4.8 Castillo di Gargonza: a) Aerial view b) Well and piazza
Source: Photographs by Phillip Tabb

its clear boundary, internal grid system, and place-marking tower. Figure 4.8a shows an aerial photograph of the whole site, and Figure 4.8b a view inside of the central well and piazza.[33]

Serene urban characteristics from resort and hospitality places usually emphasize remarkable natural places immersed within a mountain scene, lake, seaside, or agricultural landscape that:

- includes a combination of residential and mixes of use;
- is typically accompanied with compactness and density of form;
- has important interactions with the natural environment, both visual and physical;
- has identity and place-oriented form;
- is usually clustered and self-contained;
- is primarily a pedestrian environment; and
- has the possibility for business retreats and gatherings.

The primary contribution of resort and hospitality environments to serene urbanism is their relationships to beauty, comfort, relaxation, the natural environment, and the full-growth cycle from seed to beautifully prepared meals. They tend to be self-reliant, with organic and sustainable practices. They generally encourage and help facilitate participants to fully engage within the natural or cultivated environments, and become more active players rather than simply passive observers.

Agrotourism places

Agrotourism is a growing destination place that is closely associated with the hospitality industry. Such places tend to be smaller and more intimate, supporting resort activities that are blended with local agricultural production, including wineries, gardens, olive orchards, fruit, vineyards, and vegetables. It is here where "farm-to-table" is most visible and central to the function of the place. La Pievuccia, located in the Val di Chio near Castiglion Fiorentino, is an *agriturismo* and family-owned bed and breakfast serving its own products to guests (Figures 4.9a and 4.9b). It is considered a biohotel featuring authentic wines and olive oil. The estate, which covers 20 acres (8 hectares), is divided among vineyards, olive groves, seasonal crops, and forest.

Figure 4.9 Agrotourism: a) La Pievuccia Vineyard, Italy b) La Pievuccia Hotel
Source: Photographs by Phillip Tabb

During any normal year, four different types of honey are produced: acacia, castagno (chestnut), Millefiori di Campo, and Melata, from the beehives scattered around the property. Guests at the Pievuccia are offered a unique experience, living in traditional Tuscan apartments that are characteristic of La Pievuccia's rich farming history. There are wine tastings and cooking classes, and during September and October guests are offered the opportunity to participate in the grape and olive harvest. In addition, virgin-pressed oil becomes available for purchase in late autumn in many of the agro-touristic farms. According to John Ikerd, there is a need to reclaim the sacred in food and farming.[34]

The primary contribution of agrotourism environments to serene urbanism is the integration of human activities with agricultural processes and nature. This includes direct contact with a vineyard, farm, or ranch where animal husbandry, plants, growing cycles, and seasonal changes can be experienced. These "stay farms" promote economic development and help educate the public about the important contributions of agriculture to the country's economy and quality of life. It also has become an important part of the tourist sector of many places, as there are both eco-nomic and non-economic benefits. Most agrotouristic places are not large in scale and do not house large populations; however, they provide activities that educate and engage their residents. Serene urban characteristics from agrotourism places are as follows:

- they include a combination of residential and agricultural mixes;
- are typically accompanied by a strong interaction with nature;
- focus on the changes of growing seasons;
- emphasize the importance of food growing, processing, preparation, and consumption;
- emphasize the importance of agricultural education;
- have pedestrian environments;
- possess rural character and serene places;
- have quality of atmosphere and life.

Healing or wellness places

Healing environments are found from gardens to entire communities. They are designed for restorative, recuperation, and other functions associated with wellness, which includes physical activity, exercise, yoga, and other fitness activities. Often they have spas associated with water features such as oceans, rivers, ponds, pools, and fountains. These types of environments can be destination places, day places or drop-in treatment places. Healing gardens are designed to improve health outcomes through stress reduction, relief from symptoms, and an improved sense of well-being.[35] A small community example is Järna in Sweden, which is described as a constellation of busi-nesses and social activities, organized with concepts developed by the philosopher Rudolf Steiner.[36] At the beginning of the twentieth century, Steiner founded anthro-posophy, an esoteric philosophy growing out of European transcendentalism with links to theosophy. Järna is considered the center of the anthroposophical movement in Sweden. The community is nestled beside a coastal inlet of the Baltic Sea; the land-scape interweaves the Södermanland Forest, and open plains punctuated with organic

Figure 4.10 Healing places: a) Paraguay healing herb garden b) Challis well water form and
garden, Glastonbury, UK
Source: Alamy Stock Photo

farms. Buildings within the community were designed by the Danish architect Erik
Asmussen, using Steiner's principles. The community also employs biodynamic agriculture and composting, with a network of farms using these practices. The architecture expresses Steiner's qualities of heaven, earth and Man.

Other examples of wellness places include the Garden for Natural Medicine in the
Comunidad Vy'a Renda village, Distrito Curuguaty, Paraguay, which provides healing
medicinal plants (Figure 4.10a). The Glastonbury spring, well, stream, waterform cascade, and pond form an environment for contemplation and healing (Figure 4.10b).
This type of landscape is designed for a specific population, such as encouraging seniors to get outside for exercise, sunlight, and fresh air; enabling children to "blow off
steam" during a hospital visit; or helping patients learn to use a wheelchair on outdoor surfaces.

The primary contribution of healing and wellness environments to serene urbanism
is their attention to interaction with the beneficial qualities of nature. Serene urban
characteristics from healing and wellness places:

- include a combination of residential and mixes of use related to healing;
- have important interactions with the natural environment;
- emphasize the importance of elemental qualities;
- have containment and place-oriented form;
- are necessary for quiet, safe, and tranquil places;
- are often accompanied by organic gardens;
- are exclusively a pedestrian environment;
- use nontoxic building materials.

Contemplative and monastic places

Contemplative environments support a more conscious way of living, where spiritual
and/or contemplative practices are brought into everyday life. Living is concentrated

and focused within a single place, where the discipline of everyday survival functions are woven into a contained, seamless, ritualistic, and repetitive sequence of contemplative and spiritual activities. Contemplative environments generally have a strong sense of identity, a serene atmosphere, and comprehensible form.

For example, the Novy Dvur Monastery west of Prague in the Czech Republic (2004) is a good example of both historic and contemporary forms contributing to the ecclesial environment. An estate was acquired for the new Cistercian monastery, which included a Baroque manor house and three agricultural wings framing a courtyard, and was designed by John Pawson. The circular form of the contemporary church is the most distinctive exterior gesture of the design.

Serene urban characteristics of contemplative and monastic place types:

- include a combination of residential, mixes of use, spiritual practices;
- have important interactions with natural environment and elemental qualities;
- are typically accompanied by a medium density of form;
- are typically accompanied by agriculture and/or gardens;
- have containment and place-oriented form;
- have an orientation toward self-sufficiency and on-site resources;
- emphasize stewardship and conscious interactions with place;
- are exclusively a pedestrian environment.

The primary contribution of contemplative and monastic environments to serene urbanism is their attention to support of more spiritual and sustainable styles of living, their meaningful interactions with place, and their attention to quality and simplicity of function. They are designed around these functions, forming a tight-knit place with a strong emphasis on indoor and outdoor experiences. Certain aspects from each of these place type examples contribute to an overall conception of serene urbanism. Common characteristics of intentional communities, hospitality places, healing environments, agrotourism, and contemplative places include a certain coherence of design, clear and present orders, distinct boundaries, and strong inclusion of nature in many forms. There is usually a degree of compactness, yet human scale to each form. The mosque and *madrassa* at Dar Al Islam, designed by Hassan Fathy, is an example of a contemplative environment for both prayer and education. The image in Figure 4.11a shows the visiting group Architecture, Culture, and Spirituality visiting the mosque.[37] Figure 4.11b shows the remarkable abbey at Mont St Michel in Normandy.

Contemplative and monastic environments offer great models for sustainable living. They tend to be self-sufficient, agrarian, with relative density and concentration of dwellings. There is sacredness to everyday functions, along with a keen sensitivity to, and stewardship of, the land. Combining the qualities and characteristics of intentional communities, resort and hospitality places, agrotourism, health and wellness, and contemplative and monastic environments provides rich planning guides for place design. Each of these embodies qualities of the serene and urban, with the added qualities of sustainable, biophilic, and numinous experiences.

Figure 4.11 Contemplative environments: a) Dar al Islam, Abiquiu, New Mexico
Source: Photograph by Phillip Tabb
b) Mont Saint Michel, Normandy, France
Source: Alamy Stock Photo

Notes

1 Tabb, Phillip, "Sacred Places: Archetypal Patterns in Place Creation," self-published, Boulder, CO, 1995, p. 37.
2 Donat, John, *World Architecture 4*, Studio Vista Publishers, London, 1967, p. 9.
3 Casey, Edward, *The Fate of Place: A Philosophical History*, University of California Press, Berkeley, CA, 1997, p. 9.

4 Tuan, Yi-Fu, *Space and Place: The Perspective of Experience*, University of Minnesota, Minneapolis, MN, 1977, p. 6.
5 Relph, Edward, *Place and Placelessness*, Pion Ltd, London, 1976, p. 34.
6 Norberg-Schulz, Christian, *Genius Loci: Towards a Phenomenology of Architecture*, Rizzoli International Press, New York, 1984, p. 6.
7 Brill, Michael, *Using the Place-creation Myth to Develop Design Guidelines for Sacred Space*, self-published, 1985. Patterns included: making location, succession of spaces, differentiated bounding, verticality, celestial order, discriminating views, light from above, and consecration.
8 Creation Myths: www.mythencyclopedia.com/Pr-Sa/Romulus-and-Remus.html (accessed October 2015).
9 Plato, *The Republic*, Book VII, trans. A.D. Lindsay, Alfred A. Knopf, New York, 1976, pp. 197–9.
10 Campbell, Joseph, *Primitive Mythology (The Masks of God*, vol. 1), Penguin Books, Harmondsworth, 1991.
11 New Leafs, "The Purpose of Myth," January 1, 2010. Available online at http://aeoluskephas. blogspot.com/2010/01/purpose-of-myth.html?m+1 (accessed June 7, 2016).
12 Lawlor, Robert, *Sacred Geometry: Philosophy and Practice*, Thames and Hudson, London, 1982, p. 6.
13 Irwin, Terence, *Aristotle's First Principles*, Clarendon Paperbacks, Oxford, 1990.
14 Stephens, Anthony, *Archetype Revisited: An Updated Natural History of the Self*, Inner City Books, Toronto, 2003.
15 Campbell, *Primitive Mythology*.
16 Plato, *Timaeus: The Collected Dialogues*, ed. Edith Hamilton and Huntington Cairns, Princeton University Press, Princeton, NJ, 1989, pp. 1151–1211.
17 Lawlor, *Sacred Geometry*, p. 21.
18 Waterfield, Robin, *The Theology of Arithmetic*, Phanes Press, Grand Rapids, MI, 1988, pp. 22–3.
19 Wedberg, Anders, *Plato's Philosophy of Mathematics*, Praeger, New York, 1977.
20 Tabb, Phillip and Deviren, A. Senem, *The Greening of Architecture: A Critical History and Survey of Contemporary Sustainable Architecture and Urban Design*, Ashgate Publishing, London, 2013. Also, archetypes are part of a triad of concepts – *archetypal* energies, *ectypal* exemplifications and *typal* concrete examples. The five principles used here derive from semiotics related to the significance of the numbers 1, 2, 3, 4, and 5. All but the number 4 have immeasurable square roots [Pi, $\sqrt{2}$, $\sqrt{3}$ and $(\sqrt{5}+1)/2$]. Plato, *Timaeus*.
21 Doxiadis, Constantinos, *Ekistics: An Introduction to the Science of Human Settlement*, Hutchinson Publishers, London, 1968.
22 Tabb, "Sacred Places."
23 Alexander, Christopher, Ishikawa, Sara, Silverstein, Murray with Jacobson, Max, Fiksdahl-King, Ingrid, and Shlomo, Angel, *A Pattern Language*, Oxford University Press, New York, 1977.
24 Brill, *Using the Place-creation Myth*.
25 Tabb, Phillip, "The Solar Village Archetype: A Study of Energy-Integrated Planning Principles for Satellite Settlements in Temperate Climates," PhD dissertation, Architectural Association, London, 1990.
26 Lyndon, Donlyn and Moore, Charles, *Chambers for a Memory Palace*, MIT Press, Cambridge, MA, 1994.
27 Vitruvius, Marcus, *De Archituctura (Ten Books on Architecture)*, Dover Publications, New York, 1960.
28 Relph, *Place and Placelessness*; Lyndon and Moore, *Chambers for a Memory Palace*; Brill, *Using the Place Creation Myth*; Tabb, "The Solar Village Archetype"; Alexander et al., *A Pattern Language*.
29 Brill, *Using the Place-creation Myth*, p. 1.
30 Annan Jensen, Sophie, "Mexcaltitan, Nayarit: An Island City in the Swamp," *Mexconnect*, January 1, 1998. Available online at /www.mexconnect.com/articles/979-mexcaltitan-nayarit-an-island-city-in-the-swamp (accessed October 2015).

31 Findhorn Community, *The Findhorn Garden*, Findhorn Community, Findhorn, 1975. Findhorn Community, *The Findhorn Garden: Pioneering a New Vision of Man and Nature in Cooperation*, Harper & Row, New York, 1975.

32 Auroville, India. Available online at www.auroville.org (accessed October 2015).

33 Castello di Gargonza, Italy: Lyndon and Moore, *Chambers for a Memory Palace*.

34 Ikerd, John E., "Reclaiming the Sacred in Food and Farming," University of Missouri. Available online at http://web.missouri.edu/~ikerdj/papers/Sacred.html (accessed August 2014).

35 Banner Health, McKee Medical Center, "Healing Gardens." Available online at www .bannerhealth.com/Locations/Colorado/McKee+Medical+Center/Patients+and+Visitors/ Spiritual+Care/Healing+Gardens.htm (accessed October 2015).

36 In Coates, Gary J., *Erik Asmussen, Architect*, Byggforlaget Publishers, Stockholm, 1997.

37 Architecture, Culture, and Spirituality (ACS) was started in 2007 and is composed of a very diverse and international group of individuals committed to a reflective engagement of the space between architecture, culture and spirituality. Once a year the group organizes a symposium held in various contemplative places throughout the United States.

5　Sustainability

Almost everything being done in the name of sustainable development addresses and attempts to reduce unsustainability. But reducing unsustainability, although critical, does not and will not create sustainability.[1]

Sustainable measures at the urban scale are clustered around a set of interrelated planning strategies that include urban form configuration, density, mixes of use, transportation networks, infrastructure, building typologies, architectural design, and construction. So what does this really mean? On one level, it means to do development differently than the suburban sprawl model and hopefully dystopian visions of the future. According to the World Commission on Environment and Development, it is development that meets the needs of the present generation without compromising the ability of future generations to meet their needs.[2] This implies that intelligent management and responsible use must balance our contemporary lifestyle needs with both available and future resources. This includes the demand for land, food, water, goods and services, housing, transportation, communication, energy, and the functions that drive our society: residential, commercial, industrial, recreational, institutional, and spiritual.

Context for sustainable urbanism

In his research at the Open University in the UK, the architect Peter Rickaby showed that the two most efficient and desirable sustainable models for new urban growth were densification of already existing cities and the establishment of small energy-efficient satellite settlements found surrounding the urban edge in a spiderweb network.[3] This suggests that initially there should be a focus on these two contexts for implementing effective sustainable measures, which require very differing approaches. This does not mean that the suburban context should not be addressed. Ideally the entire differing territories, from intense urban center to the rural edge, should be addressed seamlessly.

Sustainable scales of application

In Susan Owens' book, *Energy, Planning and Urban Design*, varying planning measures affect certain mechanisms, which in turn have differing energy implications.[4] A settlement or development shape will influence travel requirements, especially for automobile and pedestrian movement. The interspersion of activities also will affect travel requirements, especially trip length and frequency. The density of built form affects building typologies and energy requirements for heating and cooling. The clustering of trip ends facilitates the effectiveness of public transport systems and pedestrian connections. Climate-responsive siting, orientation, and landscaping maximize the potential for ambient on-site resources, such as wind, water harvesting and solar energy.

Owens also established the association between the types of planning and design structural variables and scale. A transect of appropriate strategies occurs at differing scales of application, from the regional and sub-regional scales to the settlement and neighborhood scales, and finally to the individual building scale. These structural variables include:

- settlement patterns;
- spacing and between-place communication networks;
- settlement size;
- shape and in-place communication networks;
- density;
- interspersion of land uses;
- degree of centralization;
- orientation of streets, lots and buildings;
- siting; and
- architectural design.

This notion of scales of application also can be applied to the larger ecological contexts within which development occurs, as well as to the smaller scales of building systems, appliances, materials, and products used in the occupation of these spaces.

This was to suggest that differences in the spatial characteristics and structure of a place could contribute to a wide variation in energy efficiency. Some of the sustainable issues overlapped, repeated, and coexisted across scales, while some were distinct or present within a particular scale. For example, water was an issue that existed at the regional through systems' scales, although it was handled in different magnitudes. On-site resource utilization was confined primarily to the building scale, although in some instances it was applicable to the cluster scale and renewable energy farms. Configuration, density of built form, and mixes of use were applicable to the settlement and neighborhood scales.

The landscape architect Patrick Condon presented seven rules for sustainable communities.[5] The strategies included:

1. restoration of the streetcar city;
2. design for an interconnected street system;
3. location of commercial activities, frequent transit and schools within a five-minute walk;
4. location of employment close to affordable housing;
5. provide a diversity of housing types;
6. create a linked system of natural areas; and
7. invest in more efficient infrastructure.

Condon prefaced this list of strategies with the idea that they should not be considered as single strategies, but rather as an accumulative whole.

Sustainability transect

The term "transect" was borrowed from ecology, which described changes in habitat and plant distribution over an ecological gradient or zone, usually defined by two edges from the ridge of a wooded hill through a meadow to a water source below.[6] An urban transect was essentially a geographical cross-section between the most urban part of a settlement center or core, to the most rural area at the edge. This kind of transect articulated the agglomeration of people, buildings, roads, other urban elements, and natural features of the place in a hierarchical, spatial fashion. The concept from the most urban-to-rural was a spatial disposition of transitional development, and a good marker across applicable sustainability scales. Density, land use mix, geometric order, and proximity played a crucial role in the context-defining characteristics of place, and provided a framework for the scales of application of sustainable strategies. Later, this was adapted to articulate urban characteristics as well, which included the gradient signifying the density of built forms to the correspondent amounts of open space.

In 1971, planner Andrew Thorburn published a copy of his diagram of a transect often found in English villages, the "Thorburn transect".[7] Rather than expressed in distinct and differentiated zones, as one later sees in the New Urbanism models (Krier and Duany), this was more of a counteracting and seamless gradient between the built elements of the settlement center moving outward, and the landscape and natural elements emanating from the edge, moving inward to the most dense areas at the village center. According to the transect articulated by Duany Platter-Zyberk and Partners, a six-zone classification was established: urban core, urban center, general urban, suburban, rural, and natural.[8] New Urbanist Douglas Farr suggests that "the transect of the everyday" provides opportunities to apply sustainable planning and design strategies that affect most lifestyle and consumer choices across the transect from urban to rural territories, and that it is important to recognize that design responses take different forms throughout these different places.[9]

From these observations, it is clear that sustainable planning strategies fall into two categories of application: between-place regional planning, and in-place urban design. The physical characteristics of green urbanism follow philosopher Michel Foucault's systems of organization, as they function as both place and network architectures.[10] They share complicit roles in creating a sustainable future focused on the urban design scale. Originating settlements were simply single nucleated designs that grew outward incrementally, until they reached the carrying capacity of a particular region. However today, walkable, nucleated settlements have grown into huge, populated cities replete with counter-urban suburban areas, and ubiquitous network territories, gluing them into expansive metroplexes. So it is not surprising that these large urban areas can be characterized now as place-oriented designs and network spaces that connect them into mega-urban agglomerations.

The hybrid electric Toyota Prius (1997) is one example of a myriad of green products currently in use (Figure 5.1a), while Beddington Zero Energy Development (BedZED) in London and constructed in 2002 (Figure 5.1b) is another example. It demonstrates what sustainable measures can be employed within the context of single buildings. The photograph of the Palatine Hill in Rome, Italy shows the many historic and physical layers comprising the urban design scale: people have occupied this place from 1,000 BC (Figure 5.1c). These examples represent only three scales of this transect.

Figure 5.1 Sustainable scales of application: a) Products   *Source*: courtesy of Phillip Tabb
b) Single buildings   *Source*: Global Warming Images / Alamy
c) Urban fabric   *Source*: courtesy of Phillip Tabb

In-place

Placemaking is an internally oriented process and structure, creating a domain focused on being, rest, stasis, agglomeration, concentration, saturation, safety, dwelling, stewardship, and pedestrian scale and experience. This means *being there* and being in place, having supportive architecture and urban forms that contribute to nodes of sustainable living patterns. Conversely, "connective tissue" is characterized by flow; it is moving, fluid, linear, interstitial, infrastructural, and dynamic, focusing on interchange, accessibility, and systemic connectedness. It is the *go-between* where resources, nature, goods, energy, and people move and respond to differing kinds of speed-scale environments and between-place processes and modes of transport. Previously fragmented, this sprawling territory offers great opportunities for a new kind of reformed green architecture and eco-urbanism. The interface between urban dwelling place and infrastructure network suggests an ecological power geometry, constellation, and progressive sense of place. Constellating urbanism is a notion that unites urban agglomerations into a more comprehensive whole, where place becomes coherent and connected.

Typical among the issues which have been addressed by place-oriented sustainable urban designs are:

* higher levels of nucleation;
* more condensed configurations;
* increased densities;
* greater mixes of use, including location of commercial functions;
* varying building typologies;
* reduced numbers of single-family detached dwellings;
* narrower and more pedestrian-friendly streets;
* increased connectivity;
* integrated transit;
* greener water and infrastructure systems;
* provision of some alternative energy source-technologies; and
* incorporation of higher percentages of open space and linked systems of natural areas.

The scales of these place-oriented patterns vary extensively, from highly horizontal, spread-out suburban landscapes to more human-scaled, nucleated, pedestrian-oriented settlement designs. Suburbs are typically characterized by a predominance of single uses, single-family detached housing, along with functional zoning of activities grouped into separate enclaves of uses, such as office parks, shopping centers, schools, and recreation areas. All these land use functions are made accessible by, and are dependent on, the automobile. Nonspatial measures include:

- the use of energy-efficient products, including on-site resources;
- construction energy; and
- conservation-conscious behaviors.

Spatial measures include:

- integration of residential and nonresidential activities (mixed zoning);
- clustering of end-use or destination functions;
- density, in which residential land uses are located closer to nonresidential uses; and
- provision of pedestrian access to goods and services.

In-place settlements can take on various forms including:

- inner-city neighborhoods;
- small towns;
- bedroom communities;
- gated communities;
- suburban enclaves;
- New Urban communities;
- sustainable, agricultural and conservation communities.

The Palazzo Pubblico in Siena, and Mercato Centrale in Florence, Italy are examples of in-place catalysts (Figures 5.2a and 5.2b).

According to the Urban Land Institute, examples of in-place conservation communities include Galisteo, New Mexico, Hidden Springs, Idaho, Jackson Meadow, Minnesota and Santa Lucia Preserve, California, USA. Both central to these communities and pivotal to their success is their walkability, connections to nature,

Figure 5.2 In-place sustainability: a) Palazzo Pubblico, Siena, Italy b) Mercato Centrale, Florence, Italy

Source: Photographs by Phillip Tabb

and focus on rich mixes of use. Critical is the quantity and quality of the types of nonresidential uses, their physical designs that encourage community engagement and interaction, and their ability to respond to necessary life-support functions. Conventional suburban planning too often has placed consideration for automobile networks and access to the maximum number of plots first, while pedestrian paths and environments have been an afterthought. Absolutely critical for in-place networks is that they plan for pedestrians first, and second for multiple modes for other connections.

Between-place

Between-place, including infrastructure, is an interface for people and resources between habitable urban territories and cities globally. According to Katrina Stoll and Scott Lloyd in *Infrastructure as Architecture*, cities continue to be spatial peaks within stretching horizontal fields.[11] These fields are carved up into counter-urban places, and by the infrastructure linkages the connect them. Networks vary with geometric configuration, from linear and orthogonal grids to radial or concentric, and from spiderweb forms to random orders. They are what Constantinos Doxiadis called an "ekistic" element, that includes water supply, power supply, transportation (water, road, rail, and air), communication (telephone, radio, television, and cable), and sewage and drainage systems.[12]

Between-place contexts support a new kind of architecture, one that has systemic, fabric-oriented qualities. Sites for infrastructure architecture tend to be situated around dense urban centers, and between defined suburban residential districts. These environments are typically complex, often chaotic, and spatially fragmented, with multiple land uses, functionally zoned and separated from one another, such as:

- industrial factories;
- power plants;
- water treatment facilities;
- brownfield sites;
- sports and entertainment facilities;
- business parks;
- automobile dealerships;
- shopping malls;
- rail lines;
- watersheds; and
- patchworks of residual land.

They also tend to be dominated by automobile highway networks. Given the piecemeal nature of this territory, sustainable strategies tend toward increased levels of connectivity for ecological and pedestrian zones; increased mixes and integration of uses, densification, and far more sinuous forms. The New Urban insertions and adaptive reuse projects for this development context typically follow linear watersheds, transportation routes, and other infrastructural systems. Further, Katrina Stoll and Scott Lloyd claimed that there has been increasing demand for integrated solutions that must respond to new, complex and fragmented urban landscapes.[13]

Between-place conservation measures can take many forms designed to reduce travel distance and frequency of trips. Nonspatial, between-place measures include:

- adoption of carpooling;
- increase of online shopping;
- permanent relocation of residences to more convenient access to critical nonresidential uses, including schools and employment;
- relocation for access to mass transport; and
- increased home-based or neighborhood-based recreational activities.

Spatial measures include:

- clustering end-uses for greater numbers of multipurpose trips;
- tighter clustering of nucleated districts;
- increased efficiency of between-place transport technology and networks; and
- land use planning efforts to create more self-sustaining life-support activities, goods, and services within nucleated districts.

Between-place connections also occur within urban areas and nucleated places by a diversity of modes. For example, Namba Parks, which was completed in 2003 in Osaka, Japan, is a confluence of multiple modes of transportation, including regional rail, automobile, and a pedestrian park system (Figure 5.3a). Namba Parks was an amazing example of an infrastructural oasis within the city center. Designed by Jerde Partnership, the parks and 30-story structure replaced the former Osaka Baseball Park, and were planned with one story of activities underground and eight stories aboveground. The program called for a combination of retail and offices, with a rooftop garden complex. Included in the project were a number of different restaurants, an amphitheater for live entertainment, and spaces for vegetable gardens and wagon shops. In 2007 a second phase of activities, which nearly doubled the size of the original design, was added to include a cinema complex and specialty stores. The sensuous form was

Figure 5.3 Between-place sustainability: a) Namba Parks, Japan
Source: Photograph courtesy of The Jerde Partnership
b) Metrocable Medellin, Colombia
Source: Alamy Stock Photo
c) Millennium Bridge, London, UK
Source: Photograph by Phillip Tabb

designed to connect to local streets, which encouraged passers-by to easily engage in the natural amenities, especially with the varied outdoor functions that included stands of trees, clusters of rocks, cliffs, streams, waterfalls, ponds, and multiple terraces. The site for the project was less than a ten-minute walk from Namba Station.

Critically important is the regeneration of informal settlements, where 1 billion people presently live, with focus on the architecture of the in-between and infrastructure – as shown in Medellin, Colombia. Medellin has an innovative, above-ground gondola lift as a complementary transport system, designed to cross the dense urban fabric below. Designed by Edison Escobar and María Patricia Bustamante Architects and a host of consultants, the work opened in 2004 and, with its three cable lines, is considered the first gondola system in South America. The line is nearly 1.5 miles (2 kilometers) in length (Figure 5.3b).

The Millennium Bridge, located in central London, crosses the River Thames and connects Bankside on the south to the City of London on the north, and was opened in 2000. Designed by Arup, Foster and Partners and Sir Anthony Caro, its eight suspension cables are tensioned to pull with a force of 2,000 tons against the piers set into each bank, and to support 5,000 people (Figure 5.3c). Two concrete piers are set near the banks on either side of the Thames, and they support the three-section span totaling 1,066 feet (325 meters). Remarkable is the pedestrian experience and convenient connection linking Bankside (Globe Theatre, Bankside Gallery and Tate Modern) with the City of London (below St Paul's Cathedral).

Sustainable urban strategies

Sustainable urbanism, simply stated, is sustainability in the urban setting. It is human habitation that constantly moves toward greater levels of homeostatic balance, accommodating growth yet building toward population stabilization. This can be accomplished through:

- careful change;
- preservation of nonrenewable resources;
- prudent use of renewable resources;
- increase of accessibility, with reduction of travel distances;
- protection of biological systems;
- responsibility toward the collection, treatment and recycling of air, water, waste, and other resources; and
- building conservation through adaptive reuse, more intelligent planning and design, and improved building practices.

New communities are considered to be in a pioneering stage and generally require great amounts of energy and resources, while long-standing communities are at a climax stage and generally are more in balance with current energy and resource flows. For new development projects at the urban edge, the following are 14 guiding biophilic principles applicable to sustainable urbanism:[14]

1. *homeostasis* – climax systems of high diversity, large biomass, and high stability through protection from rapid change and shifts of energy flows away from

production and the maintenance of systems, recognizing natural change and uncertainty (including climate change);

2. *diversity* – in demographics (age, gender, ethnicity, economic background), land-use activities, density, building typologies, affordability in housing, landscapes, biomass, and scale, sizes, and types of spaces;

3. *accessibility* – increase accessibility with settlement shape, size, and land-use interspersion concepts, network efficiency, safety, connectivity and modes of transport, resulting in travel distance and trip frequency reduction;

4. *preservation* – of ecologically sensitive and agriculturally productive land, historic and archeologically significant sites, vital community places, nonrenewable resources, wildlife and endangered species, and the night sky;

5. *prudent use of land* – reforestation, open space design, climate-responsive landscaping, productive use of residual land, development of a natural settlement place, provision of pedestrian networks and places for social and cultural activities;

6. *clustering of end-uses* – provides economic, social, and sustainable synergies appropriate to economies of scale, localization of amenities, and nonresidential needs, and infrastructural efficiencies;

7. *integrated agriculture* – provision of land for the practice of cultivating, processing, and distributing food, which also can involve animal husbandry, aquaculture, agroforestry, urban beekeeping, and horticulture;

8. *on-site resources* – use of renewable energy, elemental sources (solar, wind, geothermal, tree canopy shading, etc.), fresh air, clean water (streams, ponds, rooftop harvesting), and local building materials;

9. *waste amelioration* – air and water quality (including reductions in CO_2, NO_X, SO_X, and underlying hazardous chemicals), waste treatment with both gray and black water, waste heat recovery, and product recycling;

10. *hybridity* – a mixture and alternating choices of energy sources as they either diminish (such as fossil fuels) or enter the system (such as renewable sources), and applied to heating, cooling, air conditioning, electricity production, and transport technology;

11. *community-oriented urban design* – a stakeholder participatory planning process and form of governance, containment and coherence, creation of a range of public places, cohesion, opportunities for interaction, and fostering shared sustainability interests and functions within the community;

12. *intelligent building design and construction practices* – utilizing energy conservation techniques, climate-responsive designs, higher density and smaller footprints, more effective control systems, and use of nontoxic building materials;

13. *sustainable economic development* – fostering local businesses within or near the community, environmentally sensitive economic development with balance between life-cycle and first costs, and between pioneering and climax stages of development;

14. *place-oriented design* – sensitivity and response to the natural qualities of the land, to a beneficial orientation to the sun and other natural resources, to certain geometric systems that foster community gathering and interactions, open planning and design process, and to opportunities for community-wide celebrations and sustainable behavioral practices.

Environmental sustainability is herein related to serene urbanism, with particular focus on the small-settlement scale at the edge of metropolitan areas. Its proximity to an urban center allows for interaction with urban-scale activities, including an international airport, specialist hospitals, commerce, higher educational facilities, performing arts, entertainment, and other urban amenities. At the climax stage of development, serene urban environments located at the urban edge allow for interaction with the natural environment, and for it to become more pedestrian-oriented and self-sufficient. Settlement shape, increased density, land preservation, interspersion of activities, and climate-oriented planning and design working in combination offer a locus of practices for productive sustainability. This type of sustainable urbanism is a behavior and lifestyle-driven form of development.

Land preservation

Preserving land is important in several ways. It increases the possibility of interaction with nature and provides land for a variety of uses, including ecological zones, wild animal habitation, flood zones, storm water collection, outdoor recreation, agriculture, and preservation of historic and significant archeological sites. The magnitude, function, and type of open land uses can vary along the urban-to-rural transect. At the rural end of this transect, land preservation usually involves larger territories with greater biodiversity and functions, such as forested areas, agriculture, animal grazing, larger animal habitats, scenic corridors, buffers, and other valuable natural resources. At the urban end of the transect, land preservation is smaller in area and more targeted to specific functions and civic engagements, such as parks and recreation, urban agriculture, trails, streams, wetlands, and other natural open spaces. Within the infrastructural zones of larger cities is preserved land for interconnected waterways, ecological frameworks, stormwater management, flood control, contiguous wildlife populations counteracting habitat fragmentations, and transportation corridors for varying modes.

Land use zoning and the accompanying densities targeted to each zone are important in providing provisions for land preservation. According to Edward T. McMahon, we need to create greater value of nature.[15] The Transfer of Development Rights is a useful tool to simultaneously and potentially preserve greater areas of land and create density, which is beneficial for more sustainable urban design.[16]

Urban agriculture

Agricultural urbanism or agrarian urbanism are sustainable land planning approaches applicable to both architecture and urban design scales, and can be found along the entire transect, from dense urban centers to rural land adjacent to metropolitan areas. According to Janine de la Salle and Mark Holland, it is an emerging design framework for integrating a wide range of sustainable food and agricultural systems into communities. In other words, "it is a way of building a place around food."[17] The approach goes beyond simply urban agricultural production, reducing the distribution costs associated with the movement of produce to include economic development, community-making, and education. According to Mark Schill, climate change is expected to impact the growing of certain crops.[18] Severe water shortages, such as the one that California experienced in 2015, could threaten many agricultural areas throughout the traditionally arid western USA, and is true for other areas worldwide.

In 2009, a four-mile farm was planned down the center of the Bronx Grand Concourse in New York: it was intended to transform a predominantly 180-feet (55-meter)-wide, traffic-oriented corridor into a self-sustaining boulevard. The goal of the Edible Concourse was to show how urban agricultural practices could be implanted into dense urban environments, while tackling the very real issue of access to affordable, healthy, and locally grown foods in the Bronx. The project was a proposition about simple interventions that could be accomplished incrementally over time. Similarly, the New Amsterdam Street project in Manhattan by Michael Sorkin's urban design studio transforms an urban street into a food-producing urban place (Figure 5.4a). The work of Luc Schuiten promoted the concept of a "vegetal city," which saw a city-wide eco-transformation over time of biological systems of organization, rather than a technological one. (Allotments surround the urban environment around a Berlin neighborhood; Figure 5.4b.)

Prairie Crossing, nationally recognized as a leading conservation and transit-oriented development-oriented community located in Grayslake, Illinois, is a 389-dwelling unit, Leadership in Energy and Environmental Design-Neighborhood Development (LEED-ND) that has alternative energy systems, a charter school, native landscaping, energy-efficient homes, and a certified organic farm. Of the 677-acre (274-hectare) development, 80 percent is dedicated to open space, while 20 percent of the land is dedicated to home sites. The developers George and Victoria Ranney purchased the land and initiated the project in the late 1980s. According to *New York Times* contributor David W. Dunlap, "Prairie Crossing looks serene, clean and, most of all, inviting."[19] Prairie Crossing is served by two commuter railroads with connections to Chicago and O'Hare International Airport, and there are bicycle trails and walking paths. Central to the plan is Lake Aldo Leopold, which provides serenity, recreation, and a community focus.

Figure 5.4 Urban agriculture: a) New Amsterdam Street, New York
Source: Photograph courtesy of Michael Sorkin
b) Berlin neighborhood allotments
Source: Alamy Stock Photo

The Southlands project in Tsawwassen in the south delta of British Columbia was a working development based on concepts of sustainable design, where integrating local food and agriculture were a central focus of community life. Designed by Duany Platter-Zyberk & Company, the project design was compact, with a variety of residential uses, neighborhood shops and services, education and recreational facilities. According to Andres Duany, "agrarian urbanism" is an evolving approach that weaves various food-related activities, such as small farms, shared gardens, farmer's markets, and agricultural processing, into the development model of walkable mixed-use traditional small town designs.[20] However, its application extended beyond simply new satellite settlements to include existing urban centers. For centuries, community allotments have been associated with neighborhoods, hamlets, and villages worldwide, which are formed by subdividing a piece of land into a few or up to several hundreds of land parcels that are assigned to individuals or families.

Millican Reserve, a three-hamlet sustainable community plan, was developed south of College Station, Texas on nearly 2,500 acres (1,011 hectares) of land along Peach Creek. The development was planned for approximately 1,500 dwellings, and targeted to a broad spectrum of resident users including singles, young families, professional and university faculty, and retirement families. A large function of the development was intended for the provision of equestrian activities, with a public arena, stables, barns, paddocks, and riding trails for local residents. In addition, integrated agriculture was included and connected Texas A&M University researchers. At the entrance to the development a ring of contemporary vernacular buildings was planned, designed by Lake Flato to set an image for the place and simultaneously provide specific amenities for the community that include a country store and gas station, farmer's market, outdoor amphitheater, petting zoo, and equestrian center. The three hamlets were themed with wellness, equestrian, and recreational organizing activities.

Spring Island, located in South Carolina, is a 3,500-acre (1,416-hectare) conservation community based on strict environmental standards, in which one-third is untouched. Dwelling spacing has large buffers, while houses and unpaved access roads are small. Developed by Jim Chaffin and Jim Light, the community consists of 30 percent permanent residents, 40 percent seasonal, and 30 percent second homeowners: "Oceanfront property, Mr. Chaffin said, is overcrowded and he wants Spring Island to be like a camp, with horseback riding, boating, walking, golf and bicycling available."[21] Criticism of both Prairie Crossing and Spring Island is their lack of urbanism and a more diverse collection of nonresidential functions, which inevitably would reduce the need for between-place automobile transportation.

Agricultural urbanism combined with other sustainable urban strategies and green architectural measures could be a harbinger for future development practices, as well as a potential improvement on the present food production, distribution, and grocery store system. New agricultural practices, such as urban agriculture, farmer's markets, organic agriculture, permaculture, small plot intensive (SPIN) farming,[22] community gardens, replenishing seed banks, farm cooperatives, and the 100-mile (161-kilometer) diet could all add to a growing interest in bringing healthy food closer to urban life. According to Janine de la Salle and Mark Holland, our relationship with food is an inextricable measure of our culture, and this culture connects back to nature: "Chefs, farmers, planners, politicians, designers, and citizens – we all have a role to play in shaping and participating in the new food culture."[23] Like many sustainable urban projects, agricultural urbanism has been demonstrated on sites adjacent to metropolitan cities or in somewhat isolated locations. A next step might be to bring the best practices gained by these early demonstrations to more urban contexts and the existing stock of buildings. Blending densities, mixes of use, workplace environments, alternative transportation systems, and agriculture would certainly provide opportunities for reducing unsustainability. Demonstrations such as Millican Reserve, Southlands, and Summit Powder Mountain[24] have successfully occurred at the edge of urban areas. Yet the greatest challenges for agricultural urbanism still remain within the suburban and urban contexts. (The urban allotments mentioned previously, seen surrounding a Berlin, Germany neighborhood, exemplify many such efforts worldwide.)

Settlement configuration

The shape, configuration, and distribution of density contribute to the sustainable functions of a place. It has been suggested that energy is the permitting factor in the process of urbanization, and that the nature and availability of energy sources and technologies influence the spatial structure and configurations of settlement forms.[25] Strategic objectives for sustainable configurations include planning for:

- regional climatic patterns;
- solar access;
- density and automobile use reduction;
- settlement sizes and distribution of nonresidential functions that support pedestrian accessibility; and
- efficient, in-place transportation networks.

Research by Victor Olgyay in the 1960s suggested that ideal settlement configurations varied with differing climatic contexts. In cold climates, settlements should be compact and protected from northerly winds (Figures 5.5a and 5.5b here).[26]

The architect Ralph Erskine's image for "Arctic City" amply illustrated this.[27] Temperate climate settlements should be elongated east and west, allowing for good solar access to streets and buildings that are located within. Hot-arid climates have the need for both heating and cooling, which necessitate greater attention to the northern

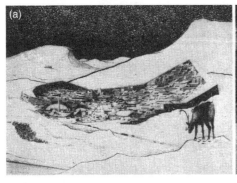

Figure 5.5 Climatic determinism:
a) Arctic City   *Source*: unknown
b) Hedesunda housing, Sweden
Source: Peter Guthrie

Figure 5.6 Urban shape and configuration in the Civitella of Val di Chiana, Tuscany, Italy
Source: Photograph by Phillip Tabb

sides of buildings, taking advantage of summer shading. Moreover, in hot-humid climate zones, designs should allow for natural breezes, both with the settlement plan and for individual buildings. Settlement shape also informs the internal order of streets, blocks, and civic places, and the ways in which it interfaces with nature.

The overall shape of a settlement is important for defensive and climatic reasons, and nucleation provides focus for cultural activities and commerce. Civitella in Val di Chiana is a sixth-century fortress located in Tuscany, and as can be clearly seen in Figure 5.6, its overall plan aspect is elongated along the east–west axis, allowing for good solar access in the colder winter months. The village is located along a ridge and features two nucleated places: to the east is the church of Santa Maria Assunta (1252), its plaza and well, and to the west is the castle (1048), partly destroyed in World War II. The village is relatively dense, supporting a healthy pedestrian network and surrounded by a stone wall and farmland beyond. The central linear axis connects the church with the castle ruins. It has a population of 9,091 (2013 census). The elliptical form is coherent, identifiable, compact, and human-scaled. While originally designed for military purposes, its present scenic views of the farmland and Arezzo Valley beyond are serene.

Density of built form

Density is a planning measure that is not without controversy. Low-density, single-family, detached housing has long been a preference for housing, especially in the United States. This is due to a desire for greater privacy, space around the entire building, flexibility to add or expand in the future, and individual control over the open space (front and rear yards). This phenomenon is coupled further with a desire to escape the negative effects of more urban living: crime, congestion, noise, pollution, deteriorating environments, and increased placelessness.

The single use, suburban, single-family, detached housing type is not without criticism. The suburban landscape requires more land, more infrastructure, and is usually a function of intense automobile use for connection to critical nonresidential functions including shopping, schools, health facilities, and employment. Increased density has long been a revered sustainable strategy, with its inherent qualities reversing the negative aspects of the suburban form.

Density is classified as the number of people within a given area, and as an urban design characteristic it affects three important influences: network configurations, building typologies, and mixed use.[28] There are three major sustainable advantages to increased density, which are:

1. the reduction of travel distance, as land use destinations tend to be located nearer to one another;
2. lower building heating and cooling loads, due to attached building envelopes area reductions; and
3. the increased economic potential for greater diversity and numbers of mixes of uses.

Typically, suburbs across the United States have densities that average four dwellings per acre (10 per hectare) compared to the density of Paris, France, with 86 dwelling units per acre (35 per hectare). The density differences can be clearly seen in Figures 5.7a and 5.7b. Increased density aids in reducing energy loads, transportation distances, and supporting pedestrian places.

Mixes of use

It is important to create a diversity of land use mixes in order to reduce travel frequency and distances from residential development to critical nonresidential functions that support everyday activities, goods, and services. Integrated mixes and the clustering of end uses contribute to reduction in automobile use, especially for the grouping of grocery markets, pharmacies, restaurants and cafes, health facilities, banks, fire and police protection, religious institutions, and schools. It is important for health

Figure 5.7 Density of built form: a) American suburbs b) Paris, France
Source: Shutterstock

Figure 5.8 Mixes of use: a) Rotterdam Market Hall b) Boulder's Alfalfa grocery market
Source: Phillip Tabb

facilities to be within easy access of residents. The health care center in Bangalore, India designed by Flying Elephant Architects (2011) is a good example of highly sustainable facilities. The Rotterdam Market Hall, designed by MVRDV Architects, is an extraordinary mixed-use building housing commercial market activities and offices, along with housing (Figure 5.8a). Large-box supermarkets are being replaced with more moderate-sized and distributed organic grocery stores, such as Whole Foods in Texas, Fresh Thyme Farmers Market in Phoenix, Trader Joe's in California and Alfalfa's Market in Boulder, Colorado (Figure 5.8b). These new mixed-use markets are providing more than just large mass products: they are including farmer's markets, arts and crafts, bookstores, cafes, and lawn and garden supplies, as well as activities for children. It is important to gather places such as these into a synergy of social interaction and critical functional service to the community. Cooking classes and instruction on nutrition are common in these kinds of markets.

Mixes of use need to respond to perennial community and individual needs as well as constantly changing ones. It is development that blends a combination of residential, commercial, cultural, institutional, or industrial uses, where those functions are physically and functionally integrated, and that provide easy and safe pedestrian connections.

Networks and connections

Networks, connections, and circulation affect sustainability in several ways. Each mode of transport has a fundamentally different technological solution, and some require a separate environment. Each mode has its own infrastructure, vehicles, and operations, and often has unique regulations; it also has separate subsystems. Typical transport and circulation networks for residential development include the following:

* roads, streets, lanes, and alleys for individual automobiles and electric carts;
* streets for public buses;
* streets and paths for bicycles;
* bridle paths and trails for horses;
* paths, sidewalks, and trails for pedestrians.

Travel to work, shopping, schools, medical facilities, social interaction, and leisure are all important in the everyday lives of residents. Strategies to reduce these travel destinations have been targeted to each of these needs. For example, elementary schools within walking distance of neighborhood residents not only save energy, but also potentially reduce obesity. Providing automobile-free or safe networks is critically important. Taken together, network architectures amalgamate into constellations of unity that give character to each settlement.

Car and van sharing startups such as Uber, Lyft, and Via are changing the in-place transportation landscape in larger cities. Car-sharing is designed to replace car ownership for people who do not need to drive to work every day, and to significantly reduce congestion and greenhouse gas emissions. Carpooling commuting is seen as a more environmentally friendly and sustainable way to travel, as sharing journeys reduces carbon emissions, traffic congestion on the roads, and the need for parking spaces. Carpooling is more popular for people who work in places with more jobs nearby, and who live in places with higher residential densities. There is a transect and scale of transportation modes that go from in-place pedestrian scale to subways, and from between-place trains and air travel. For the in-place modes, these include walking, bicycle riding, Segways, small smart cars, electric and hybrid automobiles, vans, buses and trams (in South America, even air-trams are being employed). What is important is the seamless connection among the various modes that extend and reach to each and every building and place. This includes walking, bicycles, Segways, electric carts, small smart cars, other automobiles, vans, buses, and trains (Figures 5.9a–f). Also critical is planning for the multiplication of pedestrian-focused zones as systems within systems, defined by walking distances of between 1 mile and kilometer diameters (calculated at 1.0 to 1.2 meters per second).[29]

Water and waste

Water is one of the most essential elements to health, making up more than two-thirds of human body weight: without water, we would die in a few days. Coincidentally, water comprises two-thirds of the earth's surface. It functions by transporting, dissolving, replenishing nutrients and organic matter, while carrying away waste material. Clean water sources derive from healthy waterways, wells, springs, desert desalination, and rainwater.

Wastewater is any water that has been adversely affected in quality by anthropogenic influences. It can originate from a combination of domestic, industrial, commercial, or agricultural activities, surface runoff or stormwater, and from sewer inflow or infiltration. Most urban communities utilize municipal wastewater treatment plants, where the waste is treated then discharged back into the environment. Individual wastewater systems are usually septic tank, drain field or on-site treatment unit. A constructed wetland is an artificial wetland created for the purpose of treating anthropogenic discharge such as municipal or industrial wastewater and stormwater runoff. It also can be created for land reclamation after mining, refineries, or other ecological disturbances such as required mitigation for natural areas lost to a development. Constructed wetlands are engineered systems that use the natural functions of vegetation, soil, and organisms to treat different water streams. The planted vegetation plays a role in contaminant removal, but the filter bed, consisting usually of a combination of sand and gravel, has an equally important role to play. Stormwater

Figure 5.9 Urban transportation modes: a) Segway b) Smart car c) Tesla electric car d) Bus
e) Berlin transit f) Bullet train
Source: Shutterstock

occurring from precipitation events is absorbed by surface vegetation, held in ponds
for evaporation, or runoff flows into drainage systems beneath the ground in sewers.

Sustainable architecture and construction

Sustainable architecture encompasses building design, the construction process, and
occupation and use. This includes design in response to climate, ecological flows,
energy and material conservation, the potential use of on-site natural resources,
and construction efficiency. Much has been written on sustainable site planning,
building form, envelope design, construction materials, and energy-efficient equipment. Concurrently, several certification programs have emerged, including LEED
Certification, Living Building Challenge, EarthCraft (international programs), Energy
Star (US program), and many others. Concepts such as Net-Zero[30] and Net-Positive
are instigating a new and more responsible environmental ethic related to building
construction.

The Government Canyon Visitor Center in San Antonio, Texas is situated in a
field of native grasses and restored oaks at the mouth of the canyon of Government
Canyon State Natural Area. It was designed by Lake Flato Architects in 2005 and features an elaborate water collection and storage system (Figure 5.10a). The bioclimatic
building demonstrates sustainable water use practices by conserving water: rainwater collected from the project roof is filtered and used for both landscape irrigation

and wastewater conveyance, minimizing runoff and contaminants, as well as reducing the use of groundwater. The architectural language is contemporary vernacular and appropriate to the region and context.

Another example of serene urbanism south of Austin, Texas is the Lady Bird Johnson Wild Flower Center. The Center conducts innovative on-site water usage, native plant research, and development projects in the ability of native landscapes to improve communities. When designing the water-collecting system, instead of making the roofs all the same designs, the architects wanted to incorporate as many ways of collecting water as possible. The auditorium has an inverted (i.e. butterfly-shaped) roof with the water running down towards the aqueduct, rather than being shed off into gutters, as on the gallery. Recently the Center has developed a native plants garden with planting, a children's wading creek, and a native plant maze.

The *New York Times* building designed by Renzo Piano was completed in 2007. Its sustainable features include a double-skin curtain wall, automated louver shading system, dimmable lighting system, and underfloor conditioned air distribution and cogeneration (Figure 5.10b). Considered a green tower, 95 percent of the structural steel was recycled. Most of the users of the building use public transportation. The Lawrence Berkeley National Lab reported after a year's analysis of the building that it had significantly reduced electricity and heating energy use.

Sustainable urban examples

Village Homes is a 70-acre (30-hectare) subdivision located in the west part of Davis, California. Michael and Judy Corbett planned the community for 225 homes and 20 apartments, community center, orchards, vineyards, greenbelt land, parks, swimming pool, and other common areas. Construction began in 1975.[31] The gross density was 3.5 units per acre (8.5 du/hectare), with 40 percent of the development dedicated to open space. Most of the homes were designed with either active or passive solar heating. Access streets to the houses were narrow, less than 20 feet wide, because there were distributed off-street parking bays provided in the plan. All the streets within

Figure 5.10 Sustainable architecture: a) Government Canyon Visitor Center, San Antonio, TX
Source: Photograph courtesy of Lake-Flato Architects
b) New York Times building
Source: Alamy Stock Photo

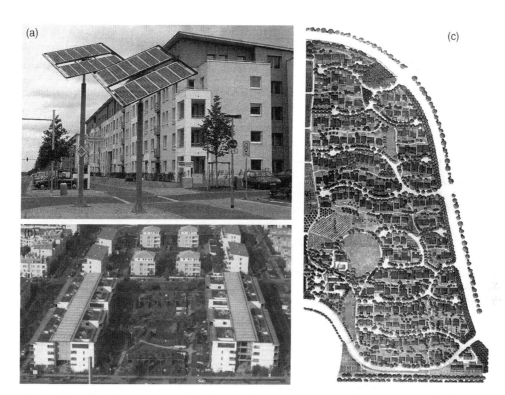

Figure 5.11 Sustainable urbanism: a) Kronsberg streetscape b) Kronsberg District, Germany
Source: Courtesy of Karin Rumming/City of Hannover, Germany
c) Village Homes, Davis, CA, USA
Source: Map by Phillip Tabb

the plan were oriented along the east–west axis, which helped enable proliferation of solar architectural designs throughout the community. Alternating the street system was an extensive pedestrian and bike path system running through the green spaces and other common areas (Figure 5.11c).

Two sustainable community projects in Germany are Kronsberg District in Hannover, constructed for the 2000 World Fair and Vauban District in Freiburg, which started in the mid-1990s. Adjacent to the Fair was the New Urban project of Kronsberg, Germany, planned by Arnaboldi, Cavadini and Hager. It was an eco-district planned for a greenfield area with high ecological standards. This was a sister project to the exposition, which went beyond focus on individual buildings to demonstrate a transit-driven sustainable community for 6,000 dwellings. The medium-density design incorporated two-story to five-story buildings with renewable technologies, and cogeneration with district heating and cooling. A density transect was used to organize the blocks in decreasing density adjacent to the northern rail line, and to the agriculture located to the south. The strong grid layout allowed for super blocks, with compact, mixed-use building types and varying courtyard designs for resident activities, community gardens, and water retention. In its center, a central square was planned, surrounded by shops, galleries, and cafes. A light rail line connected Kronsberg to Hannover city center.[32] Adjacent to the transit line a linear business park was planned, composed of a series of buildings with high-tech sustainable technologies and architectural languages (Figures 5.11a and 5.11b).

Dubai Sustainable City, located in the Arabian Desert and along the Persian Gulf, has as its objective to become an international model of sustainable living, work, education, and entertainment, and to become the first Net-Zero city in Dubai. Designed by London-based Baharash Architecture, it aligns its goals with the 1987 Brundtland Report,[33] citing the creation of a sustainable life for future generations. Included in the scheme are 600,000 square-foot (55,742 square-meter) photovoltaic electricity generation, alternative transportation systems, recycled gray and blackwater waste systems, and distributed urban farms within the 70 percent preserved land. Once considered unsustainable, Dubai is investing in reversing this trend by creating a sustainable future. Occupancy began in 2015, and it is expected to be fully built out by 2020.[34]

Sustainability at the urban scale needs to be applied across the rural–urban transect, which spans from chemical uses in building furnishings and products to urban design strategies for density, mixes of use, and modes of both between and in-place transportation. Ultimately, for sustainability to be effective, it must address fossil fuel consumption at each of the major sector uses: power production, transportation, and buildings. In the context of serene urbanism, sustainability leans towards the principles and patterns of biophilia, reinforcing processes of nature.

Notes

1 Ehrenfeld, John, *Sustainability by Design: A Subversive Strategy for Transforming Our Consumer Culture*, Yale University Press, New Haven, CT, 2008, p. 7.
2 World Commission on Environment and Development (WCED), *Our Common Future*, Oxford University Press, Oxford, 1987, p. 7.
3 Rickaby, Peter, "Towards a Spatial Energy Model," PhD dissertation, Open University and Centre for Configurational Studies, Milton Keynes, 1986.
4 Owens, Susan, *Energy Planning and Urban Design*, Pion Press, London, 1986. This book explained various scales of development from single building to regions, and the differing approaches to sustainable design at these different scales.
5 Condon, Patrick, *Seven Rules for Sustainable Communities: Design Strategies for the Post-carbon World*, Island Press, Washington, DC, 2006.
6 The transect is an ecological analysis of the abundance of terrestrial animal and plant species along a section of land. Transects can be either line, strip, or belt areas. The urban transect articulates differing mixes of use, densities, height limits, and natural land uses, from rural territories to the most urban center.
7 Thorburn, Andrew, *Planning Villages*, Estates Gazette Limited, London, 1971.
8 Andres Duany and Partners, in Steuteville, Robert, "The Transect," *Best Practices Guide*, June 10, 2009. Available online at http://bettercities.net/article/transect (accessed November 2015).
9 Farr, Douglas, *Sustainable Urbanism: Urban Design with Nature*, Wiley and Sons, New York, 2008.
10 Foucault, Michel, *The Order of Things: An Archaeology of the Human Sciences*, reissued edition, Vintage, New York, 1994.
11 Stoll, Katrina and Lloyd, Scott, *Infrastructure as Architecture*, Jovis Publishers, Berlin, 2011.
12 Doxiadis, Constantinos, *Ekistics: An Introduction to the Science of Human Settlement*, Hutchinson Publishers, London, 1968.
13 Stoll and Lloyd, *Infrastructure as Architecture*.

14 Tabb, Phillip, "The Solar Village Archetype: A Study of English Village Form Applicable to Energy-integrated Planning Principles for Satellite Settlements in Temperate Climates," PhD dissertation, Architectural Association, London, 1990.

15 McMahon, Edward T., *Conservation Communities: Creating Value with Nature, Open Space, and Agriculture*, Urban Land Institute, Washington, DC, 2010.

16 Transfer of Development Rights is a land use planning strategy designed to reappropriate allowable dwelling units to greater and lesser densities. It has two useful consequences: creating areas of lower density and land preservation, and areas of higher urban density. It is a zoning process also used to permanently protect open space, natural landscapes, productive agricultural land, wildlife habitat, and other cultural resources (sending areas), by voluntarily redirecting development to targeted, denser locations (receiving sites).

17 de la Salle, Janine and Holland, Mark, *Agricultural Urbanism: A Handbook for Building Sustainable Food and Agricultural Systems in 21st Century Cities*, Green Frigate Books, Winnipeg, 2010, p. 9.

18 Schill, Mark, "The Uncelebrated Places Where America's Farm Economy Is Thriving," *New Geography*, May 20, 2015. Available online at www.newgeography.com/content/004925-the-uncelebrated-places-where-americas-farm-economy-is-thriving (accessed November 2015).

19 Dunlap, David W., "Developing an Illinois Suburb, with Principles," *International New York Times*, July 11, 1999. Available online at www.nytimes.com/1999/07/11/realestate/developing-an-illinois-suburb-with-principles.html?pagewanted=all (accessed October 2015).

20 Duany, Andres, *Theory and Practice of Agrarian Urbanism*, Prince's Foundation for the Built Environment, London, 2011.

21 Chaffin, Jim, "Environmental Stewardship," *Chaffin/Light*, 2008. Available online at www.chaffinlight.com/enviornmentalstewardship.html (accessed October 2015).

22 SPIN farming is an organic production method of farming, usually under an acre, which was developed by Canadian farmer Wally Satzewich.

23 de la Salle and Holland, *Agricultural Urbanism*, p. 29.

24 Summit Powder Mountain is a new development designed to redefine community through entrepreneurship, innovation, and artistic achievement within the context of an American ski resort.

25 Echenique, Marcia H., "Function and Form of the City Region," in Hancock, Tom (ed.) *Growth and Change in the Future City Region*, Leonard Hill, London, 1976.

26 Victor Olgyay, *Design With Climate: Bioclimatic Approach to Architectural Regionalism*, Princeton University Press, Princeton, NJ, 1963, pp. 24-31.

27 British architect Ralph Erskine practiced extensively in Scandinavia and is known for his dramatic climatic designs for settlement proposals, large buildings, and housing clusters. His designs primarily take advantage of south orientations for solar energy, and large roofs for protection from northern winds.

28 Tachieva, Galina, *Sprawl Repair Manual*, Island Press, Washington, DC, 2010.

29 Average walking times/distances in Britain have been calculated at the rates between 1.0 and 1.2 meters per second. This translates to about a 10-minute walk over the distance of 0.5 kilometers. Source: Tabb, "The Solar Village Archetype".

30 Net-Zero is referred to as a building that produces its own energy for heating, cooling, and electrical use.

31 Corbett, Michael, "First Village, Santa Fe, NM: Living Proof," *Progressive Architecture*, April 1979.

32 Monninghoff, Hans, *Hanover-Kronsberg: A Model for Sustainable Urban Development*, Department of Economic and Environmental Affairs, Hannover, 2001.

33 World Commission on Environment and Development (WCED), *Our Common Future*.

34 Bullivant, Lucy, *Masterplanning Futures*, Routledge, London, 2012.

6   The serene, biophilic, and numinous

Although the religious question is primarily a question of life, or living or not living in higher union which opens itself to us as a gift, yet the spiritual excitement
in which the gift appears a real one will often fail to be aroused in an individual
until certain particular intellectual beliefs or ideas which, as we say, come home
to him, are touched.[1]

The numinous experience

The numinous has been a research interest of many theologians, psychotherapists,
historians, and philosophers for some time, including Rudolf Otto,[2] Mircea Eliade,[3]
Carl Jung,[4] William James,[5] Belden Lane,[6] and Ann Casement and David Tasey.[7] The
numinous is a powerful, desirable consequence that can occur with the sacred qualities of serene urbanism, whether experienced as a personal revelation in the woods,
or a feeling from a community gathering or artistic event. In serene urbanism it can
be either experience, as it is transcendent, connecting to a "wholly other." In Rudolf
Otto's words, it is personal and silent, and has an element of fascination as well as
vitality. While the overall experience can be powerful, in serene urbanism it does not
evoke terror, as suggested by Otto; rather, it creates energy, vitality, and instinctual
aliveness. Moreover, rather than the experience of nothingness, it connects, creating
"somethingness": being a part of a greater whole, whether nature or community.
The numinous is the perception of awe-inspiring, transcendent mystery, and is an
awakening. Numinous, from the Latin *numen* meaning divine presence, suggests that
the numinous in serene urbanism is the experience of a place presence or the spirit
of place, again either in community or in nature. According to the psychiatrist Lionel
Corbett, "The [numinous] experience is mysterious, tremendous, and fascinating.
The important factor is the affective quality of the experience rather than its specific
content."[8]

Great architecture and urban design also can elicit the numinous, as these places
trigger the same responses as those found in nature. These experiences occur outside the normal or usual ones. According to a study conducted by Julio Bermudez
on the extraordinary experience of the Parthenon's south facade, participants in the
survey reported that they experienced insight, beauty, joy, satisfaction, and peace (in
descending order).[9] Bermudez further posits that these kinds of profound experiences
are outwardly-driven ordinary or secular places, and that certain principles and patterns are common to both, but with the ordinary places they are less exaggerated or

emphasized. In his chapter in *The Idea of the Numinous*, Lionel Corbett identified the four characteristics of numinous experiences, as explained by William James:

- they are ineffable – defying the normal expression of ordinary conceptual language;
- they have noetic and cognitive content – they produce an overwhelming sense of clarity;
- they are transient – usually less than a half-hour, but rarely more than a few hours;
- they produce positive effects – in the grip of superior power, and can produce healing.[10]

Numinous experiences occur through a variety of channels and intimate factors. Some experiences derive through dreams, while others through visions. The natural world is a powerful source for the numinous encounter, such as feeling the life force of a blade of grass or the metamorphosing of a butterfly. It is likened to becoming aware of a presence that is normally beyond normal perception, where breezes in the trees, light reflecting off ripples in a river, the smell of fresh earth, or coming upon a wild animal in the forest, slow time down and create a heightened presence. Here the "thin space" opens and a numinous experience is possible. According to the psychiatrist Carl Jung:

> The *numinosum* is either a quality of belonging to a visible object or the influence of an invisible presence that causes a particular alteration of consciousness.[11]

If the numinous experience is about something wholly *Other* – meaning something sensed outside of oneself – then soulfulness is grounded in something more familiar found from within. The idea of soulful places does not necessarily inspire or engender more extraordinary responses; however they suggest familiarity, deep emotional stirring, and profound moving. In *Care of the Soul*, the theologian Thomas Moore suggests that soulful experiences in everyday life can cultivate dignity, peace and depth of character. As one book reviewer states:

> People who are cut off from soulful family and friendship may find themselves in a cultural void; a barren world where problems are solved with pills and the media replaces real community.[12]

These interactions reintroduce the sacred and contemporary values in daily routines and rituals through deeper experiences of place that are beyond mere superficial appearance. This might manifest in several ways, such as a walk alone in the woods, or having an intimate conversation with a community friend at a neighborhood cafe early in the morning; but what is most apparent is that place, community, family, and inner self all matter. That the environment in which we live can contribute in accessing and nurturing the soul and soulful experiences. Triggers for these experiences are found with works of public art, land art, healing gardens, parks, and other forms of natural beauty, and finally in communities, neighborhoods, and cities. Serene environments can possess both numinous and soulful characteristics.

Serene urbanism is an environmental approach that seeks to support participation in, and direct perception of, processes such as these. Numinous, charged, and soulful experiences are an integral and hopeful outcome of engagement within a serene urban

Figure 6.1 Serene experiences: a) Self-reflection b) Belonging
Source: Alamy Stock Photo

environment. This is especially numinous with the inherent dichotomy of serenity and urbanism, as they combine natural and cultural qualities. The paradox responds to two sides of human nature: the need for self-reflection, and a sense of belonging to a higher presence, community, friends, and family. Similarly, Jung describes the psychological effects as being ambiguous, in that they can be healing or destructive, and he saw them as both vital individual and social forces.[13] For serene urbanism it can support potent, compelling, and ambiguous value. To Giorgio Giaccardi, the numinous is also difficult to define:

> The psychological reflections on the experience of the numinous have often been conducted through dichotomies as an attempt to represent something un-thinkable and inherently paradoxical.[14]

Where serene urbanism is the context and setting for certain experiences, the numinous is the ultimate experience that transforms us into a unity with place. When alone, it provides opportunities for self-reflection and renewal, and can connect one with a deep sense of place (Figure 6.1a). When in the company of others, it provides a strong sense of fellowship, community, and a feeling of belonging (Figure 6.1b). The numinous experience can be a communion with a larger presence. For some this may be a religious experience, while for others it may manifest as a profound awareness and transcendence.

Biophilic dimensions

Biophilic design can improve energy efficiency and sustainability, reduce stress, and generally improve well-being. Biophilia derives from three important dimensions: nature, human biology, and the built environment. Biophilic patterns share similarities with qualities of the numinous, serene, and sustainability, and are important to the process of placemaking. For example, the "risk/peril" biophilic pattern closely resembles the numinous mysterium/tremendum. Nature certainly plays a central role in this quadrivium of concepts, as each interacts with natural processes and human habitation in site-specific ways. The three essential processes associated with biophilia are as follows.

1. *Nature* – refers to the cosmos, ecological processes and flows, overarching weather, and climatic conditions, including diurnal and annual fluxuation, flora and fauna, as well as animal habitat.
2. *Human biology* – refers to breathable air, clean water, thermal comfort, access to light, proximity to food, removal of waste of all forms, nearness to social, cultural, and institutional services, and numinous experiences.
3. *Built environment* – refers to all human-built systems, including power production, dams, bridges, transportation of resources, goods, and people, cities, buildings, and infrastructure.

The relationship between serene urbanism and biophilic dimensions is defined by the interactions of our human biology within nature, and how these interactions inform the built environment meant to serve these processes. Serene urbanism provides a supportive context within which biophilic dimensions can function. The theory of serene urbanism was, in part, informed by Edward O. Wilson's biophilic hypothesis, where there is an instinctive bond between human beings and other living systems.[15] This includes the urge for humans to affiliate with other lifeforms, an attraction to aliveness and vitality, and a certain reciprocity between humans and nature. According to research by William Browning, Catherine Ryan, and Joseph Clancy, there are 14 patterns of biophilic design.[16] The patterns are organized into three general categories: nature in space, analogues of nature, and nature of space (Figures 6.2a–c).

The intentional connections among the dimensions of biophilia generate certain design patterns that form the basis of an invigorated environmental design. The biophilic patterns developed by the Terrapin Bright Green Report (2014)[17] are organized into a series of overarching categories and design patterns that include:

- connections to nature;
- sensory stimuli;

Figure 6.2 Biophilic dimensions: a) Nature b) Human biology
Source: Photographs by Phillip Tabb
c) The built environment
Source: Shutterstock

- thermal flows and variable light;
- material selections;
- complexity and order;
- prospect and refuge;
- mystery and risk/peril.

Biophilic patterns parallel many of the serene urban and numinous characteristics, especially in regard to connections to nature and natural systems. According to the Terrapin Report:[18]

- *nature in the space* – these patterns include visual and nonvisual connections to nature, sensory stimuli activated in nature, response to the dynamic qualities of natural airflow and variable thermal conditions, the presence of solar energy, water and varying qualities of natural light, and response to ecological systems;
- *nature references* – these are patterns that do not capriciously copy nature, but rather instill and reflect their intrinsic qualities, including patterns such as authentic biomorphic forms, material compatibilities, and geometric ordering systems that foster diversity, efficiency, spatial hierarchies, resilience, and change;
- *nature of the space* – these patterns include prospect and siting positions of significance with empowering views, containment with safety and a nurturing presence, and spaces that activate natural instincts, where nature not only inspires but enlivens and awakens the senses with valorizing, conscious awareness.

Serene urbanism theory

Serene urbanism is a portrait of a living landscape for human habitation. It has been established that serene urbanism is a balanced combination of the most beneficial qualities of serene natural environments, integrated with the engaging nature and support functions of urban environments. The combination of serene qualities, urban forms, placemaking patterns, sustainable measures, and the numinous are not only desirable, but create beneficial synergetic effect. These characteristics are further explained with the following posits:

- serenity is largely missing from everyday experiences, and could become an integral planning consideration. Reduction of stress, temporal density, chaos, and dysfunction can be displaced with peacefulness, greater connections to nature, and tranquillity;
- low-density edges can be improved with appropriate densification, urban agglomerations, mixes of use, and intensity;
- high-density urban centers can be invigorated with the introduction of more serene nature, agriculture, and outdoor experiences;
- the more a place becomes a place, the greater the chance for sustainability and livability. Authenticity, context, human scale, diversity, and response to contemporary culture are essential;
- unsustainable lifestyles and behavior can be transformed with sustainable serene urban forms and placemaking systems of order. Form and function, or spatial structure and sustainable behavior, are at the consequential heart of this approach;

- the numinous is a quality that can become accessible with everyday access and experience, while it cannot be intellectualized. The provision of places for meaningful community events and gatherings are juxtaposed with the tranquillity of natural experiences, where both have opportunities to experience the numinous.

Serene urbanism is an urban design concept that emphasizes considerations of the experiential qualities of nature, and the most supportive qualities of urbanism in place-specific contexts. As a theory, it is intended to embody certain qualities and characteristics that can have broad applicability. Both the serene and urbanism vary in intensity across the rural–urban transect. At the edge, serene urbanism has greater access to nature, and is more difficult to create a critical mass for intense urban programs. In dense city centers, natural spaces are prohibitively expensive. However, urban natural places such as Central Park in New York City, Golden Gate Park in San Francisco, Hyde Park in London, Tiergarten in Berlin, and Jardin de Luxembourg in Paris all provide relief, connection to nature, and economic benefits.

The numinous expresses in dichotomist ways relative to serene urbanism, yet within either context they possess similar qualities of function and utility, along with mystery and fascination:

- *numinous serene* (*serenus*, Latin) – is a hint that nature shows us that there is something powerful, awesome, and healthy with any or all aspects of nature and the natural environment. Nature is not only something that is beautiful to observe, but also a dynamic process within which to participate and experience;
- *numinous urbanism* (*urbanus*, Latin) – is a hint that human interactions and the urban context that frames them can be extraordinary, in architecture, urban design, or settlement. Urbanism also includes the social, cultural, and institutional dimensions of society, and the ways in which they are given physical form.

The biophilic perspective flips a human-centered consciousness to one of a nature-centeredness within which we are part. It posits a more respectful and positive interactive relationship.

Serene urban examples

Serene urbanism can be seen at any scale or place along the rural–urban transect. At the edge of this transect there is more access to nature; while at the urban center, there are opportunities within the urban fabric where landscaping, parks, and urban agriculture can occur. Reinventing the single-use suburb is another territory where serene urban principles and characteristics can be put to work. In fact, this context is in dire need of diversification, inclusion of mixes of use, densification, and the introduction of more nature. Even island settlements have addressed the issues and opportunities presented by serene urbanism. The need for the serene is ever-increasing, and the application of its principles is expanding to many varied contexts and project types.

Certain existing urban territories are ripe for the application of serene urban principles and patterns. Examples can be found throughout the world with a wide variety of

Figure 6.3 Place urbanism: Monte San Savino, Italy
Source: Drawing by Phillip Tabb

project types, including existing communities (Figure 6.3), destination resorts, agro-touristic development, serene network urbanism, discrete communities, university campuses, and monastic settings. While many existing examples are found quite naturally within the hospitality sector, the concepts and characteristics are most needed in places where we actually inhabit and live our daily lives, and in those previously constructed places where the principles are missing. In many cases, it is less about going away to gain these serene experiences, and staying home to have more immediate access to them through everyday exposure.

Savannah, Georgia

James Oglethorpe established Savannah, Georgia in 1733, which has long been an excellent example of early American planning. Originally it was planned with four squares named after each ward, and by 1851 there were 20 established squares. It is through these 24 nature-filled squares located evenly throughout the original town fabric that Savannah is most recognized. Typically, the squares are surrounded by four residential and four civic blocks which, together with a square, are known as a ward. Two of the squares were demolished, leaving 22 active squares today. All of the squares measure approximately 200 feet (61 meters) from east to west, but they vary north to south from approximately 100 to 300 feet (91 meters). Buildings located along the east–west sides of the squares typically house civic functions, while north–south blocks are residential (*tythings*) (Figures 6.4a–d).

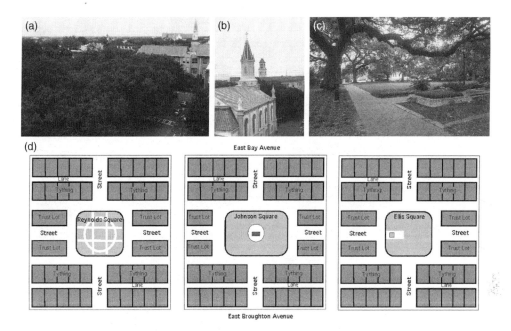

Figure 6.4 Savannah, Georgia: a) Overview of typical square b) Church overlooking Telfair
  Square c) Beneath the canopy of trees d) Diagram of three original squares
Source: Photographs by Phillip Tabb

Thesen Island, South Africa

Thesen Islands, named after a Norwegian merchant, is a multi-award winning marina
development located in the scenic Knysna Estuary on the renowned "Garden Route"
of South Africa. In the early 1980s, Barlows, one of South Africa's industrial conglom-
erates, purchased the island and its timber treatment plant. At the same time there was
growing community concern about the environmental and industrial pollution caused
by the factory's activities; as a result the plant was finally closed. In the ensuing years
the abandoned derelict buildings, machinery, and waste dumps were re-envisioned by
environmental engineer Chris Mulder in 1998. Development of Thesen Islands called
for extremely careful and sensitive planning, covering ecological, architectural, engineering, aesthetic, social, and cultural criteria. The marina is spread over 222 acres
(90 hectares) and consists of 19 man-made islands linked by 21 arched bridges, and
surrounded by 62 acres (25 hectares) of tidal waterways. The marina consists of 512
individual homes and 56 apartment units, known as the Dry Mill apartments, situated
on their own island within the marina. All the homes are built in a colonial maritime
architectural style, conforming to Knysna's vernacular architecture and its historical
maritime and timber connections. Thesen Islands is linked by a causeway and bridge
to the mainland, and is within walking distance of the scenic waterfront, yacht harbor, and town center of Knysna, one of South Africa's most picturesque and popular
coastal towns (Figures 6.5a–c).

Taken from the Thesen Harbor Town website is the following description of the
place which, interestingly, promotes both the serene and natural with the urban and

Figure 6.5 Thesen Island, South Africa: a) Harbor view b) Outdoor urban space
          c) Restaurant interior
Source: Photographs courtesy of Chris Mulder

cultural with a variety of professional, hospitality, and hotel facilities, commercial and service functions. Thesen Harbour Town is open to all, and easily accessible via the causeway linking Thesen Islands with the mainland. Many of the historic buildings, such as the Sawtooth Building, Parking Garage and Boatshed, have been adapted and modernized for reuse, retaining an authentic sense of the past:

> There is something for every family member. Being a marina development, the primary focus is of course on water activities, but confirmed landlubbers too have plenty of choice. Relax under your umbrella on the beach, take a stroll in the park, explore the maze, spot water birds from the bird hide, improve your golf putting, run your dog or take the kids to the play park. For those who enjoy racquet games, maybe a hectic game of squash or on a balmy summer's evening, mixed doubles tennis under floodlight.
>
> Thesen Harbour Town lies in the centre of the lagoon surrounded by Knysna and the Garden Route of the Western Cape. This is the hub of nature's beauty. When you think island, you think calmness, you feel the energy of nature's island

and enjoy island enchantment. When you think of Thesen Harbour Town, you think all of the above, but there's much more ... eat, shop, stay, play![19]

Los Angeles River revitalization, California

Residents of Los Angeles have been stuck in a concrete landscape, especially along the Los Angeles River.[20] The Greenway project is designed to transform a dangerous and unattractive urban network into a more living environment (Figure 6.6a). It is intended to connect existing neighborhoods, create new commuting pathways, and restore the river's natural beauty and ecological function. More than simply a transport corridor, it will become a destination and a catalyst for economic and cultural activities. Families will be able to recreate, commune, and generally interact with an invigorated waterway.[21] The Los Angeles River acted as a flood control channel until January 1, 2014, getting a new use as a navigable waterway. New public events along the river have already begun, such as bike-in movie nights (Figure 6.6b).

Figure 6.6 Los Angeles River revitalization: a) Before rehabilitation
Source: Alamy Stock Photo
b) After rehabilitation
Source: Photograph courtesy of Joe Linton

The Los Angeles River Master Plan recognizes the Los Angeles River as a body of resources of regional importance, and that those resources must be rendered less dangerous, yet protected and enhanced as a serene place. Since the mid-1980s there has been a renewed interest in the river as a valuable natural asset for the entire Los Angeles basin. As a multi-use resource, the river can serve both ecological as well as human needs in a much broader sense than it does today. Along its banks, many new, job-producing facilities can be developed, and new recreation sites can be provided for people living in the basin. Other watershed and river rehabilitation projects include the San Antonio Riverwalk, Texas, the River Thames in London, Platte River in Denver, Colorado, the Cheonggyecheon Stream in Seoul, South Korea, and Pasig River rehabilitation, Manila, Philippines. Projects such as these are doubly important because they provide not only needed green space to inner cities, but also a more vital network of connectivity for people increasing their recreational possibilities, as well as better animal habitats.

Atlanta Beltline

The Atlanta Beltline began as a thesis project by a Georgia Institute of Technology student, Ryan Gravel, in 1999, in which the railway corridor around the core of Atlanta was designed as a multi-use trail system intended to improve transportation, provide green space and public art, and encourage economic redevelopment.[22] The proposed 22-mile (35-kilometer) encircling park will include neighborhood-serving transit systems, non-motorized movement, expand existing parks, and create new parks; the 25-year plan has a 2030 completion date. The Beltline will connect 45 neighborhoods, and is considered one of the largest urban redevelopment programs in the United States.[23] The Plan includes workforce housing and job creation. The first trail was created in 2008, and by 2015 several more were opened. The Beltline's associations with serene urbanism are obvious, as creating more accessibility to nature and nodes of urban activities in Atlanta will become more possible and desirable. The miles of connectivity and inclusion of both natural and cultural places will certainly contribute to the serene urbanism characteristics of sustainability, serenity, and the numinous (Figures 6.7a–c).

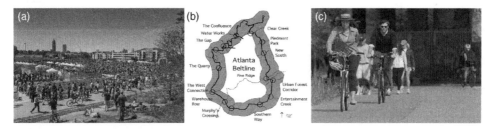

Figure 6.7 Atlanta Beltline: a) Places and nodes
Source: Alamy Stock Photo
b) Concept plan
Source: courtesy of Phillip Tabb
c) Connectors and linkages
Source: Shutterstock

Other examples

Serene Oasis is a garden adopting horticulture as a new emerging approach of therapy on an urban site in Hong Kong. Although smaller in scale than some of the other examples, its major goal is to improve the condition of people suffering from mental illnesses such as dementia and depression. The concept is to bring serenity and horticulture together with healing. Plants have life, just like human beings. Generally speaking, their life processes include seed germination, stem elongation, flower development, and maturity, which also require human effort to look after. This treatment focuses on the interaction between people and plants, and participants acquire knowledge regarding the life cycle of plants and farming practices.

Another example of serene development is Nagarjuna Serene, which is a prime residential enclave in Bangalore, India. Configured over four blocks of G+4 buildings, with four units on each floor, the apartments are spacious two and three-bedroom units spanning 1,095 to 1,448 square feet (102–135 square meters). Each apartment comes with at least one balcony and a separate utility space. The property also houses modern lifestyle amenities such as a gymnasium, swimming pool, games facilities, party hall, and more. Eco-friendly measures such as rainwater harvesting, water and sewage treatment plants are also planned within the project. Amenities include a community hall, clubhouse, library, recreational facilities, play areas, and garden.

Bucking Horse, located in Fort Collins, Colorado, is a small, mixed-use development of 240 acres (97 hectares) and constructed on the 129-year-old Johnson Farm. The program called for single-family residents, condominium apartments and townhomes, community gardens within a working farm, retailers that include horse stables, bicycle shop, yoga studio, produce and local vendors with a variety of products, a 3.6-acre (1.5 hectare) garden-to-farm restaurant, and an extensive trail system. According to the Bucking Horse website:

> Whether it is building a treehouse, learning about care of the farm animals, or growing vegetables, the project will reflect how plants, animals, and people can live and coexist.[24]

The Bucking Horse development is a good model for environmental sustainability, community-building, and fiscal sustainability, all of which are in service of neighborhood values centered on community and quality of life.

The Eco Hotel is located on roughly 100 hectares of the Encuentro Guadalupe development outside of Ensenada, Mexico, which also includes a residential area and a winery. The hotel is made up of 20 eco lofts, which are made from steel and set up on stilts. Each luxurious 20-foot square room features a bathroom, a terrace, a clay fire pit, and views of the valley below. The Hanging Gardens of Ivry-Seine, Paris, designed by architect Jean Renaudie, is brutalism bathed in nature. The urban architecture is covered in gardens that provide a serene quality of nature, additional insulation, and dead air spaces around the walls of the structures. The development of garden features such as pergolas, wall trellises, and other structures enable climbing plants to be used on vertical surfaces. Ivry-Seine is a satellite suburban town southeast of Paris, and the Hanging Gardens give life to an otherwise unremarkable place. The interesting contradiction between the modernist concrete superstructure and the abundant cascading terraces give the work added value, complexity, interest, vitality, prospect, and protection, as well as serene urban quality.

Another example, New York City's remarkable High Line Park (2009 and 2011), designed in three sections by landscape architect James Corner, Fields Operation and architects Diller Scofidio + Renfro, was a competition-winning proposal created as an aerial greenway elevated above the ground for 1 mile along Manhattan's West Side. It transformed the 1.5-mile (2.4-kilometer) section of the former New York Central Railroad spur running through the Chelsea neighborhood. Originally it was a massive public–private infrastructure project done in the 1930s called the "West Side Improvement," which elevated dangerous freight trains 30 feet (9.1 meters) off the street level, thereby avoiding conflict with pedestrians and cars on the ground below. Inspired by the Promenade Plantée in Paris, nine entrances give access to the elevated platform and the pebbledash walkways that expand and contract along the park. The design was described as part-promenade, town square, part-botanical garden, and an urban and nature integration or "agritecture." While the recycling of the freight rail line into a park was extremely beneficial to the environment, a sense of community was created and real estate development spurred adjacent to the line as a positive consequence of the success of the project.

Within the historic Pullman neighborhood in South Chicago is a remarkable 2-acre (0.8-hectare) rooftop greenhouse on top of the old Pullman rail car factory, constructed by Gotham Greens of New York. The urban farm utilizes solar energy, wind power and recycled water, and is an adaptive reuse of the existing Pullman building. It produces 10 million heads of leafy greens and herbs annually, and supplies its produce only within an 80-mile (129-kilometer) radius, thereby reducing transportation costs. In future it plans to produce kale, arugula, and bok choy, along with butterhead lettuce. As the produce is grown within the greenhouse, it is possible to better control the growing environment, creating pesticide-free greens. It employs approximately 50 full-time people from the local neighborhood.

Many landscape urbanism projects embody the principles and patterns of serene urbanism. The conflation of landscape and built structure was investigated within a larger context, with theories of landscape urbanism developed in the late 1990s. The principal post-urban themes were designed to achieved urban effects through interdisciplinarity, systemic ecology of place, adaptable territories, fluidity, spontaneous feedback of morphological development, and most importantly, through horizontal fields of urbanism (agrophilia).

According to James Corner, there are four interpractical underpinnings to landscape urbanism:

1.   ecological and urban practices which occur over time;
2.   a staging context of horizontal surface and geography with decentralization of industry;
3.   a working process across the range of scales; and
4.   the active realm of the imagination.[25]

There was a shift away from the object in space to the projective practice, with systems of distribution and density of a more organic and fluid urban form. While treating the urban environment as an ecological model had sustainable implications, landscape urbanism's tolerance of low-density and automobile-driven environment, promoting suburbanization, was inspired by ecology, but in practice was not overly ecological.

The Seattle Olympic Sculpture Park by Weiss-Manfredi is another striking example of the integration of nature and architecture within an urban setting. The public park, transformed from a contaminated brownfield, opened in 2007 and consists of a 9-acre (3.6-hectare) outdoor sculpture museum. In the words of the designers, it represents "evolutionary infrastructure," which suggests new productive connections among landscape, infrastructure, and urban territories.[26]

Another example of serene urbanism can be found in many university campuses, often associated with university towns. The natural and urban architecture can be seen in places such as Harvard University in Cambridge and Amherst College in Amherst, Massachusetts, Lewis and Clark College in Portland, Oregon, Indiana University in Bloomington, University of Virginia in Charlottesville, University of Colorado in Boulder, and University of North Carolina in Chapel Hill in the United States; Oxford University in the United Kingdom; University of Bologna, Italy; University of St Andrews, Scotland; and Katholieke University, Belgium. These environments have a balanced integration of nature and architecture, and possess a strong sense of place. Common among them is the presence of a predominantly pedestrian environment, where most student needs are accommodated within easy walking distances. The mixes of use and inclusion of cultural activities, the scale of the architecture, and omnipresent landscape are also common to these places.

The Singapore Gardens by the Bay illustrates the strong interlacing of human experiences with nature in a 250-acre (101-hectare) park located in central Singapore. Its purpose was to enhance greenery and flora in the city, and provide outdoor recreation with three main waterfront gardens. Shown in Figure 6.8 is the Supertree

Figure 6.8 Singapore Gardens by the Bay
Source: Alamy Stock Photo

Grove, comprised of tree-like structures with a height of 82 feet (25 meters), and an elevated walkway for visitors to enjoy a dramatic panoramic and engaging view of the gardens below.

Demonstrations of serene urbanism can be traced to many places worldwide, both new and old, in which a set of common characteristics exists. These demonstrations occur in dense urban areas and more remote locations at the edge of metropolitan territories. Each example has some major connection to or interaction with ecological processes or natural features of the place. Each has an agglomeration of landform art, architecture, or urban design with a wide variety of mixes of use. In the examples cited here, each has an aesthetic as well as functional connection to nature, possessing, either intentionally or inadvertently, healing and well-being qualities. Finally, each involves urban activities in creative, exciting, and beneficial ways that simultaneously serve sustainability and community objectives.

Conclusions

Given the contemporary condition and complexity now understood on a planetary scale, healthy human habitation faces important challenges – not only for present populations, but also for future generations. Can we afford to continue to lull ourselves to sleep and continue a path in either maladroitness or denial? Or are there steps that now can be taken, which will move us into an alternative future? Serene urbanism offers nuanced realignment, natural and urbanized patterns that support greater levels of sustainability, opportunities for healthy placemaking, and the inculcation of numinous experiences. With the continued shift of populations from rural to urban areas, serene urbanism has become even more important. This marriage is not new, as urban environments have incorporated nature in many various ways, including urban parks and playgrounds, zoos and botanical gardens, tree-lined streets and boulevards, landscape buffers along rivers, lakes and other waterways, and town greens. Equally, the rural environment contains many examples of urban agglomerations, from retreats and resorts to small towns, villages, and hamlets.

The ideal is to blend the best and most beneficial characteristics of both extremes – the rural and urban. As an urban design theory, serene urbanism seeks to integrate sympathetic considerations of deep ecology, landscape urbanism, agricultural urbanism, sustainable urbanism, biophilic design, serene and numinous environments, and sacred and healing places. Its application varies depending on the context, but certainly the principles, characteristics, and patterns can be appropriately applied and balanced according to the context along the rural-to-urban transect. Figure 6.9 is a pen-and-ink drawing of Castello di Gargonza, Italy where the technique blends the natural and urbanized environments into one. Perhaps Castello di Gargonza is an idealized and romanticized depiction of serene urbanism, and certainly embodies placemaking patterns, but it could serve possibly as an ectype for further development projects in the future – especially for place-oriented projects.

These same intentions, characteristics, and spirit informed the design and realization of Serenbe Community located in Chattahoochee Hills, Georgia, USA, and are explained further in Part II of this book – Serenbe: a community among the trees. The concept of serene urbanism is expressed and explained through the filters of serene, urban, sustainable, biophilic, and numinous qualities of place, which are all present in Serenbe Community.

Figure 6.9 Aerial view of Castello di Gargonza, Italy
Note: This drawing was done from a photograph taken by the author, while flying over Tuscany in a small plane piloted by Paolo Barucchieri in 2011.
Source: Drawing by Phillip Tabb

Serene urbanism is one approach to enriching and sustaining what Pope Francis calls our "common home." Inhabiting this wonderful planet of ours and accommodating increasing world population is challenging.[27] It is the way in which we go about this enormous task that will define us and be our legacy for future generations. Will we as a people continue our destructive ways, or will we find healthier and more benevolent means by which to live healthy and productive lives? In the words of Henry David Thoreau:

> In our most trivial walks, we are constantly, though unconsciously, steering like pilots by certain well-known beacons and headlands, and if we go beyond our usual course we still carry in our minds the bearing of some neighboring cape; and not till we are completely lost, or turned round – for a man needs only to be turned round once with his eyes shut in this world to be lost – do we appreciate the vastness and strangeness of Nature.[28]

Notes

1 James, William, *Faith and Morals, Classical Selections on Great Issues, Vol. IV: The Varieties of Religious Experience*, University Press of America, Cummor Hill, Oxford, 1997, p. 248.
2 Otto, Rudolf, *The Idea of the Holy*, Oxford University Press, Oxford, 1958.

3 Eliade, Mircea, *The Sacred and the Profane: The Nature of Religion*, Harcourt Brace & Company, Orlando, FL, 1959.

4 Jung, Carl Gustav, *Mysterium Coniunctionis: An Inquiry into the Separation and Synthesis of Psychic Opposites in Alchemy (Collected Works, Vol. 14)*, Routledge, London, 1970 (2nd edn, orig. pub. 1956).

5 James, William, *The Varieties of Religious Experience: A Study in Human Nature*, CreateSpace Independent Publishing, 2015 (orig. pub. 1902).

6 Lane, Belden, *Landscapes of the Sacred: Geography and Narrative in American Spirituality*, Johns Hopkins University Press, Baltimore, MD, 1988.

7 Casement, Ann and Tacey, David (eds), *The Idea of the Numinous*, Routledge, London, 2006.

8 Corbett, Lionel, "Varieties of Numinous Experiences: The Experience of the Sacred in the Therapeutic Process," in Casement and Tacey (eds) *The Idea of the Numinous*, pp. 53–67, p. 54.

9 Bermudez, Julio, "Phenomenology of the Architectural Extraordinary and Merleau-Ponty's Philosophy," in Barrie, Thomas, Bermudez, Julio and Tabb, Phillip (eds) *Architecture, Culture, and Spirituality*, Ashgate, London, 2015, pp. 39–58.

10 Corbett, "Varieties of Numinous Experiences."

11 *The Collected Works of C.G. Jung*, eds Herbert Read, Michael Fordham, and Gerhard Adler, trans. R.F.C. Hull, Routledge, London, p. 6.

12 "A Customer," review of Thomas Moore's *Care of the Soul: A Guide for Cultivating Depth and Sacredness in Everyday Life*, Harper Perennial, 1994. Available online at www.amazon .com/gp/aw/review/B01AFYCPMG/R2N8VQ8TUAIKAK/ref=cm_cr_dp_mb_rvw_ 2?ie=UTF8&cursor=2 (accessed June 18, 2016).

13 Jung, *Mysterium Coniunctionis*.

14 Giaccardi, Giorgio, "Accessing the Numinous: Apolline and Dionysian Pathways," in Casement and Tacey (eds) *The Idea of the Numinous*, pp. 137–152, p. 137.

15 Wilson, Edward O., *Biophilia: The Human Bond with Other Species*, Harvard University Press, Cambridge, MA, 1984.

16 Browning, William, Ryan, Catherine and Clancy, Joseph, *14 Patterns of Biophilic Design: Improving Health and Well-Being in the Built Environment*, Terrapin Bright Green, LLC, New York, 2014.

17 Ibid.

18 Ibid.

19 "Welcome to Thesen Harbour Town." Available online at www.thesenharbourtown.co.za/ (accessed August 14, 2015).

20 Barragan, Bianca, "Army Corps Now Reevaluating Billion Dollar LA River Rehab," *Curbed Los Angeles*, December 18, 2014. Available online at http://la.curbed.com/archives/2014/12/ army_corps_now_reevaluating_billiondollar_la_river_rehab.php (accessed August 2015).

21 Ibid.

22 Atlanta Beltline, Inc., "Committed to Fulfilling Atlanta's Promise," annual report, 2014.

23 Fehrenbacker, Jill, "Interview: Landscape Architect James Corner on NYC's Highline Park," *Inhabitat*, September 20, 2014. Available online at http://inhabitat.com/interview-architect-james-corner-on-the-design-of-high-line/ (accessed October 2015).

24 Bellisimo Inc., "Bucking Horse." Available online at www.bellisimoinc.com/projects/ bucking-horse (accessed June 7, 2016).

25 Corner, James, "Terra Fluxus," in Waldheim, Charles (ed.) *The Landscape Urbanism Reader*, Princeton Architectural Press, Princeton, NJ, 2006, pp. 21–33.

26 Weiss, Marion and Manfredi, Michael A., *Public Natures: Evolutionary Infrastructures*, Princeton University Press, Princeton, NJ, 2015.

27 Pope Francis address, September 23, 2015 at the US White House.

28 Thoreau, Henry David, *Walden: Or, Life in the Woods*, Shambhala, Boston, MA, 1992 (orig. pub. 1854), p. 130.

Part II

Serenbe: A community among the trees

7 The Serenbe concept

A woman came to buy a cupcake, and ended up buying a house.[1]

"Serenbe" is the name given to an experimental community of hamlet developments being realized southwest of Atlanta, Georgia (Figure 7.1b). The design for Serenbe was inspired by characteristics of serene urbanism, utilizing the best qualities of both the natural landscape and urban amenities. Located within an hour's drive of downtown Atlanta and a little over 20 minutes to Hartsfield-Jackson International – America's busiest airport – Serenbe is connected to larger urban amenities while being in a serene rural setting.

Created by co-founder Marie Nygren, the name "Serenbe" derives from a portmanteau word from two root terms: *serene* or *serenity*, and *be* or *being*.[2] So embedded in the very name is an affirmational or intentional quality that guides the development process. Serenity, from the French word *sérénité*, suggests a certain kind of peaceful lifestyle or rural tranquillity: one that is deeply calm, composed, reverent, respectful, and possessing grace. Also, Serenbe could be seen as serendipitous and having the propensity of discovery, delight, and magic. "Being," coming from Middle English, is about the subjective quality of a living existence and the experience of being present, which is in attendance in the here and now. In the context of Serenbe, it means being on the land and in the community, and being an integral and creative part of the life of the place.

According to Marie, when she asked the question: "What does a farm around here [Chattahoochee Hills] want to be?", the name "Serenbe" came to her, and this describes the beneficial relationships among nature, the elements, the community, the arts, and the physical place. It is this quality of serenity and being that are at the core of the desires and intentions for Serenbe Community, and this is a driving and recursive force seen in every stage of its design and development. Serenbe is an unusual and improbable community concept, and many felt that it could not be realized. Yet with a compelling vision, perseverance, and a little luck, it evolved and prospers today.

Background: context and early history

Serenbe is located in the heart of Chattahoochee Hill country, which occurs near the end of the Blue Ridge mountain range (Figure 7.1a). Most of the surrounding land encircling Atlanta has now been developed, except for a southwestern strip that includes most of South Fulton County. This area of land covers approximately 40,000 acres (16,200 hectares), about the size of the Napa Valley, and is bounded by Interstate Highway 85 and the Chattahoochee River.

The City of Chattahoochee Hills was incorporated in 2007: its purpose was the municipalization of that county, and to allow local residents to have local control of zoning. It comprises an area of 32,100 acres (130 square kilometers). The Chattahoochee Hill country underwent a planning charrette in 2004, in which the conventional zoning was changed with an overlay district allowing for the transfer of development rights. As a consequence of this planning work, three villages were identified as receivers of this transfer of density, where the constellation of villages may accommodate as many as 38,000 dwellings. Simultaneously, this allowed for greater protection of the open space already existing there. Serenbe can be seen located along the south edge of Chattahoochee Hills along the Fulton and Coweta County line (Figure 7.1c), and is being created as a model for development under these new zoning opportunities. Greater land preservation and synergetic urbanism are the intended outcomes of this kind of process.

Competitive land costs and the completion of the South Fulton Parkway have now rendered this location prime for development. The fate of this remaining area of land rests in the nature and quality of future development and the planning principles that possibly will guide it, particularly for the relatively undeveloped Chattahoochee Hill country. In this context, Serenbe Community has been conceived as a settlement model for land preservation, green building, organic farming, and clean technologies. Serenbe can be found in the lower left-hand corner of the Atlanta area map (Figure 7.1a). What makes this project important are the development goals, the power of the master plan, the integrity of its manifestation process, the geometry of place, and finally the energy of the growing community of residents. Placed in context, at the edge of a large, outwardly growing metropolitan center that unfortunately is filled with suspect suburban developments, Serenbe is different – and strives to be different. Serenbe is neither a gated community, nor a modern, low-density, single-use, suburban housing project where there is little diversity and tremendous dependence on the automobile. It shares the concept of amenity-driven development with golf communities, but seeks to employ far more diversity of sustainable functions. While Serenbe shares some of the tenets of New Urbanism, it stands somewhat apart from this movement in some important ways, as it has created its own unique qualities and

Figure 7.1 Serenbe location: a) Area map b) Entrance sign c) Chattahoochee Hills 2004 concept plan
Source: Drawings and photograph by Phillip Tabb

brand of authenticity that are difficult to label. Serenbe is in harmony with the land, is "farm-to-table," sustainable and authentic, supports active living, attracts a diverse population, and creates a permanent, vital, and alive sense of community.

Serenbe Community can be explained in differing ways from the initial intentions that informed the entire process, to the development of the master plan, which embodied the ideals, through the actual construction and realization of the physical place, to the creation of a real living and constantly evolving community of residents. The initial intentions grew from a confluence of many thought leaders who came together at the site of Serenbe at a particular time: in 2000. Yet even before this historic meeting, the pertinent experiences of key participants led to the creation of the initial impetus for the development. Two such streams are discussed here: one composed of the client–community background, desires, and influences; and the other of the designers' knowledge, expertise, and experience. The original founders of Serenbe Community, Marie and Steve Nygren, Nan and Rawson Haverty, Jr, and Ryan Gainey, each have unique histories that contributed profoundly to the initial process. The design team brought professional practice to the project, including expertise in solar energy, sacred geometry, regional architecture, environmental engineering, green construction, and village planning, especially English villages.

It is the purpose of Part II of this book to share some of the background to the creation of Serenbe, explain the planning process, and show the key components of the design, which have contributed to its success. Serenbe poses an inherent contradiction, as it seeks to be a development model with the possible transfer of universal principles and practices that may inform other projects especially at edges of metropolitan areas; yet its success is due in part to the unique and sometimes magical place-specific design responses that make it difficult to replicate. Nevertheless, hopefully there is something to be gained in understanding its beginnings, concepts, and evolving character. It is the purpose here to identify the principal serene, sustainable, urban, and placemaking concepts, to show how they influenced the master plan, and to serve as a preemptive catalyst for future development for projects in and around the urban edge. Descriptions of Serenbe are intended to delineate sacred planning concepts and the idea of geometry of place that are often missing in the modern generation of residential development. Finally, it is important to share the success in community-building that is an ineffable result of an incredible process designed to support another way to live.

The Serenbe Community planning process began in 2000, but its history is preceded by Creek Native Americans before the seventeenth century, cotton farmers after that, and a succession of property owners until the early 1990s, when the Nygren family purchased 60 acres.[3] The land came with the original 1905 country house and barn (Figures 7.2a and 7.2b). The Nygrens began visiting the place on weekends over a three-year period, eventually realizing that, in their words, they "were meant to be there."[4] They were experiencing the serene power that seemed to be missing in their busy urban lives in Atlanta. They sold their business, the Pleasant Peasant Restaurant Group, and home and moved to the land permanently. Friends began to visit, so they converted the barn into guest quarters in the mid-1990s. Having come from the hospitality business, this move to the bed and breakfast, which now is the Inn at Serenbe, was an easy transition. Concurrently, they purchased parcels of land until one day they saw bulldozers clearing trees on property adjacent to theirs. This prompted them to purchase more protective land, until they had amassed just under 1,000 acres (405 hectares). Realizing

Figure 7.2 Original farm: a) Farmhouse renovated b) Original barn
Source: Photographs by Phillip Tabb

that they could not keep buying land, they decided instead to create a demonstration of a different way to develop, in the hope that it might curb the urban sprawl that was seemingly about to happen there. By the end of the 1990s, they were poised to initiate a process that has grown into what Serenbe Community is today.

Development intentions

A charrette is a term derived from the French, meaning a cart or chariot, but more generally it refers to a collaborative session in which design professionals create work through a participatory process. The first charrette at Serenbe, led by Rocky Mountain Institute and documented by Georgia Tech, created the following goals:

- focus on the essence of community formation and the interaction of people, to foster development of their potential;
- respect for and integration of the cultural history of the surrounding area, i.e. agriculture;
- preservation of permanent open space;
- age diversity of inhabitants, from children to seniors;
- economic diversity of inhabitants;
- economic sustainability of the development effort;
- environmental sustainability of all aspects of the development;
- high-tech, connected development to allow the integration of Serenbe with the world-at-large (at minimal environmental impact);
- music, arts, and crafts as a theme for the development;
- the use of land trusts to achieve the desired character of the community;
- the development as a living laboratory;
- integration of design across disciplinary, infrastructure, and philosophical dimensions; and
- inclusion of sacred geometry, informing the planning process.

The first charrette concluded with enthusiasm, a consensual feeling of great opportunity, and a sense of the essential character for the future development. The defining characteristics gave clear direction for the next stages of the process. It was felt that the primary challenge of this development was the creation of a new set of development standards that were more environmentally aligned, new technologies that were more renewable, and new forms of living that would necessarily cross traditional disciplinary boundaries – financial, regulatory, and aesthetic. A concern was expressed that it would be important to ensure that design, lending, and construction professionals not fall prey to "business as usual," thereby diminishing the full quality of the original vision. It was important to understand the concepts of environmental sustainability and their specific impacts on development at Serenbe.

Land preservation

Preserving land and concentrating development into strategic locations was a primary objective for Serenbe. Within the 1,000 acres was hilly land where development sites could not exist at the bottom of the hills because of water runoff and flood plains. The initial development intentions and resulting concept plan were to concentrate development along lines that framed the valleys, with building moving up the slopes but not occupying the high ground. Figure 7.3a shows that rural character of the land with pasture, stand of woods, and country road, and Figure 7.3b is a more intimate view within the woods in Grange Omega center, with co-founder Steve Nygren.

Environmentally sustainable development

The initial intention for Serenbe was to create an environmentally sustainable model for residential land development in the South Fulton area of Atlanta. What does this really mean? On one level, as mentioned previously, it meant to do development differently than the suburban sprawl model. According to the World Commission on Environment and Development,[5] it is development that meets the needs of the present generation without compromising future generations' ability to meet their needs. This implies that intelligent management and responsible use must balance our contemporary lifestyle needs with both available and future resources. This includes demand for land, food, water, goods and services, housing, transportation, communication, energy, and the functions that drive our society: residential, commercial, industrial, recreational, institutional, and spiritual.

Figure 7.3 The character of Serenbe land: a) Expansive prospect and meadow b) Intimate woodland space
Source: Photographs by Phillip Tabb

In his research at the Open University in the UK,[6] the architect Peter Rickaby showed that the two most efficient and desirable sustainable models for growth were densification of already existing cities, and the establishment of small, energy-efficient satellite settlements at the urban edge. This suggests that initially, there should be a focus on these two contexts for implementing effective sustainable measures, which require very differing approaches. However, this does not mean that the urban context should not be addressed. Sustainable urbanism is sustainability in the urban setting. It is human habitation that constantly moves toward greater levels of homeostatic balance, accommodating growth yet building toward population stabilization. This can be accomplished through:

- careful change and preservation of nonrenewable resources;
- prudent use of renewable resources;
- increase in accessibility, with reduction of travel distances;
- protection of biological systems;
- responsibility toward the collection, treatment and recycling of air, water, waste, and other resources; and
- building conservation, through adaptive reuse, more intelligent planning and design, and improved building practices.

New communities are considered to be in a pioneering stage, and generally require great amounts of energy and resources, while long-standing communities are at a climax stage and generally more in balance with energy and resource flows. For Serenbe, the following 12 guiding principles of sustainable urbanism were extrapolated from the original goals and specifically applied to the master plan and design:[7]

1. *Land preservation* – the target was 70 percent, with preservation that included many of the forests, meadows, streambeds, and archeological sites. This is the reverse of most development projects of this nature.
2. *Density of built form* – development is concentrated to 30 percent of land with higher densities and attaching buildings, in contrast to existing zoning. Diverse demographics are preferable (age, gender, ethnicity, economic background).
3. *Accessibility and networks* – each hamlet has multiple automobile accesses and increased accessibility, with sidewalks, paths, trails, and bridle paths. Alternative modes are also encouraged, with bicycles, Segways, and electric carts.
4. *Diversity of mixes of use* – varies with each hamlet, and includes many life-support and community functions.
5. *Integrated agriculture* – farms are intended to provide produce for residents, local restaurants, and the farm network. The initial farm is on 25 acres (10 hectares).
6. *Use of on-site resources* – use of renewable energy, elemental sources (solar, wind, geothermal, tree canopy shading, etc.), fresh air, clean water (streams, ponds, rooftop harvesting), and local building materials.
7. *Waste amelioration* – targeted to constructed wetlands for all of the community's waste. Gray water is recycled to serve the local cattle that graze in a nearby meadow.
8. *Climatic architectural forms* – including southern vernacular forms, such as the dogtrot, porch-wrapped house cores, natural ventilation, and the use of ground-sourced heat pumps.

9. *Urban designs* – size and density are similar to European hamlets, ranging from between four and 20 dwelling units per acre. Students from Texas A&M University and Georgia Institute of Technology worked on various projects targeted to help the development process.

10. *Intelligent building practices* – construction standards are at least with EarthCraft, and increasing numbers have been designed to LEED certifications and Net-Zero levels.

11. *Economic development* – fostering local businesses within the varying hamlets, and a focus on sustainable living, with attendant support functions.

12. *Numinous considerations* – sensitivity to the land and special places that exist there in harmony with the hamlet forms. The special omega shape for the hamlet designs and other significant geometric considerations also contribute to this process.

Environmental sustainability is herein related to the small settlement scale at the edge of metropolitan areas. Its proximity to an urban center allows for interaction with urban-scale activities, including an international airport, hospitals, commerce, higher educational facilities, performing arts, entertainment, and other urban amenities. At the climax stage of development, its location at the urban edge allows for interaction with the natural environment, and for it to become more pedestrian-oriented and self-sufficient. Settlement shape, increased density, land preservation, interspersion of activities, and climate-oriented planning and design working in combination offer a locus of practice for productive sustainability. This type of sustainable urbanism is a lifestyle-driven form of development.

Amenity-driven planning

Single-use development programs focus singularly on residential housing – sometimes there can be a variety of housing typologies, from single-family detached to attached townhomes and condominiums. The architect Leon Krier calls this kind of development "functional zoning," where the sectoring scheme isolates urban activities into distinct districts in separate locations.[8] If the urban activities are toxic, then this kind of zoning can be useful. However, in most modern residential developments this process has a disintegrating effect on many important land uses, including the exclusion of retail, commercial, work, schools, recreational, and religious functions. In addition, this has the consequence of creating travel distances that require greater dependence on the automobile in order to connect these activities. In many communities today, one's "village," which contains the home, bank, grocery store, medical center, dentist, coffee shop, favorite restaurant, church, recreation center, and place of work, can be as large as five or ten miles in diameter or more. This makes it impossible to be pedestrian with accessibility and on an appropriate scale, and it is certainly counter-productive to the principles of environmental sustainability. In a study done by Texas A&M University students, their average village size was 6 miles in diameter (9.7 kilometers) – six times the size of a pedestrian-oriented village.[9]

Golf course communities are a good example of an amenity-driven development concept, where residential uses are organized around the nonresidential asset of a golf course, clubhouse and bar. Residential properties are sold because of their proximity and attraction to these amenities. However, the single-use focus and

Figure 7.4 Amenity-oriented development: a) Golf course community b) Golf course
         condominiums
Source: Alamy Stock Photo

reliability of a large, manicured, and water-intensive landscape are not sustainable.
Places such as Google, Apple, Facebook, Adobe, and Yahoo – all located in Silicon
Valley – offer possibilities to form employment-based community development
(Figures 7.4a and 7.4b).

An obvious riposte to this kind of zoning is allowing the interspersion of nonresidential activities, especially those that are frequented daily and/or weekly, within the
residential zone. The geographer Susan Owens suggests that the spatial strategy for
interspersion of activities can greatly affect travel requirements, especially through
reduction in travel distances.[10] Key to the effectiveness of this planning measure is
the quality and sustainable nature of the activities that are being included. For example, many new urban communities provide nonresidential land uses and activities,
yet many of them do not service the basic or life-support functions and needs of the
community. Therefore, the settlement design generates little transport energy savings.
As an instrument of sustainable development, integration requires rigorous programming and strategic interspersion placements in the fabric of the place. The closer to
the actual golf course, the more valuable the property. Many golf communities are
also gated communities. This idea of creating a magnet that attracts homebuyers can
be applied to environmentally sustainable communities as well. The golf course and
associated activities are replaced with a complement of nonresidential functions that
contribute to a more community-oriented and sustainable lifestyle.

As mentioned previously, there is renewed interest in "agriculture urbanism" and
the concept of farm-to-table. Typical among sustainable food and agricultural systems
are urban farms, farmer's markets, organic farming, and permaculture, SPIN farming
(under an acre of urban vegetable farming), the 100-mile (161-kilometer) diet (food
produced within 100 miles of consumption), artisan agriculture, and the slow food
movement. Agricultural urbanism is a perfect complement to amenity-driven development projects that seek higher percentages of land preservation, and it was a perfect
match for Serenbe.

The architect Douglass Farr suggests that a vibrant mix of uses will create a strong
node of activity.[11] According to researchers Robin Best and Alan Rogers, there are
five small-settlement land use categories – housing, industry, open space, education,
and residue.[12] These, along with the addition of agricultural and health care, form

a community composed of the major land uses that are key interspersion functions, which can lead to a more sustainable, amenity-driven place:

- *housing diversity* – with mixes of residential housing types (starter, family, independent, assisted living), different sizes, forms (attached, detached, aging in place), and costs;
- *food production* – agriculture (vegetables, herbs, farm crops, landscaping, animal husbandry), grocery stores, farmer's markets, and landscaping material;
- *medical care facilities* – doctor, dentist, veterinarian, pharmacy, health and wellness facilities, fitness, other healing practices;
- *industry* – light industry (if appropriate), office, retail, financial, real estate, hospitality, beauty, entertainment, professional services, gasoline station, etc.;
- *educational* – daycare, kindergarten, elementary school, middle school (if possible), and masterclasses in the arts and crafts;
- *open space* – recreational (parks, dog runs, playgrounds, swimming pools, trails), and open spaces (for wetlands, protected areas, site drainage and water retention);
- *residual* – catch-all category for miscellaneous functions (such as municipal, fire protection, police, post office, religious, maintenance, power production, etc.); and
- *agriculture* – community-supported organic agriculture with farms, greenhouses, farm store, and farmer's market.

The inclusion of nonresidential activities is necessary in rendering a community more sustainable, but there are several functions that are essential in this process, and more likely impossible – or at least difficult – to achieve. The obstacle in providing these key amenities is economy of scale, with its resulting effect on the financially determined size of the population base and corresponding catchment area, which most often far exceeds the resident population and recommended distances necessary for walkable communities. Research has shown that the size of a walkable community is contained in a one-mile diameter area. At an average walking speed of about 3.5 feet per second (1 to 1.2 meter per second), from center to boundary is a little over a 12-minute walk.[13]

Two such critically important functions that should be included in this area are the grocery store, kindergarten, and elementary school, because they are frequented daily and weekly by local residents. Grocery stores very greatly in size and type of product, and range in size between 5,000 square feet and 70,000 square feet and upwards. The larger the grocery store and product shelf size, the greater the catchment area. School size (classrooms per grade level and students per classroom), density of population, and percentage of families with school-aged children determine an elementary school catchment area.

According to the 2009 National Household Travel Survey, the average travel distance for shopping was 6.4 miles.[14] Social and recreational purposes were high, with an average of 17.4 miles per trip. To go to a local restaurant was about 4.4 miles; for schools, daycare, and religious activity, it was 9.1 miles for each purpose; and for medical and dental purposes, about 10.6 miles. For many of these important purposes, this is between ten and 20 times the distance compared to a walking community. The 2009 National Household Travel Survey went on to report that 44 percent of children (aged 5–14) arrive at school by automobile, 40 percent by bus, and only 13 percent walk. In rural and developing areas, these distances are even greater. The annual average trip length to work is nearly 21.4 miles, which remains another issue altogether. So it becomes a challenge for new communities to find creative and economically feasible solutions to both a decrease in catchment area, and an increase in access to these functions. When traveling for shopping, grocery store, restaurant, schools, recreation, and social purposes, medical and dental facilities, what if one were able to walk there, rather than drive for 20 minutes?

Health and wellness

Social isolation, fear of crime, disrupted family life, and unhappiness are bad for health. Air pollution, contaminated water, poor food supplies, heavy road traffic, dislocated neighborhoods, and poorly designed buildings are also bad for health. Other important functions that could be considered as an amenity in a development to counteract these negative effects are health and wellness. Health is considered the absence of disease, but more than that, the term comes from the Middle English "hale," and also means "wholeness". Therefore, it is a combination of physical, mental and social balance and conditioning. According to research by Roland Strum and Deborah Cohen in 2014, there is a robust relationship between increasing sprawl and physical health, with an approximate 10 percent increase in chronic medical problems, which suggests that suburban design may be an important new avenue for health promotion and disease prevention.[15] In Georgia, for example, an American Planning Association publication in 2012 cites that children between the ages of ten and 17 had an overweight and obesity rate of 37.5 percent.[16] This is astonishing, and raises questions about the patterns of urban growth and subsequent lifestyles that it seems to create. According to exercise and wellness scientist Charles Corbin, wellness is a multidimensional state of being, describing positive health effects as exemplified by quality of life and sense of well-being.[17]

Some also include environmental and spiritual health as a part of wellness. Health and wellness tourism is now an international trend set by consumers seeking to either protect and enhance or improve their health or medical conditions, as well as those interested in maintaining their well-being. Spas, beauty and fitness facilities, various physical therapies such as massage, yoga, Rolfing, Ayurvedic therapy, acupuncture, Jin Shin Jyutsu, and Pilates, and healthy cuisine are common avenues usually accompanied by beautiful, tranquil, and natural settings.

Applied to amenity-driven development, the kinds of programmatic functions include a health spa, small fitness center with therapy pool, small doctor's offices, a pharmacy, local organic farming, and health-oriented restaurant. The American Planning Association (APA) adopted a definition of smart growth, with one of the six critical elements:

1. have a unique sense of community and place;
2. preserve and enhance valuable natural and cultural resources;
3. equitably distribute the costs and benefits of development;
4. expand the range of transportation, employment, and housing choices in a fiscally responsible manner;
5. value long-range, region-wise sustainability rather than short-term, incremental, or geographically isolated actions;
6. promote public health and healthy communities.

Figure 7.5 Health considerations: a) Access to organic agriculture b) Healthy food
Source: Shutterstock

They seek to eliminate negative health effects, protect healthy community characteristics, promote healthy behaviors, and assure quality health and wellness services
(Figures 7.5a and 7.5b). An important aspect of healthy communities is the concept of
active living: a way in which a community integrates physical activity into daily routines. These typically manifest with 30 minutes of activity each day through walking,
bicycling, playing in the park, walking the dog, working in the yard or garden, taking
the stairs, and using recreation facilities. Circulation networks should be safe, clean,
varied, and preferably completed cycles, connecting nodes and places of interest in
continuous circuits. Following are some principles for the design for a health-oriented,
active living community:

- physical activity is a behavior that can improve health and quality of life, and a
  community plan should take every opportunity to encourage it;
- everyone in the community should have safe, clean, convenient, and affordable
  choices for physical activity;
- places should be designed to provide a variety of opportunities for physical activity, and should accommodate an inclusive and wide range of preferences and
  abilities – including opportunities for social interaction, and low traffic levels;
- development patterns should encourage mixes of use, compact design, safe interconnectedness, and completed circulation cycles, including streets, to encourage
  active living;
- parks and green spaces should incorporate trails, be accessible and part of the circulatory network of the community, connecting to destinations such as housing,
  schools, cafes, urban agriculture, and other places of interest.

Role of the arts

One of the initial stakeholders' defining characteristics was the role of the arts as a
theme of the development, which includes culinary, visual, performance, and crafts.
This is somewhat unusual, as the arts are rarely a formative force in contemporary
development projects; rather, at best they are an additive element after the fact. The
relationship between culture and the development plan certainly can be seen as an

amenity and something contributing to quality of life. The presence of the hospitality and culinary arts functions of the Inn at Serenbe and its conference facilities are an example of this commitment. In fact, they played an important supporting function in hosting and shaping the experience for the first charrette, providing on-site facilities for all the participants (this support continued throughout many of the physical planning charrettes that followed). Besides adding to the economic vitality of the community, the arts can be innovative and creative, as well as reflective and archival. According to the Mississippi Arts Commission, the arts make money, give students an edge in school, attract visitors, bring the community together, celebrate culture, and provide a high rate of return on investment.[18] For Serenbe the arts can further a more authentic and enriched sense of place, and contribute to its evolutionary growth.

The arts can integrate into the community in many stimulating and practical ways. The culinary arts provide skillful sustenance through international and local cuisine. Food prepared in a healthy, conscious, and pleasing manner will be a magnet for visitors and community residents alike. When the culinary arts are linked to local organic farming, as in what Jessica Prentice termed "locavore" or the eco-conscious food movement,[19] then there is a cycle throughout the food chain (growing, production, distribution, preparation, consumption, and recycling) which can foster learning that is healthy, visible, and educational – from farm to table.[20]

The visual arts provide many benefits to the community through drawing, painting, photography, digital media, sculpture, and environmental works of art. These forms help in the qualitative development of the community in both reflective and formative ways. The performing arts have always been an important cultural instrument, and in the case for Serenbe, this was true for both adults and children alike. Craft, of course, is a more pragmatic art form that tends to be local, artfully constructed or handmade, and useful. These may include fiber-optic art, street furniture, lighting standards, benches, treehouses, footbridges, and other community artifacts. All the arts can become an integral economic part of the community. Serenbe can promote both cutting-edge and vernacular forms of art, thereby reflecting the character of the place and time.

According to Christiane Crasemann Collins,[21] the boldest conception of art occurs not only with individual works of art or single buildings, but also with the entire community form. Sacred geometry seems to have informed large cities such as Paris, London and Washington, DC, as well as in smaller, cloistered environments. This is a powerful idea, and brings up the question of how a community design can actually become an art form in itself. The integration of urban design elements and the way in which they are composed into a comprehensive whole might be considered an art form; a sense of coherence and beauty of design woven in the landscape also may contribute. Geometric design has the potential to embody aesthetic, semiotic, and philosophical concepts as well; and the quality and care in construction can endear and ensoul the physical manifestation of the place, especially in the use of materials and attention to craft. Seen in this way, the arts are more than an appliqué; rather, they are integral to the whole, becoming a container to encourage an artistic way of life – however that might evince. This suggests that the settlement design for Serenbe could be elevated to an environmental form of art, as well as a support for thriving artistic activities:

- *visual arts* – it was important that the first hamlet be visually compelling and offer art not only through galleries and live–work studios, but in the development itself. This included all art and craft forms (Figure 7.6a);

Figure 7.6 Integrated arts: a) Visual b) Performing c) Culinary
Source: Photographs courtesy of Serenbe Development Corporation

- *performing arts* – these offer an opportunity for community members to gather and share in cultural experiences. Performance venues occur outdoors, utilizing the natural environment (Figure 7.6b);
- *culinary arts* – food production, health, education, and the concept of "farm-to-table" is another community amenity and opportunity for interaction. Healthy, organic food is connected to creative, delicious food preparation in homes and restaurants (Figure 7.6c).

The land and preservation

Response to the land was extraordinarily important in the planning process: there are both physical and qualitative explanations of it. The general geology in this area of Georgia is the Piedmont Region, which consists of igneous and metamorphic rocks resulting from ancient sediments that were subjected to high temperatures and pressures, and reexposed. The geology typically found in this area includes minerals (schists, amphibolites) and rocks (gneiss, migmatite and granite).[22] The region is more hilly than mountainous, and is made up of low hills and narrow valleys that are punctuated with occasional granite outcrops. Serenbe is considered to be in the Brevard Fault Zone, which generally runs in a southwest–northeast direction. Piedmont soils consist of the minerals kaolinite, halloysite, and iron oxides that are commonly red in color, for which Georgia is famous. The original forests of the southern Piedmont consisted of oak and hickory trees; today they mainly consist of oak, hickory, and pine forests. The pines usually occur on the less favorable or disturbed areas, while sweet gum, beech, red maple, elm and birch are found in river valleys. Fauna commonly found in and around Serenbe include white-tailed deer, muskrat, raccoon, opossum, squirrel, beaver, gray fox, and armadillo. Ancient Native American peoples occupied the land 10,000 years ago, and as recent as AD 1200 developed a hierarchical palisade (fortified) village pattern, where they grew corn near floodplains. Later European settlers established cotton plantations and dairy farming. Growing southwestward of Atlanta, the present-day settlement pattern ignores these geographic and cultural layers of the past, generally levelling the land and destroying the vegetation, making way for single-use, detached, single-family residential developments.

As mentioned previously, Serenbe is located on the southern edge of Fulton County. In fact, the southernmost portions of Serenbe's property lie in Coweta County. Of the 1,000 acres that comprise Serenbe, the development target for land preservation was

70 percent, thereby allowing only 30 percent for development. At a gross allowable density of one dwelling unit per acre, this produces a total of not more than 1,000 dwelling units on approximately 300 acres of land. The Serenbe property is mainly small, forested, rolling hills with some meadows strung along the southeastern and western edges. The topography varies from an elevation of about 800 feet (244 meters) to 970 feet (296 meters) above sea level. At the lower elevations there are usually water features: streams, lakes, or wetlands. The climate in this area is a humid subtropical zone (Köppen Climate Classification), which is nearly always located in the southeast region of a continent. This is characterized by hot, humid summers and cool winters, with significant amounts of precipitation occurring in all seasons. This is a challenging climatic context, as there are three distinct seasons in which a building design must respond: overheating in the summer season; underheating in the winter season; and the swing seasons (spring and autumn), which behave dynamically between these extremes.

The land at Serenbe is beautiful and expresses through the feminine principle. It tends more toward intimate experiences, such as narrow forest paths, small streams, and lakes, punctuated by magical nurturing places discovered along the way. There are pastures with farm animals on them, two small waterfalls, wildflower meadows, and the Cedar Creek basin that is full of wildlife. It is common to find special places deep in the forest, and experience quiet moments. Certain places open to the night sky, where one can see myriads of stars unobstructed by urban night light pollution. The land has a compelling quality, and a feeling of what the philosopher Martin Heidegger termed "aletheia," or truth experienced in a primordial sense of the place.[23] The deeper you go into the forest, the more immersing this feeling becomes. In his "Axiom for Sacred Place," the theologian Belden Lane wrote that a sacred place might be tread upon without being entered.[24] He says further that the place chooses and is not chosen. This suggests that a sacred realm may exist, but may not necessarily be readily accessed or initially revealed. The land at Serenbe has such a quieting and serene quality, which some say allows for it to communicate. The land speaks to those who can hear it.

The master plan

Initially, the master plan was created in a three-day charrette, then later progressed through a process of design refinements and feedback from the owner and engineers. The development program was loosely defined at the beginning, as the right balance between the natural and urbanized portions of the design needed to be determined through the land planning process. The zoning did not allow for more than 1,000 dwelling units, and it was felt that a build-out with that many dwellings would either be too dense, given the rural context, or occupy too much of the land. One of the important design objectives early on was the preservation of land, which meant that a somewhat reduced program was used to accommodate the settlement portion of the project. Intuitive sieve mapping was implemented to determine the best place to urbanize the design. According to urban planner Nan Ellin, a kind of "vulnerable urbanism allows for things to happen,"[25] and the design for Serenbe was an unforeseen and spontaneous design.

The design for Serenbe Community then grew from what the land had to offer, which was a set of interconnected hills and valleys that formed a pattern of natural places in which to situate the developed parts of the plan (Figure 7.7). So, rather than a single massed development scheme, what emerged was a constellation of inter-connected hamlet sites that were situated in the gently defined valleys. While each place was visually separated from one another, they were within very close walking proximity. The developed areas of the master plan used only 30 percent of the land, leaving 70 percent for open space. The original concept plan was developed in a three-day charrette, and essentially delineated this schema of constellating hamlets gently grafted into the natural landscape. At first, the urbanized areas were shown some-what conceptually, and did not fully express the full magnitude of the development program. Later iterations allowed for more detailed programmatic developments, fit-ting the specifics of each selected hamlet site.

As the concept developed, both pedestrian and automobile connections were also carefully considered on the natural contours, and with minimal negative impact to the overall site. The design for Serenbe was neither intended to be New Urban, nor a copy of traditional village forms. Rather, it was conceived as responding to the given landforms and the variegated density and land use mixes characteristics of each of the four urban agglomerations. It, too, was in response to contemporary housing and nonresidential programs, including space types, variable sizes, degrees of privacy, con-temporary vernacular technologies, and materials. As posted on the Serenbe website, the hamlets express differing themes:

> Each of Serenbe's four hamlets have complementary commercial centers focused on the elements of a well-lived life: arts for inspiration, agriculture for nourish-ment, health for wellbeing and education for awareness. The "one row urbanism" built here is remarkably attractive, and even with just the first few buildings built in the first hamlet it jumped close to the top of the list of recently built places in terms of interest and inspiration value.[26]

Each of three hamlet sites tended to be positioned in a slight, landformed bowl, at the interface between sloping, forested portions of each of the naturally formed sites, and the flat meadows or waterways below. This created a sense of place and allowed for both the ridge tops and valley bottoms to be free of development. As in ecosystems, these interface locations tend to be vital bottoms to be free of development. They also tend to be vital and dynamic places, mediating between the differing subsystems – meadow and hill. These locations were the most benign and, at the same time, engaging places to site the settlements. The sites were generally oriented to the north–south or southwest–northeast, and transitioned from a more enclosed character on the northern portions of each site to a more open landscape to the south. A fourth hamlet site was given on the northeastern side of property adjacent to Atlanta Newnan Road, and was large enough to accommodate a slightly larger hamlet, which cascaded down the slope from the county road down to a streambed below. Given these site conditions, it then became the challenge to create an appropriate settlement form for each of the hamlets, and an interconnection network that would bind them all into a coherent whole.

The curvilinear hamlet forms resembled the omega or horseshoe shapes, and have interesting characteristics of this particular typology. The hamlets were connected by a serpentine road system that followed closely the contours and shapes of the natu-ral landform omega sites. Rather than gating or isolating each of the omega ham-lets, there was an effort to create porous and open-ended entrances and exits, with between three and four ways into them. A path system was created to connect the

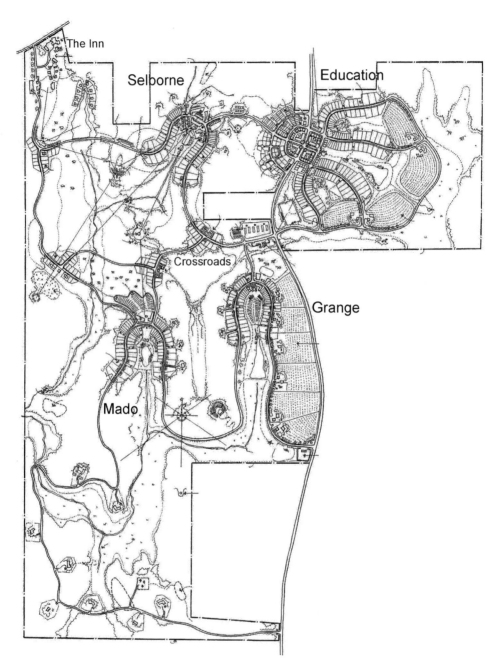

Figure 7.7 Original concept plan (2001) with four hamlets and feathered-in farmettes
Source: Drawing by Phillip Tabb

hamlets through the woods and along riverbeds. In the interstitial or in-between areas, special event places were located such as the bonfire site, wildflower meadows, tree houses, interfaith chapel, waterfalls, and labyrinth. The hamlet roads are designed to follow the transect from more rural to urban. Each hamlet is designed with a 60-foot right of way containing roads, parking, sidewalks, and planting areas. As the roads enter the hamlet, there are no curbs, which maintain its rural character. Once past the tree filters and estate houses, it transitions into granite curbs and sidewalks on each side. On-street parking is present, and in the center of the hamlet is double-sided perpendicular parking to accommodate the more dense use.

A transect was used to further give definition and spatial organization to the omega-shaped hamlets. Each of the omega legs then have a density gradient that culminates at the top or apex of the omega, where there is a concentration of density and mixes of use. Housing follows a similar pattern (as described earlier under the transect illustrated in Figure 3.1a). Dwellings are set back from the roads at the entrances to the hamlets, and separated from one another, then gradually move closer to one another and closer to the serpentine road; this also provides a context for varying sizes of plots and homes of differing levels of affordability. The landscape counterveins the process by decreasing as it moves into the hamlet center. There was a concerted effort to maintain the rural character of the area, and transition into each of the hamlets. Parallel parking occurs along the omega street, in remotely located, small parking lots, and in detached garages with dwellings on the outside of the omega. Automobiles are not allowed to enter the inner omega, as it is designated a natural area and a safe place for pedestrians. Also, it was important for it to be quiet and tranquil. Figure 7.8 shows the revised master plan, representing previously constructed hamlets and revised design for future ones.

The omega forms

In order to increase the population catchment areas for amenity at Serenbe, a scheme was developed where repetition of nonresidential uses was kept to a minimum, and each hamlet gathered together a different complement and mix of uses appropriate to its identity. It was intended that these varying distributions would serve to create a greater diversity of use, thereby reducing the need to shop outside of the community. According to Nan Ellin, people are asking for greater mixes of use in their settlement in order to generate synergies and efficiencies as well as higher revenues.[27] For Serenbe, the mixes of use then became the basis for hamlet theming, or establishing individual character through programming, purpose, and use. However, each hamlet has a similar range of differing dwelling types, from estate houses to cottages, live–work units, townhomes, and condominium flats. Four distinct themes were paired with the hamlets, which guided the development program and details of the master plan: the arts, the farm, health and wellness, and education. Each of the hamlets was programmed and designed to house activities that supported these place-defining themes. The driving concept is that developing complexity, especially in nonresidential land uses, contributes to sustainability by providing more goods and services, thereby reducing between-place automobile use and encouraging pedestrian movement and outdoor activities:

- *Selborne Hamlet* – oriented toward the arts, especially the culinary, visual and performing arts;

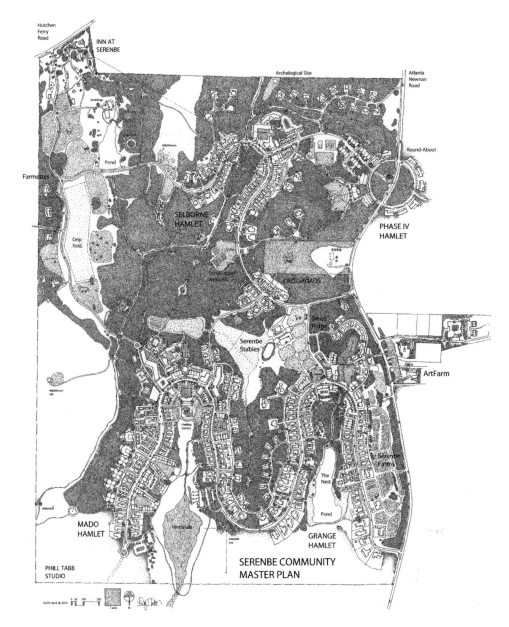

Figure 7.8 Serenbe Master Plan with Serenbe Farms (2014)

Note: The 2014 version of the Serenbe master plan was created to include changes and additions to the design, as well as to document what had been constructed at that time. This includes the evolution of Mado Hamlet.

Source: Drawing by Phillip Tabb

- *Grange Hamlet* – oriented toward organic agriculture production, farmer's market, and equestrian facilities;
- *Mado Hamlet* – oriented toward health facilities and wellness activities, both indoor and outdoor;
- *Education Hamlet* – oriented toward greater levels of commerce and educational facilities;
- *Crossroads cluster* – smaller grouping of cottage homes, estate houses, and townhomes;
- *ArtFarm* – a context for artistic productions and affordable housing;
- *Interstitial space* – natural and architectural sites for a variety of activities.

The artist hamlet, later named Selborne (center–north on the plan), was the first hamlet to be constructed, with its mixed-use activities surrounding the visual and culinary arts. The first nonresidential building to be constructed in Selborne Hamlet was the Blue Eyed Daisy Bakeshop. It was built when the west leg of the omega had a built-out of some 30 homes. The land uses initially planned for Selborne were focused on visual art production, display, and education, and included artists' residences, live–work studio space, and a center for art education. The culinary arts were seen as an important magnet as well as a supportive ingredient to the development of this first hamlet. So, the inclusion of a small cafe and bakeshop would provide residents and visitors alike with an opportunity to meet and enjoy one another, especially in the pioneering stage of Serenbe's growth. In addition to the designated retail areas of the hamlet are two live–work clusters, where shops and services on the ground level are combined with residences above. The hamlet center is seen as a large village green surrounded by arts-related activities.

The Farm Hamlet, later named Grange (east on the plan), has associative activities such as Serenbe Farm, the equestrian center, and a farm market. In the original master plan the farms were divided into 5-acre small farmettes, each with its own farmhouse, barn, and pastureland. However, it was more pragmatic to manage one single farm, so the agriculture at Serenbe becomes one management system. A 25-acre (10-hectare) organic farm area was designated adjacent and to the east of the hamlet, with a farm produce market located within the hamlet, but close to the farm. The equestrian center is planned to the north or top of the hamlet, and serves as an entrance into the hamlet, giving it a rural character. The stables are planned for 20 horses, an arena, and associated paddocks that cascade down to the hamlet center. At the center of the hamlet a green open space is planned, with a band pavilion and mail collection. Commercial activities include a restaurant, tack shop, and small hardware store.

The Health and Wellness Hamlet, later named Mado (west on the plan), has activities and facilities supporting many different kinds of healing arts and practices. This includes a fitness center, therapy pool, community swimming pool, daycare facilities, east–west pharmacy, greenhouses, doctor's offices, spa, recuperative hotel, various small therapeutic practices, and vegetarian restaurant. What is unique about this scheme is the way in which these activities have been woven into the actual fabric of the place. There are assisted living and independent living buildings planned near the apex of the omega shape that add to the uniqueness and theme of this hamlet. Rather than being concentrated like a shopping center for health, the activities are spread throughout the hamlet, making it a truly integrated scheme. These facilities are within walking distance of the other hamlets at Serenbe, and an easy automobile drive if necessary. Located around the wetlands a 1 mile (1.6 kilometer)-long running or walking track is planned.

The Education Hamlet, yet to be named (northeast), is intended to have educational facilities from kindergarten through higher education, and to house more business and commercial activities. These facilities would include a fire station, police house, bank, library, small grocery store, offices, and more retail. Its location provides access from the other hamlets, but also from neighboring communities, so it can have a slightly greater outreach function and interface with Chattahoochee Hills. This may help realize some of the purposes such as the grocery store and schools, which may need larger catchment areas. It was envisioned that a facility for higher education, located adjacent to the hamlet, could bring on-site environmental programs to Serenbe that focus on sustainable urbanism, green architecture, organic farming, and also include a design-construct component. Those uses planned in the interstitial spaces are activities that either require greater privacy or intimacy, are very special and unique, or situated on site-specific places within the open space. At Serenbe they include an interfaith chapel, the labyrinth, the bonfire, Camp Serenbe, an elementary school, equestrian center, outdoor recreation field, treehouse, and celestial observation site. These activities are generally located in special places in the landscape, and some are on connecting walking paths throughout the forested areas, while others are destinations found deeper in the woods. The large green space along Cedar Creek is a natural destination that usually only residents visit. This interstitial space, and the activities that occur within it, add to the richness and connectivity of the community. The interspersion of these activities, along with the woodlands and meadows, serves as an amenity-driven land use design to unite the various hamlets.

Taken together, this grouping of nonresidential activities and uses forms a network of interrelated sustainable functions. They become of increasing complexity and a cross-program, allowing people and activities to converge and comingle, creating a functional synergy. While the groupings intended for each of the hamlets can give particular character and identity to them, it is a greater intention to be able to provide a wider range of functions that can be spread among the hamlets, ultimately reducing automobile travel and encouraging pedestrian movement. Therefore, increasing complexity of use is encouraged. For example, the Serenbe farms can provide produce for the grocery store, all nearby residents, and the restaurants and cafes within each of the hamlets. Residents from around the Chattahoochee Hills can also use the facilities. The equestrian center is located in the center of Serenbe, offering easy access to all. Arts activities, including a farmers' market, attract people from around the Chattahoochee Hill area.

The Thorburn transect was observed by Andrew Thorburn, and was seen as a spatial organization of density and landscape distribution for English villages.[28] Density increases as the country road approaches the village center. Buildings move closer to the road and to one another, while the landscape does the reverse, with buffers between the road and dwellings at the perimeter, progressing to rear, walled-in gardens and mature trees along paths approaching the center. Common to many English villages is a pinch point that occurs at the perimeter of the settlement, usually bounded by a stone wall, archway, or even structures placed close to the entrance road. This marks the threshold of dispersion, where dwellings outside of this boundary are no longer considered part of the village agglomeration.

For Serenbe, this transect was used to transition from the rural character of the land to the more urban parts of the omega apex (Figure 7.9a and 7.9b). Estate houses on larger plots are positioned away from the country road, and spaced away from

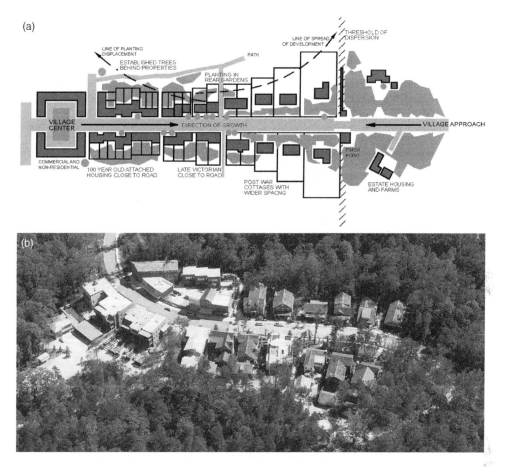

Figure 7.9 Thorburn transect: a) Transect in diagram form
Source: Diagram by Phillip Tabb
b) Transect applied to Selborne Hamlet
Source: Photograph courtesy of Serenbe Development Corporation

one another. Cottage homes occur after the pinch point, which consists of a change in road paving material, granite curbs, and a slightly raised crosswalk. Parking along the street occurs on the omega center side, with the landscape along the sidewalks. The omega center serves as a landscape buffer and amenity. At the apex buildings are attached, positioned next to the sidewalk, and mixes of use with higher densities. Housing progresses from estate homes, to cottages, to townhomes, and finally to live–work units. In Mado, condominiums with units stacked will also accompany independent and assisted living.

Geometry and shape grammar

Curvilinear shapes provide a natural, open-ended system that contains an inner area bounded by urban form. At Serenbe this inner area is kept natural, with a stream in Selborne, a pond in Grange, wetlands in Mado, and a forested streambed for the

Education Hamlet. For these forms used at Serenbe, the curves at the top of the hamlets enclose greater than a half-circle. This is done to create a greater feeling of enclosure or sense of place, which is unlike a "U-shape," which does not suggest completion. As distinct from linear and nucleation geometry, the curve defines a larger territory or place of dwelling. There is a domain that is articulated within it, that becomes known as the place or hamlet in this case. The circular top is designed to provide a destination and identity for each hamlet. The greatest intensity occurs at the curve apex or top, where there is a higher density and a concentration of mixes of use that correspond to the primary function of the hamlet.

The omega is a symbol for the last or 24th letter of the Greek alphabet, and means the completion of a sequence. It also suggests the volume of an object and the containment of an open-loop system. Therefore, the geometry related to this form has two qualities. The first is the creation of a sense of place through its embracing nature, where center, boundary, and domain are given clear form. The shape is not a "U," but an "Ω," which supports greater containment. The second occurs with the open end of the omega, which allows for natural ecological flows; solar energy, water, clean air, resident animals, and people. That which is contained is also allowed to escape and refill. In the ancient I-Ching, the *Chinese Book of Changes*, the omega may be equated to the caldron or a bronze-cooking vessel called the *ting*, as it provides nourishment and transformative powers.[29]

The omega shape slowly opens outward to create both a sense of entry and exit, with connectedness to the neighboring hamlets; a gated community or completely enclosed plan does not allow for natural flows to occur, and both ecological and human systems are not permitted to enter. According to Edward Blakely and Mary Gail Snyder, gated communities create a form of intense suburbanization, discrimination, and privatized public spaces.[30] However, in the case of Serenbe, water is collected from the surrounding and sloping hills and flowed into small streams that move through and eventually empty into Cedar Creek. Each hamlet has at least three open roads entering and exiting. At the top or apex of each omega form are a collection and an intensity of activities that give focus and identity to each hamlet. The curvilinear roads give an ever-unfolding perspective of the hamlet as one moves through it, which adds both mystery and visual interest.

The geometry of the omega form is strong, provides a powerful presence and memorable spatial organization, and adds qualities that are very identifiable, understandable, and coherent. There is a general "democracy" of housing placement relative to the omega center, in that half the homes are placed adjacent to the center, and the other half are only a short distance away on the other side of the omega road. There are five major urban design ramifications of this form:

1.   creating a sense of place (circle);
2.   opening back to the community (legs);
3.   concentrating activities at the top (apex);
4.   connecting to the interstitial space (open end); and
5.   the omega-shaped road with its varying width and functions (omega).

It is perhaps ironic that the meaning of the omega is often to denote "the last" or "the end," as Serenbe is a model for future development – and ends always lead to new beginnings, especially within living systems (Figures 7.10a and 7.10b).

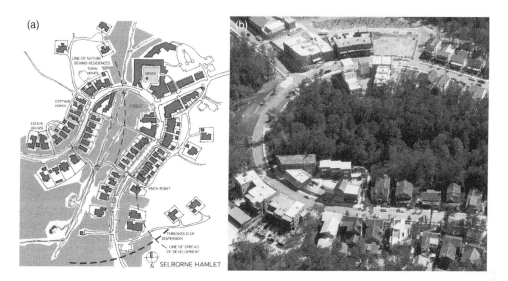

Figure 7.10 Selborne omega geometry: a) Conceptual omega plan
Source: Drawing by Phillip Tabb
b) Selborne omega apex
Source: Photograph courtesy of Serenbe Development Corporation

The shape and width of the omega road are extremely important for the function of sustainability and pedestrian safety. It was once thought that wider suburban streets would be safer, but recent studies have found the opposite – that in fact they are more dangerous. This is caused by the easier passing of cars, which has the consequence of faster speeds. A wider street that has seamless, free-flowing, two-way traffic and speed limits of 35 miles (56 kilometers) per hour, is a cause for higher levels of pedestrian deaths. According to a 1997 study by Peter Swift,[31] these wider suburban streets produced four times pedestrian deaths per unit population as traditional narrow urban streets.[32] According to the landscape architect Patrick Condon, there is no single feature of sustainable community design that is more important than road width.[33] Many suburban residential streets are between 40 and 45 feet (12 and 14 meters) wide. Sustainable communities seek to support safer, more pedestrian environments, especially with the streets. Therefore, road widths are planned to be narrow, creating what is called an increase in "side-friction," which describes the degree of activity, complexity, and spatial constriction for these activities along a residential street that contribute to slower automobile speeds.

The properties and function of the Serenbe omega roads vary, depending on their location within each hamlet. The Selborne omega road begins at 22 feet (7 meters) wide, and increases in width as it is organized along the Thorburn transect. It has the following typical properties:

- *entrance-edge* – rural, two-way, narrow road with no curb, gravel, or drainage on both sides of the road, and a parallel forest path on one side (the road is 22 feet wide);
- *estate area* – rural road, no curbs, with periodic access, drives to estate homes are set back into the landscape, and the forest path adjoins the sidewalk at threshold and pinch point;

- *thresholds* – pinch points with slightly raised pavers crossing the street. They also connect to paths passing through the omega centers (22 feet apart). Natural paths and no curbs transition to granite curbs and sidewalks;
- *cottage area* – a wider street, one side with parallel parking, granite curbs, storm sewers, trees between the street and sidewalks, and sidewalks on both sides (30 feet wide). There are intermittent views between cottages to the hamlet center;
- *townhouse/live–work area* – bordered by thresholds, parallel parking on both sides, and buildings close to sidewalks (38 feet, with double-side parking), and paths going to the hamlet center. Live–work units transition to nonresidential functions;
- *hamlet apex* – the street at its widest is bordered by thresholds and perpendicular parking on both sides (22 feet at stream and 58 feet wide at parking). This area has the greatest concentration of nonresidential functions.

Constellating urbanism

The combination of the four hamlets and crossroads clusters evolve as proximate urban areas, creating the larger development whole and sphere of influence that is referred to as Serenbe Community.[34] The Gestalt effect is the experience of the entire community as a self-organizing unity or complete place, and it is the higher order of sustainability that is intended for, and results from, this process. On a physical level, the constellation of the settlement parts is meant to help operationalize sustainable practices, sustainable businesses, and sustainable technologies; yet on a social level it is meant to help create coherence, identity, and a greater sense of community. The centers are magnets that attract people, and the multiple pathways safely support pedestrian movement. Serenbe was designed for sequential phases of construction: generally, one hamlet at a time. Therefore, there can be an incremental set of changes from one to another.

This is a kind of evolutionary, built-in intelligence that allows for adaptation to market preferences, economic pressures, the introduction of greater levels of sustainable technologies, the creation of additional housing or nonresidential types, and the inclusion of more community-wide activities.[35] There are three components to this phenomenon:

1. the individual places themselves;
2. their connections to one another and to the interstitial spaces; and
3. the whole settlement or constellation.

In comparing the master plan with the celestial chart (atlas) by Alexander Jamieson (1822), the effect becomes clearer. Three urban design processes taken together at this scale help to form a more sustainable context:

1. *nucleated settlement* – each settlement has a coherent form and focus on non-residential functions with sustainable goods and services; these functions vary in order to create a larger number of uses available to the resident population;
2. *interconnections* – each nucleated settlement has multiple means of connection including paths, trails, roads, and public transport in denser places (Chattahoochee Hills), that help to form interdependent cross-programming and sustainable services;

3. *constellating urbanism* – the combination of nucleated settlements, their multiple means of connection, and quality of interstitial space of the in-between, all contribute to a greater experiential, serene, urban, sustainable, and symbolic whole.

Sustainability at the scale of each settlement is a focus on:

*   form compaction and density;
*   land preservation;
*   the quality and essential nature of integrated, nonresidential uses;
*   the degree to which the community is pedestrian-friendly;
*   interconnectedness;
*   sustainable technologies;
*   green materials; and
*   efficient construction practices.

The systemic and accumulative interactions among the settlements further the sustainable objectives through an increase of catchment areas, with the consequent provision of more nonresidential land use, support for safe and easy pedestrian access, introduction of integrated agriculture, and community-wide recycling. The provision of land use purposes such as the visual, culinary and performing arts, organic agriculture, the health and wellness functions, and the educational and increased commercial purposes will certainly help facilitate this process. Taken as a whole, Serenbe develops greater opportunities for social interaction, more complex programmatic elements, and a more intense sense of community.

Serenbe is connected to greenways that connect to the heart of Chattahoochee Hills and the proposed three village sites to the north, and to the city of Palmetto to the east. Most residential developments promote a kind of repetition of homogeneous parts, such as ever-increasing numbers of housing units, or providing only a single amenity. The Serenbe design, on the other hand, promotes ever increasing complexity of land uses and a cross-programmatic interdependence. The intentional hybridity of programmatic genres creates a spatial and temporal complexity, giving greater depth and opportunities for interaction. The constellation effect gathers these levels of complexity into a comprehensible whole that was designed to create a greater sense and use of place. As a constellation, Serenbe arises from both the unity and generative principles, where multiplication and wholeness find expression. The master plan for Serenbe is unfettered by the overly pragmatic consideration normally associated with suburban practice. The site was not leveled and deforested in order to accommodate the maximum number of dwellings in the most economical way; rather, the master plan responded to what was there, and whether it formed an interesting settlement plan. The hopeful view is that Serenbe is a harbinger for positive change in the ways in which we create places to live that are more harmonious with nature.

The idea of a constellating urbanism can have both literal and symbolic presence. Commonly applied to human systems such as families or organizations, there is usually a hidden dynamic at work. Applied to physical systems such as community design, it takes on a slightly different function: that is, to create a unity experience with the place and, in some instances, a union of mythology and archeology, or a physical design and a cosmological presence. Hence the concept "as above, so below," as connected by the *axis mundi*. This suggests that higher principles can be expressed on Earth. The Egyptologist Anthony West writes that these are subconscious representations of archetypal concepts, or what he calls a pipeline to the "intelligence of the heart." Therefore, the symbols become a pathway to a deeply seeded understanding of the forces of a living system.[36] According to Graham Hancock, heaven's mirror is a way of remembering the phenomenal action of the sun, moon, and constellations, as they become a common source through time for reflection.[37]

Systemic constellation theory, originally developed by the psychotherapist Bert Hellinger for family dynamics,[38] suggests that independent yet interconnected parts of a system create a combination of actions affecting the collective whole. For Serenbe, this means that the interrelated hamlets, and the individual placemaking practices that they employ, can support even greater constellating, synergetic, and programmatic relationships. On a symbolic level for Serenbe, the constellation effect is focused on the name Serenbe, the resident community, and affection for the place. It embodies the higher ideals and encompassing qualities of nature, humanity, and charity. In this vein, Virgo is a fitting constellation reflecting the Serenbe master plan, as it is an Earth and feminine sign of the Zodiac, representing fertility and the abundance of harvest. Its brightest star, Spica, is associated with the ear of wheat. This has significance at Serenbe, as it is correspondent with Serenbe Farms and the proposed market in Grange.

For Serenbe, this concept also serves far more pragmatic purposes. It represents the social network distributed spatially throughout the community, which is accessible, identifiable, and operationally integrated. This constellating effect allows for the complexity of dwelling and place to be codified into a comprehensible fabric. There is a shift in focus from a single urban place to a field of places. The nonresidential clusters, organized natural areas, and the circulatory networks that connect them, all fit into this constellation construct. The layers of this construct can be seen in the master plan for Serenbe, and the combinations of master plan elements constitute what is being referred to as the "Serenbe Constellation".

The sign and name "Serenbe" are a symbol of the wholeness of the community. When we gaze up at the night sky, the complexity and sheer number of stars, planets, and other celestial bodies can be overwhelming. To understand this complexity, constellations have been identified as cosmic placemarkers in the sky as well as the passing of time. Once we see a figure or shape we recognize, it is difficult to see that pattern as part of a larger random agglomeration. The constellation Virgo is easily recognized in the southern sky as the "Wheat-bearing Maiden," and associated with the late summer harvest (Figure 7.11a). Finally, for Serenbe, the constellation is the atmosphere of the place, the residents, and the sense of community that dwells there. The major nonresidential functions that are of use to the entire community are indicated in the constellation in Figure 7.11b.

The Serenbe concept is described sometimes as being utopian, New Urban, sustainable, environmental, biophilic, or agrarian – but whatever it may be called, it is a unique blend of the serene and urban. Some residents refer to Serenbe as "urbal," meaning a blend from the best qualities of the urban and rural environments. Following is the vision statement as shown on the Serenbe website:

> At Serenbe we value nature, passion, creativity and community.
> We believe people can live more fully when connected to the wonder of nature.

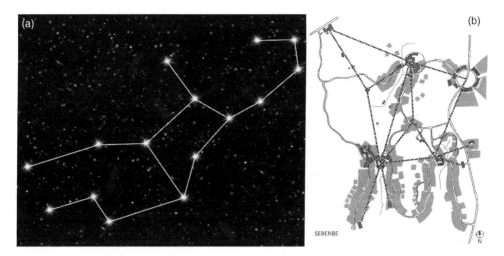

Figure 7.11 Constellating urbanism: a) Virgo constellation
Source: Shutterstock
b) Serenbe constellation
Source: Drawing by Phillip Tabb

This is a community where people live, work, learn and play in celebration of life's beauty. A place where connections between people, nature and the arts are nourished.[39]

Notes

1 This quote was often given in presentations about Serenbe by co-founder Steve Nygren, suggesting that when newcomers visited Serenbe, it was very compelling, especially when the Blue Eyed Daisy opened.
2 The word *Serenbe*, while initially created by co-founder Marie Nygren, is now a common or more general term used to describe the entire community at Serenbe. This includes the land, inn, hamlets, crossroads, interstitial spaces and functions, activities and residents. Serenbe is the broader whole or constellation that comprises the larger place.
3 After the initial charrettes of Serenbe, the larger context of Chattahoochee Hills was looked at: more than half of the landowners participated, where a conceptual land use plan was created, forming three villages of approximately 10,000 residences each through the Transfer of Development Rights process. This later was adapted by Fulton County.
4 CD interview with Steve and Marie Nygren; Todd, John, *From Eco-cities to Living Machines: Principles of Ecological Design*, North Atlantic Books, Berkeley, CA, 1994; Pearce, A.R. with Vanegas, J.A. and Browning, W.D., "Serenbe: A Project Planning Charrette," summary analysis report submitted to Serenbe Development Corporation, Palmetto, GA, 2000.
5 World Commission on Environment and Development, *Our Common Future*, Oxford University Press, Oxford, 1987.
6 Rickaby, Peter, "Towards a Spatial Energy Model," PhD dissertation, Open University and Centre for Configurational Studies, Milton Keynes, 1986.
7 Tabb, Phillip, "Placemaking as a Sustainable Planning Strategy: Serenbe Community," paper presented at the Architectural Research Centers Consortium (ARCC) conference, San Antonio, TX, April 17, 2009; Tabb, Phillip, *Serenbe and the Geometry of Place*, self-published, College Station, TX, 2010.
8 Krier, Leon, "Architectural Design," in *Leon Krier: Houses, Palaces, Cities*, Architectural Design AD Editions, London, 1984, pp. 32–3.

 9 Student study exercise given by author in a graduate seminar course titled "Theory of Placemaking, ARCH 624," fall of 2010, Texas A&M University.

10 Owens, Susan, *Energy Planning and Urban Design*, Pion Press, London, 1986.

11 Farr, Douglas, *Sustainable Urbanism: Urban Design with Nature*, Wiley and Sons, New York, 2008.

12 Best, Robin and Rogers, Alan, *The Urban Countryside: The Land Use Structure of Small Towns and Villages in England and Wales*, Faber & Faber, London, 1973.

13 Tabb, Phillip, "The Solar Village Archetype: A Study of English Village Form Applicable to Energy-integrated Planning Principles for Satellite Settlements in Temperate Climates," PhD dissertation, Architectural Association, London, 1990.

14 US Department of Transportation, Federal Highway Administration, *National Household Travel Survey*, US Department of Transportation, Washington, DC, 2009.

15 Strum, Roland and Cohen, Deborah, "Proximity to Urban Parks and Mental Health," *Journal of Mental Health Policy and Economics* 17(1), 2014, pp. 19–24. Available online at www.ncbi.nlm.nih.gov/pmc/articles/PMC4049158/ (accessed November 2015).

16 American Planning Association, "APA Policy Guide on Smart Growth," April 14, 2012. Available online at www.planning.org/policy/guides/adopted/smartgrowth.htm (accessed June 18, 2016).

17 Corbin, Charles B., "Dimensions of Wellness: Seven Dimensional Model," University of Illinois Wellness Center, Champaign, IL. Available online at http://wellness.illinois.edu/dimensions/ (accessed June 18, 2016).

18 Mississippi Arts Commission, *Seven Compelling Reasons to Increase Funding for the Arts in Mississippi*, Jackson, MS, 2012.

19 In Michelle K. Glowa, "Critical Sustainablities: Competing Discourses of Urban Development in California," June 1, 2015. Available online at https://critical-sustainabilities.ucsc.edu/locavore/ (accessed December 2015).

20 "Farm-to-table" is a food production process referring to seamless stages, from agricultural planting, harvesting, storage, processing, preparation, and consumption. At Serenbe it occurs from Serenbe Farms to the various on-site restaurants and residents' homes.

21 Crasemann Collins, Christiane, "Cartographers of an Imaginary Atlas," in Hegemann, Werner and Peets, Elbert, *Introduction to American Vitruvius: An Architects' Handbook of Civic Art*, Princeton University Press, Princeton, NJ, 1988, pp. xii–xxii, p. xx.

22 Department of Geology, University of Georgia, "The Geology of North Georgia." Available online at www.gly.uga.edu/railsback/GAGeology.html (accessed October 2015).

23 "Martin Heidegger on *Aletheia* as Unconcealment." Available online at www.ontology.co/heidegger-aletheia.htm (accessed November 2015).

24 Lane, Belden, "Axiom for Sacred Place," in *Landscapes of the Sacred: Geography and Narrative in American Spirituality*, Johns Hopkins University Press, Baltimore, MD, 2001, pp. 19–20.

25 Ellin, Nan, *Integral Urbanism*, Routledge, London, 2006, p. 121.

26 "About Serenbe." Available online at http://serenbe.com/about (accessed June 20, 2016).

27 Ellin, *Integral Urbanism*.

28 Thorburn, Andrew, *Planning Villages*, Estates Gazette Limited, London, 1971.

29 The I-Ching is *The Chinese Book of Changes*, and expresses 64 hexagrams or patterns that describe certain energies and phenomena. The Caldron is Hexagram 50, which describes the nature of sacred containment and nourishment, symbolic of the preparation of food.

30 Blakely, Edward and Snyder, Mary Gail, *Fortress America: Gated Communities in the United States*, Brookings Institute Press, Washington, DC, 1997.

31 Swift, Peter, "Narrow Streets Are Best," *Better Cities & Towns*, November/December 1997, p. 1. Available online at http://bettercities.net/article/narrow-streets-are-safest (accessed June 8, 2016).

32 Swift, Peter, "Residential Street Typology and Injury Accident," *Sierra Club Environmental Update*, 1997. Available online at http://vault.sierraclub.org/sprawl/articles/narrow.asp (accessed September 2015).

33 Condon, Patrick, *Seven Rules for Sustainable Communities: Design Strategies for the Post Carbon World*, Island Press, Washington, DC, 2010.

34 The idea of a constellating urbanism can have both literal and symbolic presences. Torsten Preiss, Indra, *Family Constellations Revealed: Hellinger's Family and Other Constellations Revealed (The Systemic View, Volume 1)*, CreateSpace Independent Publishing, 2012. Tabb, Phillip, "Constellating Sustainable Development: The Serenbe Communities," Making Cities Livable Paper, Carmel, CA, 2005, p. 4.

35 Kahn, Andrea, Cannon, Charlie, Duong, Phu and Verbakel, Els, *Constellations: Constructing Urban Design Practices*, Graduate School of Architecture, Planning, and Preservation, Columbia University, New York, 2007.

36 West, Anthony, *Serpent in the Sky: The High Wisdom of Ancient Egypt*, Julian Press, New York, 1987.

37 Hancock, Graham, *Heaven's Mirror: Quest for the Lost Civilization*, Three Rivers Press, New York, 1999.

38 Hellinger, Bert, "Systemic Constellations". Available online at www.systemicconstellations. com (accessed August 2015).

39 Serenbe Community website: https://serenbe.com/ (accessed October 2015).

8 Master plan elements

Each of Serenbe's four hamlets has complementary commercial centers focused on the elements of a well-lived life: arts for inspiration, agriculture for nourishment, health for wellbeing and education for awareness.[1]

The project objective of developing only 30 percent of the land was challenging. The rolling hills and resulting valleys with flood plains running down the middle presented even greater restrictions and limitations. The result was to build along the interface between the sloping woodlands and the natural valley floors below. As a consequence, there were three prime development sites that fitted these conditions. A fourth site was identified at the highest elevation, adjacent to the prime access road. The master plan of Serenbe was made of hamlet-scaled forms positioned around edges of each of the valley bottoms. Furthermore, each hamlet seemed to form a unique sense of place with its particular omega center, individualized set of amenities, and nonresidential functions.

Selborne Hamlet

The name Selborne is taken from the linear village in the south of England with the same name.[2] Originally it was referred to as the "Artist Hamlet," with an intended focus on the visual, performing, and culinary arts. A charrette was organized in 2002 to focus on further developing the design for Selborne Hamlet and the Crossroads. The purpose was to respond to the overall master plan and to develop Selborne in greater detail in terms of the overall form, further implement the Thorburn transect, establish more accurate plot sizes and building-to-plot relationships, get an accurate dwelling count, and refine the hamlet center program with associated land use mixes. In addition, there was design work done on the hamlet center at the top of the omega, and the center enclosing space of the omega was established as a building-free open space. Selborne was planned as the smallest of the four hamlets with an estimated dwelling count of about 120, yet it was extremely important, as it was the first to be developed. Therefore, Selborne became the model for the remaining hamlets of Serenbe, and it expressed characteristics such as density, use mixes, and the Thorburn transect. Selborne is 600-feet (183-meters) wide from center-line of each leg of the omega road (Figures 8.1a and 8.1b).

As mentioned previously, the thematic focus of the hamlet was on the culinary, visual, and performing arts, and the ways in which these activities could contribute to the vitality of the place and community life. This was especially important in this

Figure 8.1 Selborne Hamlet: a) Aerial view
Source: Photograph courtesy of Serenbe Development Corporation
b) Live–work courtyard
Source: Photograph by Phillip Tabb

first hamlet in order to demonstrate the concept of community originally intended for Serenbe. In addition, the activities help as a visible amenity, which was attractive to future homebuyers, and helpful in growing the hamlet. In the plan the lower densities can be seen at the omega ends, while at the apex there is compactness. The omega road is double-loaded, with the houses aligned along it having access to the woodlands, either in the center or around the perimeter.

The Thorburn transect was implemented in organizing the lotting scheme, which can be seen with the larger estate homes on bigger plots at the edges of the omega road, and the transition of dwelling proximities growing closer to one another and nearer to the road as they approach the omega apex. It was intended that the hamlet center be organized by interesting geometry and more extraordinary architecture to give it distinction, and to communicate its quality and function in promoting the arts, including architecture. The constructed wetlands were created to process waste for the community and located downhill, south of the hamlet just before its entrance.[3]

Selborne Hamlet is approximately 30 gross acres (12 hectares), including the open space center. The hamlet is oriented on a north–northeast and south–southeast axis. This coincides with the overall geology of the Piedmont region, of which it is a part. This is good for solar access. Nearly all of the detached residences are aligned along the omega roads with an east–west aspect to the dwelling form.[4] This is to provide shading in hot summers, and rooftop access for the south-facing photovoltaic arrays along the long axis ridges year-round. Attached and commercial structures are located at the top of the omega form. The small stream runs down the middle of the hamlet, then makes an immediate left-turn. This particular site is extremely wooded and many of the trees have been saved (Figures 8.2a–c). Special geometry was used to organize some of the functions at the top of the omega road; part of it aligns with the stream, and another with the incoming perpendicular road (Selborne Way). The internal geometry forms a Fibonacci kite.[5] Significant points of this geometry are situated in the site, including the hamlet center green. The kite converges to a point which is on

Figure 8.2 Selborne Hamlet center: a) Central path b) Omega stream c) Selborne lighting
        standard
Source: Photographs by Phillip Tabb

axis with the omega center, where there is a small gathering place in the woods. The axis terminates with the bonfire site, further in the woods to the southwest.

Grange Hamlet

The second hamlet is called Grange: it is approximately 50 gross acres (20 hectares), including the center open space and lake, and 750 feet (229 meters)-wide from the centerlines of the omega road (Figures 8.3a–d). The hamlet is oriented to more pragmatic matters of the land and community, including the equestrian center, Serenbe Farms, Montessori elementary school, and general store. In the center of the hamlet is a 5-acre (2-hectare) lake that provides a focus of activity and tranquil view. Planned at the apex of the omega road is more commercial property: a bookstore, a restaurant, a general store, and a few related shops.

Opposite the commercial area is a small hamlet green with a neighborhood mail pavilion that serves as an urban gathering place for the local residents of Grange Hamlet. A trampoline was placed level with the ground, which is popular with resident children. It is intended that lessons learned from the first hamlet, Selborne, be applied to subsequent hamlet developments, and as a result to initiate more sustainable dwelling designs and on-site technologies, especially geothermal systems. Initially, two residential projects were constructed, demonstrating intensive green design principles. One was by a local designer who speculatively built the house with passive solar heating, while the other was sponsored by *Dwell* magazine and later constructed by a private resident. During the 2008 recession, the nest cluster focused on both affordability and sustainability, with smaller cottage designs (900–1,700 square feet; 84–158 square meters), utilizing earth-sourced heat pumps and, in some instances, photovoltaic electricity. The Bosch Experience Center residence was the first at Serenbe to achieve Net-Zero energy performance, where it employed a ground-sourced heat pump for heating and cooling, photovoltaic electricity, and energy-efficient appliances. The Home and Garden Television (HGTV) green home was certified as LEED Platinum, and it too incorporated photovoltaic electricity and energy-efficient equipment.[6]

An important part of the Grange Hamlet is Serenbe Farms, located on land adjacent to the east omega leg. Initially planned for about 30 acres, the Farms uses approximately two-thirds of the available land, while the other one-third is being used for the staging and storage of construction materials. It is a certified organic farm with more than 350 varieties of vegetables, herbs, flowers, fruit, and mushrooms. All the produce is distributed within a 40-mile (64-kilometer) radius, through a community member's program. The land was used originally for commodity cotton farming decades ago, and was cause for the erosion of large quantities of topsoil. Consequently, the farm now uses red clay as a foundation for organic matter, community compost, and small amounts of rock dust, trace minerals, and sea salts reintroduced to the soil. There are three organic farming methods employed at the farm: composting, cover cropping, and crop rotation. The farm utilizes drip irrigation and mulches to minimize water usage. It serves the local restaurants, general store, Serenbe residents, nearby neighbors, and the farm cooperative. Many of the Grange Hamlet homes back right up to the farms for easy access and views to the growing areas.[7] As Mado Hamlet becomes developed in 2016, there are plans for additional farming and community gardens, with easy access for independent and assisted living residents (Figures 8.4a–d).

Figure 8.3 Grange Hamlet: a) Aerial view b) Grange Lake
Source: Photographs courtesy of Serenbe Development Corporation
c) Live–work cluster model d) Grange lighting standard
Source: Photograph by Phillip Tabb

Figure 8.4 Community food: a) Serenbe Farms b) Bosch Experience Center cooking class
c) General store exterior d) General store interior
Source: Photographs by Phillip Tabb

Mado Hamlet

The Mado charrette in April of 2007 was specifically targeted on the development of the third hamlet form and theme of nonresidential functions. In the center of the hamlet are natural wetlands and the 100-year flood plain, which are part of the Cedar Creek basin. The eastern leg of the omega is on fairly sloping forested land, while the west leg is on relatively flat land, which is easier for development. The name "Mado" comes from the Creek Nation Native American word meaning "things in balance," which seemed a fitting name for a focus on health and wellness.[8] Consequently, the theme for Mado was health and wellness, so a cluster of activities was determined and dispersed throughout the fabric of the hamlet plan (Figure 8.5a).

Mado was planned for a slightly larger population, especially if one considers the provision for assisted and independent living, with approximately 380 dwelling units with seven different dwelling types: live–work units, townhomes, cottage homes, affordable cottages, independent living boarding houses, terraced condominium units, and estate dwellings. Several more affordable housing clusters were planned within the hamlet, with smaller dwelling footprints aligned along a greenway. This includes dispersed independent living units, with an assisted-living facility located near the hamlet center. The natural wetlands occupy the lower elevations in the center of the hamlet, and are terminated with a circular pool which marks the omega center (Figure 8.5b). The commercial area at the hamlet apex features an open air square that has parking

Figure 8.5 Mado Hamlet: a) Mado plan (2014)
Source: Photograph by Phillip Tabb
b) Aerial view of site (2015)
Source: Photograph courtesy of Serenbe Development Corporation

below, and is surrounded by a vegetarian restaurant on the south edge, two three-story medical buildings on the east and west sides, and live–work shops and services to the north along the omega road. Mado is approximately 55 gross acres (22 hectares), including the open space center and wetlands, and is 700 feet (17 meters) wide from the centerlines of each leg of the omega road. Figure 8.5a shows the concept plan for Mado and the initial construction of the omega road started in 2015.

Rather than concentrating the health and wellness activities, there was an attempt to disperse the functions throughout the hamlet, so that they were more integrated into the fabric of the place. Planned near the entrance of the east leg of the hamlet is the spa complex, with several associated live–work units that could house various physical therapies. The spa complex has an approximate site area of 1.8 acres (0.73 hectares), and comprises a single-story spa center with a footprint area of 10,000 gross square feet (929 square meters). The formal entry is from the east. Planned for the facility is a visitor parking lot at the side of the building, with approximately 60 parking places. There are pleasant views to the omega center along the wetlands. It is envisioned that a series of hot tubs might be placed among the high grasses, affording great views and privacy. The west leg houses the recuperative hotel. It has an approximate site area of 2.5 acres (1 hectare), and the footprint of the hotel is 6,000 gross square feet (557 square meters) with 12 cabins at 625 square feet (68 square meters) each. With the hotel having four levels, this totals approximately 28,375 gross square feet (2,636 square meters), including the cabins. The hotel is designed to accommodate high-end users and those who require discreet privacy for recovery from medical procedures received from other facilities within the hamlet.

Being sited at the edge of the hamlet affords a great deal of privacy and nearness to the natural beauty of the wetlands in the hamlet center, and the waterfalls further to the west. Other health and wellness facilities include a fitness center, therapeutic swimming pool, and a pharmacy. A couple additional housing types are being introduced into Mado, which include horizontal independent flats, V-shaped affordable housing units, and the assisted living facility. Figures 8.6a–c show building schematics for the various health and wellness functions, and a model of the recuperative cabins, which originally were designed for the first plan for Mado.[9]

There is a concentration of health and wellness related activities planned for the apex of the omega form. The fitness center is located at the corner of the top of the omega and the west T-junction loop. The footprint is slightly trapezoidal in shape, with a gross area of 21,875 square feet (2,903 square meters). As a two-story building, a bridge is planned that connects to the assisted living facility for direct access. The therapy pool is located to the northwest of the fitness center, on the west side of the omega. The footprint is rectangular in shape, with a gross area of 7,500 square feet (697 square meters). The northwest façade has large movable doors that open

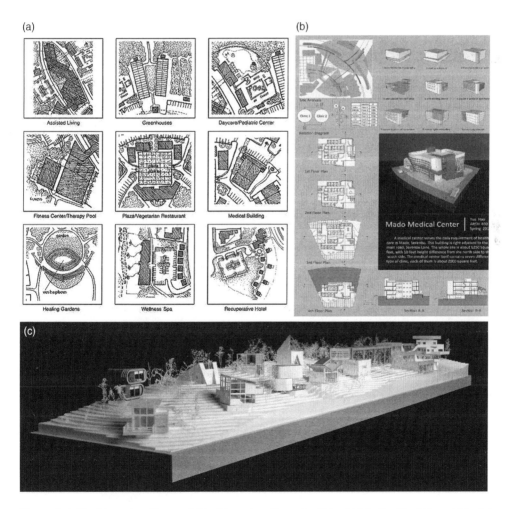

Figure 8.6 Health and wellness: a) Health and wellness facilities b) Medical building c) Model of healing retreats

Source: Photographs by Phillip Tabb

out to the natural forest behind the building. The footprint of a typical building is rectangular in shape, with a gross footprint area of 7,200 square feet (669 square meters). As a three-story building, it could utilize 21,500 total gross square feet (1,997 square meters). The building efficiency is planned at approximately 82 percent. There is a small visitor parking lot at the rear of each of the buildings, with approximately ten parking places in each. There are an additional ten parking spaces along the street in front of the building, and there will be parking beneath the plaza. The vegetarian restaurant is located in the very center of the hamlet, with the square plaza to its north and the circular pond and gardens to the south. The gross footprint of the restaurant is 10,000 square feet (929 square meters). This includes dining areas, bar, kitchen, storage, and related retail.

The assisted living complex, planned as a three-story building of approximately 125,000 square feet (11,613 square meters), is located in the northwest corner of the omega in a Z-shaped form. Its recessed spaces overlook the Montessori school and community swimming pool on one side, and the fitness center and green on the other. The complex has the potential for 80 rooms at an average of 750 square feet (70 square meters) each. The building has two courtyards, one being a soft green space and the other a hard-surfaced, outdoor dining area that overlooks the daycare center. The dining room, kitchen, game rooms, and offices are located on the ground level.

The running trail that surrounds the wetlands has lengths of 1-mile (1.6 kilometers), with changing rooms provided at the beginning. The hamlet benefits from specialized and thematic programming, which introduces unexpected uses blended into a residential environment, such as the pediatric clinic, swimming pool, and daycare. The hamlet is designed to accommodate active living and a variety of housing choices for aging in place.

The spa complex is approximately 10,000 square feet, with associated and smaller live–work units or 625 square feet each. The fitness center is planned for 22,000 square feet (2,044 square meters), in which two-thirds are on the ground level with a mezzanine above. It is to be connected by a bridge to the assisted living complex. The therapy pool is 7,500 square feet (697 square meters), and adjacent to the fitness center. The medical office blocks accommodate a gross area of 21,500 square feet (1,997 square meters) on three floors. It is planned with an efficiency of 82 percent. The recuperative hotel is designed for approximately 6,000 square feet on a 2.5-acre site (1 hectare) to the southwest of the hamlet plan. The vegetarian restaurant is planned for 10,000 square feet (929 meters squared), replete with all associated functions. To the north of the hamlet are two commercial greenhouses related to the Serenbe Farms West, planned to produce healing herbs and flowers year-round.

Education Hamlet

The fourth hamlet, the Education Hamlet, is still in the planning process. The site for this hamlet is generally located along Atlanta Newnan Road to the east of the other hamlets, and therefore has fairly easy access from these other places in Serenbe. The site is fairly level along the road, but then dramatically slopes downhill from west to east to a streambed below. The exact size and location of properties are still undetermined, which makes any design somewhat speculative. Its accessible and visible location along Atlanta Newnan Road suggests a larger number of nonresidential functions that normally might not be appropriate for the more intimate omega hamlets.

Additional purposes that are being considered for this hamlet include a small grocery store, restaurant/cafe, bank, post office, fire station, retail shops, and office space. There was even discussion about including a small gasoline station. Adjacent to the hamlet is space allocated for higher educational facilities for on-site classes at Serenbe, where students could learn about Serenbe within a living-learning environment, work on planning and architecture projects, spend time at Serenbe Farms, and construct some permanent works for the community, such as bridges, benches, shelters, and other small structures. This facility is envisioned to be similar to the Rural Studio at Auburn University in Alabama started in 1992 by architect Samuel Mockbee, where design, construction and community work are combined. This is a wonderful opportunity to engage in community work within Serenbe, as well as the undeveloped countryside surrounding the Chattahoochee Hills area.

This hamlet was probably the most challenging to plan, due to its location and proximity to Atlanta Newnan Road. Instead of being sited in a defined valley, this hamlet is on a hill with a county road passing right through it. Additionally, the contours to the east fall quite dramatically, making automobile access challenging to develop. Despite the difficulties that this site presents, there are certain advantages. Its location and connection to the outside can be a benefit to Serenbe residents as well as those living nearby, and this hamlet could be planned with more commercial and educational functions, especially those that normally require larger catchment areas. An initiating feature to the design of this hamlet is a proposed circular roundabout occurring at the intersection of Atlanta Newnan Road and Selborne Path. The roundabout serves as a placemarker, directing traffic along Atlanta Newnan Road both to the hamlet and Selborne Hamlet. Adjacent to this circle would be a series of commercial and educational buildings, reinforcing its form. A village green would occupy its center. Residential building types would be generally higher in density, with condominiums, townhomes, and semi-attached housing. On the downhill side of the site could be some estate houses, providing an appropriate transition to the forested open space and streambed below (Figure 8.7a).

Along this traffic circle a study-away facility is planned, designed to accommodate undergraduate and graduate programs in architecture, urban design, landscape architecture, land development and horticulture. The design in Figure 8.7b shows a campus-like scheme by Texas A&M University students. Serenbe is envisioned to be a laboratory for studies in the areas of sustainability, biophilia, and environmental community planning. A pilot program occurred in the fall of 2015, with undergraduate and graduate architecture students from Texas A&M University (Figure 8.7c) who conducted planning, architectural design, and design-construct work for various projects within Serenbe.

A charter school was approved in December of 2010 and initially sited adjacent to the Education Hamlet. However, a site located near the center of the city of Chattahoochee Hills was selected instead, as it was in a more convenient location for a larger catchment area. This was constructed in 2013, and occupation occurred in fall of 2014. A goal of the school is for students to cultivate the capacity to achieve a meaningful, healthy, flourishing life that embodies responsibility, stewardship, and experiential engagement with the arts, agriculture, and the environment in informed, imaginative, and rigorous ways. The school features a hands-on, thematic, and instructional approach that uses its unique surroundings as a framework in which students can learn, and positions agricultural, environmental, and artistic themes as lenses

Figure 8.7 Education Hamlet: a) Hamlet center plan b) Study-away facilities c) Serenbe study-
          away program, fall 2015
Source: Photographs by Phillip Tabb

through which the Georgia Performance Standards can be achieved. Additionally, research suggests that students who engage in environmental-based investigations in their own community often experience better performance on standardized tests, reduced discipline and classroom management problems, and increased enthusiasm for learning. The charter school will use the abundant, rural nature of Chattahoochee Hills as a vehicle for experiential learning.

Other land uses and interstitial spaces

Other land uses comprise a variety of activities and functions, which are considered amenities and add to the experience of living in Serenbe. The articulated functions include the Crossroads Cluster, ArtFarm, Serenbe Stables, Serenbe Inn and Farmhouse, animal village, and eventually estate housing development south of Cedar Creek. The interstitial spaces are those considered between each of the developed hamlets and generally situated in the forested areas of Serenbe: they further add to the quality of the serene, and provide direct connections to nature. These areas amount to 70 percent of the allocated land, and possess special natural and community-oriented activities within the forests, wetlands, recreational areas, greens, equestrian functions, and meadows.

The Crossroads

In conjunction to Selborne Hamlet, this charrette addressed the first crossroads cluster that was originally developed for 25 dwellings. This settlement pattern is quite common in Georgia, and the result of buildings agglomerating at road crossings or T-junctions. A model for this small settlement type was the Historic District of Roscoe, Georgia, located in Chattahoochee Hills. White-painted, southern vernacular houses are grouped along curving crossroads, forming this intimate community. Houses also included front and wraparound porches, swings, and picket fences. At Serenbe the crossroads clusters are more densely packed, single-family residences, with a central green space, four townhomes, and two live–work dwellings, presently housing flower and bicycle repair shops. On the original design, one of the corner properties of the first crossroads cluster was designated a common structure that possibly could be used by the entire cluster community for gatherings, birthdays, parties, and other shared occasions. At the end of the cluster is a small children's play area tucked into the woods next to the community mailbox pavilion. To slow traffic, raised crosswalks and stop signs were placed at both ends of Selborne Lane, which enters the crossroads. Tabb Way, the leg of the "T," extends and eventually will connect to Mado Hamlet (Figures 8.8a–c).

Interstitial land uses

Interstitial places are the domain of the in-between space. They are residual and the natural remains of the unurbanized portions of the land at Serenbe. According to architect Aldo van Eyck, the in-between was tied to the concept of twin phenomena. The hamlets focus both inward and outward simultaneously, constituting a twin-phenomena (urban–rural interface).[10] The interstitial spaces are in-between the omega legs and hamlets, creating a sense of separation as well as integration. The separation contributes to the identity of each hamlet, and the integration homogenizes the

Figure 8.8 The Crossroads: a) Street view b) Concept plan c) Townhouse square
Source: Photographs by Phillip Tabb

urban and nonurban territories into a whole. A few structures have been constructed in the interstitial areas as well as a few purposeful landscapes, but the interstitial areas are primarily left open and natural. Formal structures inside the interstitial areas include the pavilion and labyrinth, which are part of the Inn at Serenbe, the treehouses near Selborne Hamlet, the bonfire pavilion, the various sites for Serenbe Playhouse, Serenbe Stables, and the proposed interfaith chapel. Various temporary sites are located throughout this interstitial space for productions by Serenbe Playhouse.

The ArtFarm could be considered in the interstitial area as well. It is an important addition to Serenbe, in that it contributes to the original goal of introducing the arts to the development.[11] The Artist in Residence (AIR) program brings in various visual artists to live and work, and share their creative works with the community. There is a path leading from the ArtFarm to Grange Hamlet. Eventually the ArtFarm master plan shows development further away, with proposed condominium studio spaces and a gallery clustered together in a compound and residential sites (Figures 8.9a–d).[12] In 2015 Serenbe, in partnership with Auburn's Rural Studio, began construction of two of its 20K houses[13] at the ArtFarm. Two additional 20K houses are planned in the near future. Both Serenbe Farms and the stables are located outside of the hamlets, but have been discussed elsewhere. There are many natural areas that are also considered part of the Serenbe experience.

Near Selborne Hamlet center is the treehouse that serves as a wonderful place for children to discover and use. In fact, there are two treehouses connected by a bridge. In summer it has been the backdrop for one of the Serenbe Playhouse theatrical productions. The recreation area accommodates a soccer field, two tennis courts, and a

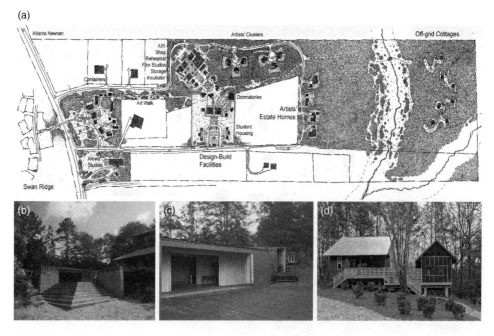

Figure 8.9 Serenbe ArtFarm: a) 2015 Master plan b) Main house and outdoor stage c) ArtFarm
        containers d) Auburn–Serenbe Rural Studio 20K house at Serenbe
Source: Photographs by Phillip Tabb

basketball court. Adjacent to this area is an outdoor dog run. Planned for the future is the interfaith chapel, which is sited at the end of the long meadow between the Inn and Selborne Hamlet. It is on the highest piece of land in that area, and looks over the forested area below. In addition, the farm next to the Inn includes 100 animals with several enclosures, and fenced areas holding the animals. There are goats, sheep, llamas, pigs, chickens, and rabbits, and an adjacent fenced field for cows and horses. To the southwest of the pastures is located the wildflower meadow, which originally was a deforested area on the side of one of the hills that was enlivened with a mass of wildflowers. This is remarkable to see, especially in the spring. Another landscape intervention occurs on the meadow along the road that lies between the labyrinth and Selborne Hamlet. The land was slightly sculpted and also planted with wildflowers, to help create a more seamless connection between the two areas of the site. Trails meander throughout the interstitial spaces for approximately 7 miles. Some simply connect the hamlets to one another, to the animal area and the Inn, but others lead deeper into the forested areas of the site. One of the more interesting trails begins in the center of Selborne Hamlet and follows the stream past the treehouses and near to one of the cow pastures. It presses on through the woods, past the west side of the proposed Mado Hamlet, to the larger of the two waterfalls. Then the path leads further down the stream until it spills into Cedar Creek, which is a magical and extremely natural part of the site. This basin is filled with lush meadows with tall grasses and a variety of tree species including sweetgum, sourwood, oak and southern pine. It is common to come across a beaver dam, armadillos, turtles, many varieties of birds, and to spot white-tailed deer.

This interstitial territory is also integral to creating serene connections to nature, providing residents' engagement in outdoor activities, which not only contributes to health and well-being, but also allows for enjoyment and discovery. Figures 8.10a–d show a sample of the activities within the interstitial space, including the Serenbe Inn horse barn, Serenbe Farms feathered in-between residential portions of Grange Hamlet, an instructor and student of dressage at the Serenbe Stables next to the Crossroads cluster, and children horseback riding as a part of the Serenbe Camp activities. The interstitial spaces at Serenbe are one of its greatest amenities and assets, and will continue to evolve over time. It will be important to preserve some of this space without purpose for future generations. The land south of Cedar Creek still remains wild, mysterious, and serene. While many visitors to Serenbe do experience the hamlet centers, the more permanent residents further south generally explore the land.

The master plan layers

The updated master plan (2014) illustrates several important layers that include articulation of the open spaces, meadows, forest land, and organic farmland, mixes of use in the urbanized areas within the developed hamlets, the interspersion of uses throughout the open space, and both automobile and pedestrian circulation networks. The last plan simply identifies key special places within the master plan.

- *Natural layer* – identifies generally the natural areas of the site that include: forests, meadows, wetlands and water, and special features. The special features include the pond, lake, streams, labyrinth, chapel and celestial sites, the larger and smaller waterfalls, wildflower hill and rock garden, and the archeological site.

Figure 8.10 Interstitial land uses: a) Interstitial aerial view
Source: Photograph courtesy of Serenbe Development Corporation
b) Serenbe Farms interface with Grange housing c) Serenbe Stables d) Bridle trails throughout Serenbe
Source: Photographs by Phillip Tabb

- *Urbanized layer* – the three prime omega-shaped hamlets, the Crossroads cluster, and the counter-urban ArtFarm compound are designated with varying land uses that include: commercial, attached housing, cottage homes, estate homes, urban greens, and urban water features.
- *Circulation layer* – indicates all automobile networks that include roads, drives, alleys, and on- and off-street parking, and all pedestrian networks that include paths, trails, bridle paths, sidewalks, and plazas. There are about 7 miles of trails throughout Serenbe.
- *Interstitial layer* – identifies all the land uses and activities that occur in the in-between or interstitial spaces among the urbanized areas, including: the forest path systems, natural waterways and features, meadows, paddocks, agriculture, recreation, archeological site, and special structures.

The master plan embodies the ideals and intentions of the original charrette in a process of ever-expanding understanding of what makes an environmentally sustainable community at Serenbe. The plan layers combine concepts of preservation of land, fitting into the land, creating coherent places with diverse activities, integrated agriculture, and all the amenities that are intended to support emerging and healthier lifestyles. The geometry is an integral part of the design and helps enable the articulation of these ideas.

At this stage of the process the master plan certainly furthered the manifestation process, but also provided the emerging community with a potent symbol of change.

Geometry of place served to fit with the land, form an overall placemaking spatial structure, organize the architecture into a coherent and interesting unfolding, and frame ceremonial patterns of use. The linear, nucleated, transected, curvilinear qualities of the omega are strong contributors to the character of the design. The constellation concept binds everything together into a unified place. The role of geometry was important in giving the plan an ecological response to the land, a community-oriented function and spatial structure, as well as formal distinction and character.

The master plan layers reflect important planning considerations, indicating the magnitude of open space (as seen in Figure 8.11a). The large expanses of woodlands, meadows, pastures, and streams are shown in the light and darker gray tones. The pond (upper center) and lake (lower right) are shown in black. The urbanized areas are indicated in Figure 8.11b. Shown in black are all the existing and proposed buildings comprising the hamlets. Both roadways and paths are presented in black lines in Figure 8.11c, where the networks of connectivity can be clearly seen. Figure 8.11d shows in black on the map locations of various facilities, natural areas, and special places within the interstitial space between each of the hamlets.

Architecturalizing the plan

Building types as well as architectural languages vary at Serenbe. Rather than specify one style or approach to design, it was felt that multiple expressions would reflect personal preferences and community diversity. Rural values – such as love of nature, respect for all life, honoring the wisdom of elders, acknowledging our responsibility to future generations, self-sufficiency, financial prudence, tolerance, generosity, neighbors helping neighbors, thriftiness, living simply, gratitude, and finding joy every day in the wonder of existence – are important. Serenbe Community members sympathize with these, yet do not view them nostalgically. Rather, they are contemporary in their views, lifestyles, and tastes.

So, how are all these values translated into architectural expression? First, there is no single style of architecture that is imposed by the development process. This means that the architectural design process honors individual rights of personal style – within reason. There are certain standards of construction quality, design integrity, and the use of an appropriate range of materials.

Second, there is the general interest in climatic and authentic southern vernacular design. This means that vernacular forms are used to perform a particular function appropriate to the climate of north Georgia. Third, there is the recommendation for front porches and friendly entrances to each dwelling aligned along the omega roads. These are cultural as well as functional interventions to the designs. Fourth, there is the desire for diversity of building types, massing, and design. In order to attract diversity, it was felt that it was important to reflect diversity, especially in the architecture. Finally, there is the notion that the strength of the omega geometry and amount of preserved natural landscape would be preeminent and homogenize the differing architectural languages, yet what would still remain would be an overall coherence of community. In other words, the urban form would "tame" the varying expressions of the aggregate architecture to a certain extent.

New Urbanism developments, for example, set fairly strict design guidelines so that there is far more consistency of architectural style: they are less tolerant in allowing

(a)

NATURAL AREAS

Figure 8.11 Master plan layers: a) Natural layer b) Urbanized areas c) Networks layer
              d) Interstitial uses
Source: Drawings by Phillip Tabb

for individual expression. Gated communities want houses to be similar in size and
quality, so that all the properties within the community conform and maintain high
value. Many suburban developments have a very limited range of housing products
for economic reasons – the economy of repetition. Often, variations in style are simply
a function of adding different stylistic dormers, garage door designs, or the flipping
of plan types. While most suburban designs emulate some sort of vernacular style, the

(b)

URBAN AREAS

Figure 8.11 (cont.)

increase in house size and multiple car garages render them somewhat out of scale, or unfortunately out of proportion. Whereas in the past roof slopes were a function of climatic determinants, suburban roof slopes are generally low for economic reasons. At Serenbe there are multiple architectural design processes that are intended to achieve the goals of an emerging "rurban" architecture.[14]

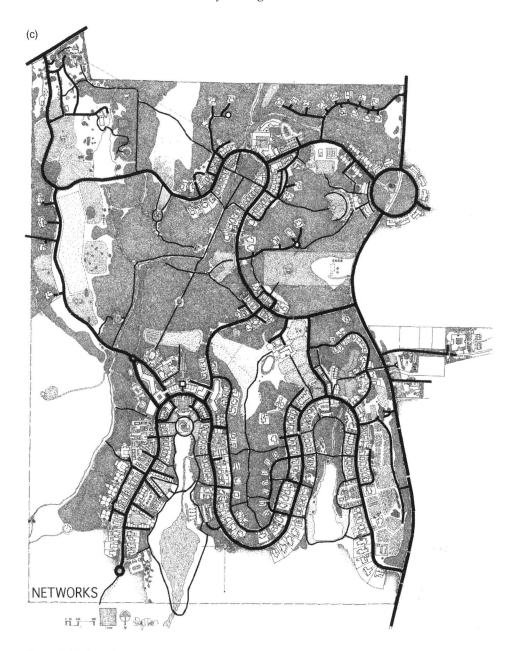

Figure 8.11 (cont.)

Building types

Three basic building types describe and make up most of the constructions at Serenbe: residential, nonresidential, including retail, and restaurants, and special building types. Residential buildings include single-family, detached estate houses, detached cottage homes, townhomes, live–work units, small nest homes, condominiums, and

(d)

INTERSTITIAL

Figure 8.11 (*cont.*)

independent and assisted living (Figures 8.12a–c). The commercial building types include small shops, cafes, restaurants, school, community swimming pool facility, medical buildings, stables, fitness center, pharmacy, spa, and hotel and inn. Special types include the proposed interfaith chapel, celestial observation site, labyrinth refractory structure, and children's treehouses.

Figure 8.12 Housing typologies: a) Estate homes b) Cottage homes c) Townhomes
Source: Photographs by Phillip Tabb

Architectural languages

It has been the objective within Serenbe to create an architectural character that reflects diversity and individual choice, while at the same time respecting a certain continuity of the overall aesthetic of the community. As with more established neighborhoods that have evolved over decades, this variable character expresses homeowners at varying stages of life, family functions, and individual tastes. The omega form is powerful enough to accommodate these differences without damaging the overall unity of the place. Many new developments employ similar building types, sizes, and architectural languages which are rather boring, characterless, and overly conforming. However, many architectural languages are typically expressed at Serenbe, from traditional to contemporary (Figures 8.13a–c). Initially, southern contemporary vernacular architecture was constructed at Serenbe, as it combined climate-responsiveness and character, appealing to new homebuyers. The scale, proportions, and materials provide an attractive aesthetic. Because the type of architectural language is open, within reason, many homeowners bring their own preferences and experiences of the kind of home that they feel most suits their lifestyle, family structure, and the character with which they feel comfortable. The omega spatial organization and bulk plane zoning allow for both the freedom of architectural character, and a formal urban design order along the rural–urban transect.

The architectural languages for nonresidential uses vary, and while they are relatively small in scale because of the size and function, they possess some relationship to residential and commercial forms. They do tend to be slightly more urban in character and material selections. Typical among these uses are the restaurants, shops, office structures, and even the live–work units, especially at the ground level (Figures 8.14a–c). Exterior materials tend to be constructed with brick, block, stone, steel and glass, and roofs are usually flat compared to the residential gable type. Other uses include building types located outside of the hamlets, such as the Serenbe Stables, barns and the container structures at the ArtFarm.

In 2004 the west leg of Selborne Hamlet went into construction and after approximately 20 houses were built, the Blue Eyed Daisy was constructed. This marked the beginning of community-oriented amenities, and provided a context for residents to meet outside of their private homes.

The relationship between sustainability and placemaking is important, and this occurs on multiple levels: overall planning, urban centers, infrastructure, architectural

Figure 8.13 Variations in architectural languages: a) Contemporary live–work b) Contemporary cottage c) The Waterfall Estate House
Source: Photographs by Phillip Tabb

Figure 8.14 Live–work languages: a) Southern Engineering Incorporated office b) Live–work retail shop c) Serenbe cluster
Source: Photographs by Phillip Tabb

programming, design and construction.[15] Many of the sustainable measures are embodied within the overall planning scale, while individual property owners apply other green strategies to the designs, construction methods, and equipment choices. It is clear that the Serenbe planning elements contribute to a direct interaction between the natural and urbanized areas. Serenity is clearly possible within the interstitial spaces, while community is encouraged within the urbanized areas of the omega forms.

Notes

1 Tabb, Phillip, "Placemaking as a Sustainable Planning Strategy: Serenbe Community," paper presented at the Architectural Research Centers Consortium (ARCC) conference, San Antonio, TX, April 17, 2009; "Serenbe and the Geometry of Place," self-published, College Station, TX, 2010.
2 Hoskins, William G., *The Making of the English Landscape*, Hodder and Stoughton, London, 1955.
3 The constructed wetlands were designed by engineer Michael Ogdon and landscape architects Reed Hilderbrand. Several wedding photographic shoots have taken place in this wetlands.
4 Sharp, Thomas, *The Anatomy of the Village*, Penguin Books, Harmondsworth, 1946.

5 A Fibonacci kite is a shape created by pentagonal geometry, where one of the five sides is projected outward to a point. At Serenbe the geometry was derived from particular points on the master plan at the omega apex.

6 The Home and Garden Green Home (HGTV) of 2012 was constructed in Grange Hamlet and received thousands of visitors. It was Serenbe's first LEED platinum house. The HGTV Green Home is an annual demonstration project constructed in different places throughout the United States, which is placed in a competitive sweepstake and given away to a winning subscriber.

7 de la Salle, Janine and Holland, Mark, *Agricultural Urbanism: A Handbook for Building Sustainable Food and Agricultural Systems in 21st Century Cities*, Green Frigate Books, Winnipeg, 2010.

8 This name was give by one of the Serenbe residents, Karen Reed. In the context of this work "health" was seen as a relative state of the physical, mental, and social condition of a person, while "wellness" was seen as being in a relative state of positive health.

9 Mado Hamlet is an interesting experiment of blending health and wellness nonresidential functions with residential development. Residents will have easy access to the services that these functions offer.

10 The concept of "twin-phenomena" in architecture was first developed by architect Aldo van Eyck, where two independent actions occur through one architectural device.

11 The ArtFarm was originally developed in response to local artists, who suggested that the hamlet live–work units were too small and not conducive to the needs of practicing artists. Live–work units were better suited for galleries and shops.

12 This version of the ArtFarm master plan was developed in a charrette conducted by Texas A&M University students in October of 2015. The program called for rehearsal space for the Serenbe Playhouse, artists' studios, a film lab, residences for the Artists in Residence (AIR) program, and facilities for design-construct programs.

13 The 20K house was a low-income program launched in 2005 for housing developed by the Rural Studio of Auburn University in western Alabama. It was designed to provide small housing units of approximately 500 square feet (50 square meters) at a cost of $20,000.

14 The terms "rurban" and "urbal" are portmanteaus of two root terms of rural and urban, or urban and rural. These are meant to suggest a blend of the beneficial qualities of the two contexts.

15 Tabb, "Placemaking as a Sustainable Planning Strategy."

9 Placemaking as a sustainable strategy

> Emerging backlashes – from nature, from social movements, from politics – reveal this widening gap between standard policy approaches and dynamic systems.[1]

Sustainable applications at Serenbe

The sustainable approaches employed at Serenbe follow both recommendations for sustainable urbanism and green architecture, affecting two scales appropriate for these scales of development. In 2008, Serenbe received the Urban Land Institute Inaugural Sustainability Award, which cited seven general categories of sustainability found at Serenbe for this award:

1. land preservation;
2. density of built form;
3. mixes of use;
4. integrated agriculture;
5. innovative water-waste systems;
6. networks and circulation; and
7. efficient architectural designs and construction practices.

Principles applied to ecological urbanism, conservation development, sustainable urbanism, and biophilia were applied as appropriate to the scale and context of Serenbe.

Land preservation and agriculture

According to the US Department of Agriculture in a National Resource Inventory study, in the two-decade period between 1982 and 2010, 43 million acres (17.4 million hectares) of land were converted to developed uses – and one-sixth of this was prime agricultural land.[2] In that most of the Serenbe land is second-growth forest and pasture land, it was important to preserve as much as possible. Also important was to demonstrate that development could be concentrated to create undisturbed land without compromising livability. As previously discussed, Serenbe preserves 70 percent of its land for open space, agriculture, forested land, and other natural features. The remaining 30 percent is planned for residential development and comprises the hamlets and Crossroads cluster. The remaining open space is a great amenity to residents, providing a context for interaction with nature, recreation, and exercise – serene experiences as well as those of the numinous.

Figure 9.1 Land and agriculture: a) Gainey Lane b) Serenbe Farms
Source: Photographs by Phillip Tabb

Initially, approximately 25 acres (10 hectares) were allocated for Serenbe Farms, of which about 5 acres are now being harvested. Another 2 acres have been planned adjacent to Mado Hamlet for resident allotment gardening. The farm participates in the Community Supported Agriculture program and the Serenbe farmer's and artist's market; it also serves local restaurants and residents. It offers many opportunities for farm education, from school farm tours through corporate tours, to seasonal classes and an apprenticeship program. Typically, a farm manager and several interns from all over the United States operate Serenbe Farms. As mentioned previously, they employ three organic methods: composting, cover cropping, and crop rotation. Composting is commonly known as the process of collecting and recycling organic matter that has been decomposed and then used as an organic fertilizer. Cover cropping is the practice of growing rich green grasses and legumes for incorporation of organic matter back into the soil. Crop rotation of vegetables and cover crops is a seasonal practice designed to disrupt the disease and pest cycle, and to ensure that nutrients are not depleted. The Serenbe website refers to the farm thus:

> A source for local organic food, a place for nurture and nature, a place to get your hands dirty, a place of inspiration and reflection, a place to celebrate the seasons and their bounty, a farm to create and sustain the future.[3]

The character of the land is preserved as both rural and settled. Common are stands of forest, meadows, black fences, and winding rural roads (Figure 9.1a). The idea of utilizing some of the land for productive organic farming is both an aesthetic and healthy amenity for the community. Figure 9.1b shows Marie Nygren consulting with the farm manager for the produce of the day. This is a valuable reminder that we are not separate from our environment, but an integral part of the greater whole.

Density and mixes of use

The urbanized portions of the project comprise building properties, buildings, roads, sidewalks, trails, parking, and space for other urban activities. The zoning for Chattahoochee Hills is 1.0 dwelling unit per acre (0.4 per hectare) which, for Serenbe, translates to a maximum of 1,000 dwellings allowable by codes. However, the master plan calls for approximately 900 dwelling units to be distributed on 300 acres of land. This generates a gross density of approximately 3.3 dwellings per acre (8 units per hectare), and net densities are certainly higher, especially at the omega apexes. This approach to density distribution is accomplished through the Transfer of Development Rights, and the receiving areas are designated to the hamlets and cross-roads cluster. A Transfer of Development Rights program is a market-based technique that encourages voluntary transfer of growth or development: it preserves landown-ers' asset value by moving the right to build dwellings from a location where develop-ment is not desired, to a location where development is more preferable and usually higher in density. The resulting effect is that of creating more beneficial open space with correspondingly compact development.

Residential net densities within each hamlet range from estate homes at an average of 2.5 dwellings per acre (6 per hectare), to townhomes at 20 dwellings per acre (50 per hectare) in the live–work clusters. The density has two effects. The first is concen-trating residents within closer proximity and walking distance of one another. The second is in providing greater numbers of residents who can support nonresiden-tial functions. Providing greater numbers of mixes of use within walking access also reduces between-place transportation energy. The sustainable consequences of density are shorter travel distances with reductions of transport energy, and reductions of heating, ventilation, and air conditioning (HVAC) loads due to more compact and efficient building types. For example, apartments in condominium buildings require about half the energy for heating and cooling. Figure 9.2a shows a density of one dwelling unit per acre distributed throughout the entire site, while Figure 9.2b has a more concentrated density that correspondingly creates more open space.

Networks and infrastructure

The hamlets are connected with the curvilinear omega roads, side streets on the larger hamlets, and alleys. Automobile parking is along one side of the omega road and in small remote parking lots woven into the fabric of the hamlets. Residents on the uphill side of the omega road can have garages accessed by rear alleys. In the cottage and omega apex zones there are sidewalks; outside of these zones are pedestrian paths that lead into the nearby woods and meadows. Multiple paths connect each of the hamlets, providing many ways to physically connect. Throughout the Serenbe property, there are approximately 7 miles (11.2 kilometers) of trails. The automobile roadways tend to be curvilinear, while the pedestrian network is more gridded. Multiple modes of movement include walking, bicycles, electric carts, and automobiles.

Gray and black wastewater are collected in individual cisterns located on each residential property, where primary treatment is designed to separate solids from li-quid effluent, then through gravity feeds delivered to the constructed wetlands as a biofilter system that uses the natural functions of vegetation, soil, and organisms to treat anthropogenic discharge and remove sediments and pollutants (as pictured in Figures 9.3a–c). Constructed wetlands are engineered systems that are described by other terms, such as reed beds, soil infiltration beds, constructed treatment wetlands, and treatment wetlands. The associated filter bed, consisting usually of a combin-ation of sand and gravel, has an equally important role to play. The treated water is

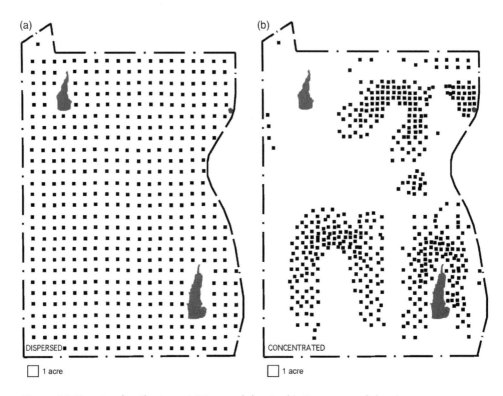

Figure 9.2 Density distribution: a) Dispersed density b) Concentrated density
Source: courtesy of Phillip Tabb

then piped to a nearby meadow where local cows graze. The system was originally designed by John Todd,[4] who is credited with inventing the Living Machine, and then adapted by engineer Michael Ogden for Serenbe.[5] It is located on low ground between Selborne Hamlet and the Crossroads cluster.

Networks are important at Serenbe, especially with its constellation concept of individual hamlets and all the activities that occur within the interstitial space. With 7 miles of trails, connectivity is ubiquitous among the many destination places within Serenbe. An efficient and safe pedestrian network allows for easy access between the hamlets and their nonresidential functions; often, the distance is shorter between places by using the pedestrian paths rather than the roads. According to Serenbe resident, Karen Reed:

> My husband, Tom and I appreciate the planning done here at Serenbe. We have walked all the trails, and been aware of the beautiful symmetry of the master design. We have a feeling of extremes being brought together – there is a rural, expansive, solitude that balances with the points of connection. We love living here.[6]

Sustainable benefits of the omega form

The characteristics of the omega form offer certain physical, experiential, and sustainable benefits. Linearity is a spatial ordering system created by a line that serves

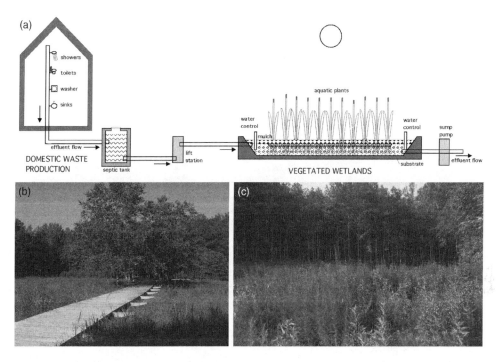

Figure 9.3 Constructed wetlands: a) Sectional diagram b) Pedestrian boardwalk c) Vegetated wetlands
Source: Photographs by Phillip Tabb

to function through the process of additive linkages. The omega is generally double-loaded with buildings on both sides of the circulation, that are usually determined by the interface between the sloping hills and the forest or meadowland below and a common contour. Double-loading creates more efficient organization. The English village, for example, was often sited paralleling a river or roadway, the sea or a transport roadway, and consequently evolved in a linear fashion.[7] A common reason for this type of development was a constriction caused by mountains or the sea. Open-field strip farming also facilitated this kind of settlement form. While not always the case, linear hamlets and villages are usually double-loaded with dwellings and shops located on both sides of the road, forming a main street. Typically, each dwelling was situated along the circulation spine, giving equal access to it, giving a kind of democracy of proximity. Commercial and other nonresidential activities usually occurred in a random manner also along the spine. This included the parish church, public house and a variety of shops. The road became the main public space, uniting the hamlet or village. For Serenbe, the linear development is due to elongated valley floors and the sheer length of the interface between the valley and hills.

Nucleation occurs where there is a central focus or function, and in the case of small hamlet or village settlements, this usually takes on the form of a center green, market square, or church, and plaza. In Continental Europe these centers were usually generated by the church, and the central space accompanying the church. However,

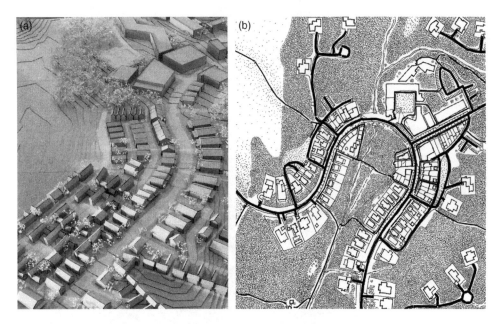

Figure 9.4 Networks: a) Model of omega road in Mado Hamlet
Source: Photograph courtesy of Carlos Reimers
b) Circulation network in Selborne Hamlet
Source: Photographs by Phillip Tabb

in England, Christianity came after the major village formation period – Anglo Saxon settlement from about AD 500 to AD 1066 – and the central market space was a market square that later was connected by Church Street to the parish church. These places are usually public, and serve to provide a common space of activities that support the community as a whole. In Serenbe, these nucleated centers reflect different functional themes and tend to be eccentrically nucleated, as the centers of concentration are at the apex of the hamlets.[8]

Selborne is planned with a campus-like green surrounded by arts facilities. It is intended to be used on Saturdays for the farmer's market and other outdoor community activities. Grange has a small commercial cluster of activities reflecting the agricultural activities of the hamlet. Mado has a concentration of health-oriented functions. The Education hamlet is organized with a larger provision of commercial activities and educational facilities. Each hamlet is planned to have a restaurant or cafe to serve both local residents and visitors to Serenbe. The more intense and diverse the nucleation for each hamlet, the more interdependencies occur, which contributes to greater levels of place-boundedness and fewer trips outside of the community for necessary shopping for goods and services.

The transect gives a hierarchal expression to the linear spatial structure. As described earlier, this hierarchy is a gradient from a blending of more natural landscape features at the edge of the omega road, to more urban ones at the center. The estate housing types are those designated in the lowest density area at the beginning of the transect. They are positioned on larger properties, and set back from the road to allow for the forested landscape buffer between the dwelling and entry road. Next to estates are the cottage-type dwellings that occur on smaller plots, usually 60-feet wide by 100-feet deep. The location of dwellings is determined by the positioning of the buildable areas within the designated setbacks, and they progress closer to the road as they move closer to the hamlet center.

The townhomes are attached building types and located close to the sidewalk and street. The live–work clusters have units that are considered zero-lot lines or right against the sidewalk, usually with an interior courtyard. Commercial functions were planned to be located at the apex of the omegas, where the greatest density, mixes of use and intensity occurred. It is here that the hamlet themes are given identity. In Selborne the commercial did not occupy the omega center, while in Grange and Mado, the commercial was planned for both sides of the omega road. Each hamlet has a "public room," or an open space dedicated to public use and gatherings. The farmer's market, for example, occurs at the top of the omega in Selborne. In Grange it is a public green, and in Mado it is a plaza with parking below, and a restaurant and shops above.

The curvilinear shape provides a natural open-ended system that contains an inner space bounded by the form. At Serenbe this inner area is kept natural, with a stream in Selborne, a pond in Grange, and wetlands in Mado. In the case for these forms used at Serenbe, the curves at the top of the shape are greater than a half-circle, so that they begin to close. This is done to create a greater feeling of enclosure or sense of place – unlike the "U-shape," which does not suggest completion.[9] As distinct from linear and nucleation geometry, the curve defines a larger territory or place of dwelling. There is a domain articulated within it that becomes known as the place or hamlet, in this case. The circular top is designed to provide a destination and identity for each hamlet.

The omega shape slowly opens outward to create a sense of entry–exit and connectedness to neighboring hamlets. A gated community or completely enclosed plan does not allow for such natural flows to occur: both ecological and human systems are not permitted to enter. As mentioned previously, in the case of Serenbe, water is collected from the surrounding and sloping hills and collected into small streams that flow through and eventually empty into the Cedar Creek. Each hamlet has at least three open roads entering and exiting. The curvilinear roads give an ever-unfolding perspective of the hamlet as one traverses through it, which adds both mystery and visual interest. The geometry of the omega form is strong and gives a powerful spatial organization to the place that is very identifiable, placemaking, and coherent – and ends always lead to new beginnings, especially within living systems.

As mentioned previously in Chapter 7, the shape and width of the omega road are extremely important for the function of sustainability and pedestrian safety. It was once thought that wider suburban streets would be safer, but recent studies have found the opposite, that they in fact are more dangerous.[10]

Sustainable architecture

There are many sustainable architectural languages evident at Serenbe. A living vernacular architecture is in constant interpretation, but responds to certain consistent principles. This means that the architectural response is to phenomenal causes rather than static formal effects. For example, a cause could be the response to the sun in a hot climate: therefore, covered porches, verandas, overhangs, and sun-shading devices would help keep the sun off the conditioned spaces inside. The sun angles will be particular for the latitude within which it exists, and these design elements should be designed accordingly, rather than simply being a copy from buildings that are likely to exist in different locations. A contemporary vernacular will respond to these causes and consequent sun angles to create form-shading, rather than simply copy a traditional porch for purely aesthetic reasons. The works of architects Lake and Flato in Texas demonstrate form shading without directly mimicking a southern porch. The large overhangs employed by architect Glenn Murcutt, and operable shutters offer another method of shading. The form, technologies, and materials change and evolve over time, refining their designs and integration. Vernacular architecture seems well-suited to housing located in rural locations, which in part is due to the low density that allows for more flexibility in form-responses to climate.

Typically, traditional vernaculars evolved with smaller space and use programs than are common today. As a consequence, overall forms were on a smaller scale, and tended to be designed by self-dimensioning systems of construction and with more pleasant proportions. Designs grew from archetypal forms and simple geometry. As space programs grew, dwelling forms did not grow in height but in width, which is cause for less favorable proportions. Façades stretched sideways, and roofs became flatter. The introduction of the two-car garage also contributed to this transformation. In a study conducted by the architect Robert Naismith, images of 1,000 residences in the Scottish countryside built between 1750 and 1900 were entered into a computer and analyzed for their geometric proportions.[11] Most were organized by the use of multiple squares, and this not only generated the overall form, but also informed the size and placement of dormers, windows, and doors. Roofs were typically 45 degrees and derived from the square. Living principles of residential contemporary vernacular architecture used at Serenbe are as follows:

- *climate responses* – architectural form responds to climatic determinants, including temperature, precipitation, wind, and solar energy. The form seeks to take advantage of natural resources and limit the negative effects. For the Serenbe climate, this means a response to both overheating and underheating conditions;
- *solar form response* – project forms either encourage solar energy utilization in cold and temperate climates, reject solar energy in hot climates, or respond to both – especially in the swing seasons. For Serenbe, this includes some passive solar heating and photovoltaic electric generation. The majority of dwellings have a long axis with east–west orientation, and are positioned next to one another on the north–south axis (Figures 9.5a and 9.5b);[12]
- *geothermal* – ground temperature heating and cooling is readily available at Serenbe through the use of the ground-source heat pump system. Ground temperatures below approximately 20 feet remain a constant 50–60°F, and well depths are determined at 200 feet per ton of air-conditioning – warmer than the air above during winter and cooler than the air in summer;
- *cultural responses* – considerations of lifestyles, patterns of use, and local cultural idiosyncrasies contributing to the spatial organization, exterior space design, functional use, and new family types. This includes emerging technologies. A common preference at Serenbe is to have the complete complement of adult spaces on the ground floor: living, dining, kitchen, utility, master bedroom and bathroom, and home office;

- *historical responses* – incremental development of forms, technologies, and materials that maintain the tradition and continuity with the past. Yet contemporary needs, technologies, and material systems modify older forms. There is an evolutionary integration of the new with the old, as the new contemporary vernacular becomes hybrid. For example, in the United States, wraparound porches protect gable vernacular house forms from the intense summer sun;
- *materiality* – use of local and common materials that are easily obtained, constructed, manipulated, and changed over time. This includes modern materials such as concrete, concrete block, drywall, solid fiber cement siding, and modern roofing materials such as standing seam metal roofing;
- *contemporary vernacular* – drawing from vernacular traditions yet planning for contemporary spatial use patterns, technologies, and construction techniques. This typically involves integration of larger and more spaces;
- *domesticity* – vernacular architecture tends to occur at the residential scale and accommodate domestic functions. This includes ancillary structures such as detached garages, workshops, barns, home offices, and other small buildings;
- *scale and proportion* – vernacular architecture has primary, secondary, and tertiary forms that are in scale and generally well proportioned. This means that the building massing is scaled to express favorable universal proportions. This is particularly applicable to downsized homes.

An authentic vernacular architecture is honest in its form responses and use of technology. It attempts to use the form of the building to mitigate the deleterious climatic effects of a particular region, rather than relying solely on fossil fuel-driven electrical and mechanical technologies. Permanently fixing a narrow metal shutter alongside a large picture window on the façade of a house does not render it vernacular. If employed, a shutter should actually function, as it was originally intended. The principles of a living vernacular architecture and current sustainability measures share

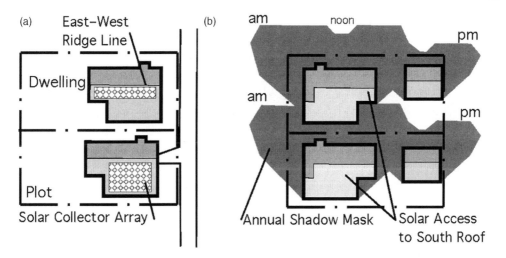

Figure 9.5 Solar access: a) Ridge line orientation b) Annual solar shading masks
Source: courtesy of Phillip Tabb

common objectives and means.[13] An example is the Marika-Alderton House designed by Australian architect Glenn Murcutt in 1994 for an Aboriginal client in northern Australia. It is powerful in its simplicity, and becomes a vernacular animation with its response to weather and climate. The overhanging gable roof provides shelter; the faces contain operable windows and shading devices for modulation of airflow and ventilation, and the raised platform contributes to underfloor cooling.

Contemporary architecture modeled by vernacular and climate-driven languages is a good example for many of the homes at Serenbe. The challenge has been to respond to environmental effects, rather than predetermined images of the past. This is not an easy task, as mentioned previously, the climate of Atlanta has complex environmental factors with three distinct climatic seasons: winter, summer, and the swing seasons. In winter where there is underheating, the vernacular forms want to respond to good solar orientation for passive heating at least six hours of the day. Passive solar heating with adequate glass and thermal mass can accomplish this. However, in the urban context, a six-hour solar window is difficult to achieve because of the lower winter, spring, and autumn sun angles and higher density of buildings. In summer, this density and large roof overhangs are welcome, as they provide shading in response to overheating and high humidity. The vernacular form responds by becoming a thermos where the exterior envelope tightens up against direct solar gain and infiltration of outside warm air and humidity. This is opposite to the winter condition, where shading and density are welcomed. In the swing periods, spring and autumn, the vernacular form of this region wants to open up and close down in response to the conjunction of both overheating and underheating. Heating can be provided by solar gain in daytime, and cooling can be accomplished through natural ventilation. Since electricity is needed year-round, photovoltaic systems need to be placed high on rooftop residences, with good solar access during at least six hours of the day. The geothermal systems are a good match for the vernacular form of this region (Figures 9.6a–c).

Critical regionalist architecture

Regionalism is considered by several defining factors – history, culture, climate, customs, geography, and physical context – all of which give specific characteristics and meaning to a region, including the love of a particular locale or setting. Its sensibility looks to the uniqueness of site and location when deriving the formal aspects

Figure 9.6 Contemporary vernacular architecture: a) Nest houses b) The White Cottage c) The Red Cottage
Source: Photographs by Phillip Tabb

of any given project. Typically, critical regionalism seeks to mediate the spectrum between the universal characteristics of a civilization, and the particularities of place. Critical regionalism modifies this to include the avant-garde and innovation, pushing the boundaries of historical precedents while maintaining some connections to modernism, mainly its progressive qualities. It arose in response to placelessness and a lack of meaning in the modern environment. There was a confluence of authentic climatic and regional characteristics with the needs of contemporary culture, and the modern means by which to construct hybrid architecture in response to it.

The research of Alexander Tzonis and Liane Lefaivre into design cognition and regionalism contributed to notions that problem-solving should de-empathize imported universal solutions, in favor of the reflective, local, and unique qualities of a region.[14] They saw critical regionalism as not needing to draw exclusively from the context; rather, that elements of a place could be stripped of context and used in unfamiliar ways. There was a confluence of local (centripetal) and global (centrifugal) considerations in developing a contemporary synthesis. Critical regionalism and the greening of architecture shared a common interest in becoming modern, while returning to sources. It addressed questions of sensitivity to local contents with the implications of globalization, and with new configurations of analytical and discursive techniques. These were directed to give appropriate expression to emerging culture and contemporary conditions. It also considered the specifics of local climates and materials, topographies, and building methods.

In his 1983 essay, "Towards a Critical Regionalism," Kenneth Frampton called for an architecture that would strive to overcome placelessness and lack of identity by utilizing a building's geographical context.[15] According to Frampton's proposal, critical regionalism should adopt modern architecture *critically* for its universal progressive qualities, but at the same time, value should be placed on the geographical context of the building. Emphasis, Frampton noted, should be on topography, climate, and light – on tectonic form rather than "scenography". He further stressed that architecture was neither a vacantly "international" exercise in modern technology, nor a 'sentimental" imitation of vernacular buildings, arguing for a propinquity of place cultivated between the universal and local. The "critical" in this proposition of regionalism meant a questioning and critique of the cliché, inappropriately picturesque, and superficial. Steven Moore saw in Frampton's call a powerful "proto-environmentalist discourse" that helped legitimatize the next green phase in architecture.[16]

The critical regionalism principles employed at Serenbe are similar to those of a contemporary vernacular, but differ in several ways. A prime example of this difference is in the attitude of critical regionalism to refrain from copying historic forms and to fully engage with contemporary culture, including new materials and advanced technologies used in climate responsive ways (Figures 9.7a–d):

- *climate and regional responses* – architectural forms respond to climatic determinants of either overheating or underheating, including temperature, precipitation, humidity, wind, and solar energy. The forms seek to take advantage of natural resources, and limit negative weather effects;
- *response to contemporary culture* – space sizes and functions relate to contemporary activities and technologies, communities respond to aging in place, and architectural forms and character reflect the diversity of users;

- *blend of historically relevant forms and new technology* – architecture responds to climatic determinants and historically relevant forms. Construction utilizes new materials, technologies, appliances, security systems and equipment;
- *scale and proportion* – critical regionalist architecture has primary, secondary, and tertiary forms that are in scale and generally well proportioned, given the fact that space programs tend to be larger than the inspiring vernaculars that preceded them. Porches, defined entries, and dormers are among the measures;
- *individuated architecture* – unlike typical suburban housing and New Urban developments where architectural language is generally controlled and limited to one language, at Serenbe the character is encouraged to respond to specific sites, location along the transect, and the aesthetic tastes of individual owners.

The Grange Nest

During the 2008–9 recession, five estate properties were subdivided into 15 smaller, cottage-sized lots adjacent to the lake in Grange Hamlet. This tripling of the density was done in response to a slowdown in housing construction nationwide, and the sense that the American public might like smaller, less costly homes. Initially, a

Figure 9.7 Critical regionalism: a) Model of Selborne Hamlet center
Source: Photograph courtesy of Serenbe Development Corporation
b) Selborne live–work units c) Model of Tabb Crossroads residence d) Tabb residence
Source: Photographs by Phillip Tabb

Figure 9.8 Nest developments: a) Street view of First Nest b) Second Nest prototype house
       c) Second Nest cluster of 12
Source: Photographs by Phillip Tabb

prototype cottage of 1,250 square feet (116 square meters) was constructed. When the Nest was complete in 2014, cottages varied in size from 900 to 1,700 square feet (158 square meters). The two-story gable vernacular forms were designed for economy and energy efficiency. Dwellings were typically one, two, or three-bedroom units. Cottages along the omega road have presence, and street-facing porches with narrow spaces between the dwellings that frame views to the lake (Figure 9.8a). The other cottages deeper within the cluster tend to be larger and feature more dominant views to the lake. A commons gazebo was placed in the center of the cluster of houses. Many of the homes typically used ground-sourced heat pumps for heating and cooling. Some of the cottages incorporated photovoltaic electricity. In 2012, a group of Texas A&M University architecture students created designs for an additional 12 smaller cottage units for another site on the other side of Grange Hamlet (Figures 9.8b and 9.8c).

Urban architecture

The hamlets at Serenbe are organized by the omega form and by the Thorburn transect. Therefore, there is an intended transition between the rural landscape of the Chattahoochee Hill area, and the initial buildings that introduce the hamlet. Conversely, the more urban buildings are found at the apex of each hamlet. At the edge there is an attempt to nestle the hamlets into the natural landscape, and at the center of the hamlets there is the more urban and dense form, that is meant to help support community-based activities and create a more intense and vibrant social environment. It is here that there are clusters of commercial functions, urban open spaces, and higher populations of residents. Both of these extremes are seen as valuable design

Figure 9.9 Urban architecture: a) Selborne apex b) Grange apex c) Grange center green
          d) Selborne live–work cluster
Source: Photographs by Phillip Tabb

approaches at Serenbe. One Serenbe resident, John Graham stated, "Serenbe seems to be about the 'urbal' amenity and the quality of life."[17] Pictured in Figures 9.9a–d are a series of images depicting some of the more urban locations within Selborne and Grange hamlets. The three architectural styles are described as follows:

- *Rural architecture* – at the scale of Serenbe this is generally in isolated structures, detached housing of two or three stories, and made with stick construction and wood finishes. Roofs are pitched, often with gable forms. The architecture is kind, plain, substantial, pragmatic, using low technology and local materials.
- *Urban architecture* – at the scale of Serenbe it is generally mixed use, attached buildings of three or four stories, and made with masonry construction. Roofs are typically flat. Urban architecture responds to the urban setting with more multi-use programs and higher technology.
- *"Rurban" ("urbal") architecture* – is a strangely new, mainly residential hybrid and shared habitat that blends both rural and urban characteristics. While recently viewed as a kind of landscape urbanism bringing agriculture into the city, it also suggests bringing urban characteristics into the rural environment. This new architecture certainly includes the latest in technology, with the benefit of hybrid sustainable systems.

Figure 9.10 Nonresidential sustainability: a) Blue Eyed Daisy b) LEED certification
Source: Photograph courtesy of Serenbe Development Corporation
Source: Photographs by Phillip Tabb

Whereas the rural architecture at Serenbe is oriented to accommodating functional family space requirements, as well as enhancement for interacting with nature, the urban architecture focuses on internal functions and the external role as a contributing urban design element, forming outdoor rooms and gathering places.

Sustainability with nonresidential building types – particularly with the smaller scales found at Serenbe – generally require both skin and load-dominated conservation strategies. This means designing for overheating in summer with daylighting, natural ventilation, geothermal cooling, and sunshading, and in winter, passive solar heating, geothermal heating, and effective insulation levels. Serenbe's Blue Eyed Daisy was the first small commercial building to be certified by LEED (Figures 9.10a and 9.10b).

Sustainable construction

Energy-efficient construction is an important part of the sustainable strategies for Serenbe. EarthCraft is a voluntary, residential green building certification program of the Greater Atlanta Home Builders Association and Southface Energy Institute, which was created in 1999 to address the challenging energy, water, and climate conditions of the southeast. In 2004 and 2008, together these were named Green Building Programs of the Year by the National Association of Home Builders. To achieve compliance, new homes must meet both EarthCraft and Energy Star certification criteria: this means achieving passing scores from diagnostic tests for air infiltration and duct leakage. The criteria include:

- resource-efficient site planning;
- energy-efficient building envelope and heating and cooling systems;
- resource-efficient design and use of building materials;
- effective waste management;
- indoor air quality; and
- water conservation.

In the Atlanta Metro area there are more than 4,000 single-family EarthCraft homes and 1,500 multifamily EarthCraft homes. There are five pilot EarthCraft communities as well. Following is a listing of the principal strategies:

- advanced energy-efficiency capabilities, including Energy Star lighting and appliances to reduce energy consumption;
- water conservation capabilities, saving potable water and water harvesting systems to collect and reuse on site;
- resource-conserving architectural design and materials to minimize impact on landfill;
- healthy indoor air quality for occupant health and comfort;
- good site location and planning for transportation convenience; and
- an education program for homeowners to ensure optimum benefit from living in an EarthCraft building.

The EarthCraft Community Program was initiated by the Greater Atlanta Home Builders Association, the Atlanta Regional Commission, the Urban Land Institute, and Southface in 2003, and officially launched in 2005. A goal was to bring sustainability to regionally specific development, and support smart growth and green living. Consideration at the community scale includes:

- site selection;
- land disturbance;
- water quality;
- stormwater management;
- energy, water and transportation infrastructure;
- community design;
- open space;
- green space preservation;
- pedestrian design; and
- transportation.

Serenbe is one of the five pilot Georgia EarthCraft Communities. The other communities include Longleaf, Harris County, Clark's Grove, Covington, Glenwood Park, Atlanta, and Vickery, Forsyth County. Presently there are an additional seven projects enrolled in the program. The EarthCraft Community initiatives include the following. Sustainability must:

- include sound building practices, and all buildings must be EarthCraft certified;
- be true to its place – every development must respond to its unique site and the broader community within which it lies;
- begin with integral planning that includes sustainability goals and community outreach – this includes a community participation charrette and site analysis planning workshop; and
- be verified in the field.

The EarthCraft building and community programs offer a good opportunity to create models and ongoing development practices that support environmentally friendly and resource-efficient housing and communities. This has been a major goal for Serenbe from the beginning, and this process is a demonstration of its commitment. Potentially, thousands of homes could follow this lead in the Chattahoochee Hills in the near future. Key to energy-efficient construction is the foundations, the envelope design, fenestration orientations and sizes, along with the tightness of the construction itself. For the remainder of all new homes constructed in Grange Hamlet, and all homes in Mado Hamlet, geothermal heating and cooling systems will be utilized.

The Bosch House performs at the Net-Zero level, and the HGTV House (2012) is certified LEED Platinum. Both houses have high levels of insulation, a ground-sourced geothermal heating and cooling system, photovoltaic arrays for electricity production, and utilize energy-efficient appliances. The Bosch House is designed using a trad-itional, southern vernacular form with gable roof and wraparound porch. The HGTV House is contemporary vernacular, also using the gable roof form and a U-shaped courtyard plan, creating an outdoor room. The Solar Ready House was constructed along the east–west axis for excellent passive solar heating and the roof ready for a photovoltaic array. Sustainability at Serenbe is integral to its mission and is progres-sively increasing in practice.

Figure 9.11 illustrates a few of the common sustainable architectural measures used throughout Serenbe – photovoltaic array installation (Figure 9.11a), geothermal heat-ing and cooling (Figure 9.11b), insulation beneath a slab-on-grade (Figure 9.11c), a passive solar and photovoltaic-ready house adjacent to the Grange lake (Figure 9.11d), the energy-efficient Nest cottage (Figure 9.11e), and the Bosch and HGTV houses (Figures 9.11f and 9.11g).

Place and sustainability

The creation of place or place-boundedness suggests certain inherent sustainable ben-efits, which include denser planning organization, building efficiencies, and behavioral opportunities that otherwise might be excluded with dispersed suburban schemes. As mentioned previously, according to Susan Owens, at the planning scale these benefits take the form of improved configuration, increased density, network efficiencies, and greater mixes of use.[18] These advantages are clearly seen at Serenbe, where hamlet sizes are within a half-mile diameter, and there is intentional inclusion of nonresiden-tial land uses within each hamlet, reducing the need for automobile trips outside the settlement.

At the building scale, denser building typologies can lead to building energy effi-ciencies for heating, cooling and electric power. Semi-detached townhomes and apart-ment blocks can reduce energy loads over the less efficient single-family detached house. Additionally, building plot sizes can be reduced, which produces two conse-quences: land preservation, and travel distance reduction.

Perhaps the greatest benefits attributed to placemaking come in the form of the creation of supportive pedestrian environments of all kinds. The combination of plan-ning efficiencies, denser building typologies and mixes of use, and pedestrian net-works supports greater pedestrian activity. The introduction of integrated agriculture also contributes to reduction of between-place transportation and automobile use in general. In-place focus for sustainability provides greater opportunities for direct interaction between resources and consumption or use. Direct participation, place stewardship, and interaction with local ecological flows and systems all contribute to

Figure 9.11 Green construction: a) Photovoltaic installation b) Geothermal system c) Insulated
         slab-on-grade d) Photovoltaic house e) Solar-ready house f) Bosch Net-Zero house
         g) HGTV Green Home
Source: Photographs by Phillip Tabb

this enriched potential for community-level sustainability. Each of these placemaking
strategies is present and operative in Serenbe, which contributes not only to sustainability, but also other cultural and numinous experiences.

Notes

1 Leach, Melissa, Scoones, Ian and Stirling, Andy, *Dynamic Sustainabilities: Technology,
  Environment, Social Justice*, Earthscan, London, 2010, p. 1.

2 US Department of Agriculture Natural Resource Conservation Service, "2010 National Resources Inventory Summary Report," p. 8. Available online at www.nrcs.usda.gov/Internet/FSE_DOCUMENTS/stelprdb1167354.pdf (accessed June 19, 2016).

3 Serenbe Farms website: www.serenbefarms.com/ (accessed October 2015).

4 Todd, Nancy Jack and Todd, John, *From Eco-Cities to Living Machines: Principles of Ecological Practice*, North Atlantic Books, Berkeley, CA, 1993.

5 Campbell, Craig and Ogdon, Michael, *Constructed Wetlands in the Sustainable Landscape*, John Wiley and Sons, New York, 1999.

6 Email communication from Karen Reed to author, July 15, 2009.

7 Sharp, Thomas, *The Anatomy of the Village*, Penguin Books, Harmondsworth, 1946; Tabb, Phillip, "The Solar Village Archetype: A Study of English Village Form Applicable to Energy-integrated Planning Principles for Satellite Settlements in Temperate Climates," PhD dissertation, Architectural Association, London, 1990.

8 Tabb, Phillip, "Placemaking as a Sustainable Planning Strategy: Serenbe Community," in *Proceedings of the Conference of the Architectural Research Centers Consortium (ARCC)*, College of Architecture, University of Texas at San Antonio, San Antonio, TX, 2009, pp. 405–13.

9 Tabb, "The Solar Village Archetype."

10 Condon, Patrick M., *Seven Rules for Sustainable Communities: Design Strategies for the Post Carbon World*, Island Press, Washington, DC, 2010.

11 Naismith, Robert, *Buildings of the Scottish Countryside*, Victor Gollancz, London, 1985.

12 Tabb, Phillip, *Solar Energy Planning: A Guide to Residential Development*, McGraw-Hill, New York, 1984.

13 Oliver, Paul, *Dwellings: The Vernacular House Worldwide*, Phaidon, London, 2007.

14 Tzonis, Alexander and Lefaivre, Liane, *Critical Regionalism: Architecture and Identity in a Globalized World*, University of Michigan, Prestel, MI, 2003.

15 Frampton, Kenneth, "Towards a Critical Regionalism: Six Points for an Architecture of Resistance," in Foster, Hal (ed.) *The Anti-Aesthetic: Essays on Postmodern Culture*, The New Press, Port Townsend, WA, 1983, pp. 16–30.

16 Moore, Steven, "Environmental Issues," in Mitcham, Carl (ed.) *The Encyclopaedia of Science, Technology, and Ethics*, Macmillan, New York, 2005, pp. 262–6.

17 Interview with Serenbe resident John Graham, October 2015.

18 Owens, Susan, *Energy, Planning and Urban Design*, Pion Press, London, 1985.

10 Cultural and numinous moments

The spirit remains the same, yet its language and expression have changed.[1]

The cultural dimension of Serenbe is important not only for sustainable objectives, but also for community-building. In many ways it is the most important accomplishment achieved by the development. At Serenbe the sacred and numinous share important ideas, and often are confused with having strictly religious or spiritual purposes. However, they are intended to describe inspiration that derives from positive experiences of the land, and interactions among the community members themselves. They also engender fascination, mystery, and an everyday connection to the land and nature. They are places that beguile and inspire, sedate and stir. By having these kinds of experiences, it is possible to support greater engagement, caretaking, and stewardship of both land and community. Similarly, "thin places," a Celtic concept where the veil between the natural world and spiritual realm seems especially transparent, are present at Serenbe.[2] Thin places can be experienced deep in the forest, along the streams or in a resident's backyard. They evoke beauty, mystery, and serenity; and soulfulness is a quality that is growing as Serenbe grows, evolves, and continues to mature.

Community

The word "community" is another portmanteau with the terms *common* and *unity*, which means that there are most likely places, support functions, local economy, infrastructure, an appropriate scale and size, and a configuration that fosters community where residents can interact. Many urban design projects have the goal of creating community, but many fall short of this goal for various reasons. Sometimes it is unfavorable zoning regulations, or they are too large or too dependent on the automobile to become accessible. Perhaps there are no community places to foster social interaction sufficient to build community relations. Sometimes, other urban forms – especially infrastructural ones such as freeways, waterways, or industrial zones – can separate residential areas from one another, or from social gathering places. Therefore, how can community really be accomplished? In the case of Serenbe, this can be only partially explained. For many who have moved there, community was a latent intent that became realized through the quality of the place, and a willingness to participate by the residents who chose to reside there.

Community-building

The creation of community is important at Serenbe, and was one of the original goals. To new property owners, Serenbe is a friendly place with many social activities and opportunities to interact with fellow neighbors. As time goes on, the full range of events unfold throughout the year. Several times a year there is a special dinner at the owner's home, where potential homebuyers dine and mix with established community members. This is a wonderful opportunity for existing and potential new members to meet and interact. Every year Serenbe hosts the Serenball, a formal dress event where the community spends an evening together. "Les Dames d'Escoffier" is an afternoon culinary event where many of the resident's favorite chefs from Atlanta's restaurants come with scrumptious gourmet creations. In addition, Georgia's organic farmers share their wine and organic produce. Marie Nygren hosts the Serenbe "Southern Chef's Series," where guest chefs come and prepare a special lunch for those in attendance. In the spring is the Holiday Bazaar, where special vendors, live music, marshmallow roasting, and raffle prizes are given from the local Serenbe shops. It is held at the Selborne courtyard and spills into some of the live–work units as well. One-of-a-kind arts and crafts are displayed for sale.

The Saturdays from May 8 to October 30 host the Serenbe farmer's and artist's market. It is a wonderful venue for purchasing organic produce, fruit, culinary treats, and arts and crafts from local vendors. One of the purposes of the market is to improve the production and marketing of local agricultural and artisanal products, and in turn, stimulate community interest. Often there is music and games for the children, and it is a good place for community members to mix. The temporary tents and vendor stalls are pictured on the Selborne center green, and people are seated all along the omega road. Everything at the market is seasonal, which adds to its authenticity and utility. Along with the market activities are organized farm tours. Usually the market is held in the mornings and finished by lunchtime.

The Serenbe Institute is a nonprofit, tax-exempt community organization that supports an Artist in Residence (AIR) program, where advanced visual artists (including ceramics, drawing, environmental arts, and mixed media) or performing artists (theater and music) are selected to reside in the community and produce work to be shared by everyone. It is funded through a property transfer fee. The purpose of the program is to provide uninterrupted space and time for artists in creating their work, to contribute to educational outreach to the community, and to participate in other Serenbe activities.

Figure 10.1a shows the view from the top of one of the Selborne live–work units of the performance of Serenbe Playhouse, in its inaugural season in the summer of 2010. The Selborne west courtyard was transformed into an outdoor theater, with the stage literally surrounding the existing fountain. All of the Serenbe Playhouse performances use the outdoor environment as a theater and stage, and most often they are in the woods or meadows ("The Ugly Duckling" was performed on a stage constructed a foot below the top of one of the Serenbe ponds). *The Secret Garden*, *Oklahoma!*, *The Snow Queen*, *Evita*, *A Midsummer Night's Dream*, and *Jungle Boy* have been among the performances of the Playhouse. In Figure 10.1b construction of the stage set for the production of *Evita* in the woods can be seen.

Figure 10.1 Community-building: a) Serenbe Playhouse b) *Evita* stage set
Source: Photographs by Phillip Tabb
c) Serenbe Films d) Fourth of July fireworks at Grange Lake
Source: Photographs courtesy of Serenbe Development Corporation

Serenbe Film Society is another opportunity offered to residents for entertainment and enjoyment, and is created in various forms, from drive-in to film and dinner venues (Figure 10.1c). The films shown include classic, world-renowned movies, and elite shorts. The Fourth of July is important at Serenbe, and community residents participate in the annual parade that later is completed with fireworks over Grange Lake (Figure 10.1d). Residents sit along the lake's edge on a grass hill, watching the fireworks above. These venues, along with other more spontaneous events, support an environment of community – something that is missing from many modern suburban developments.

The three restaurants and the pavilion provide opportunities for culinary delights, which of course, bring the community together. These places are occasions to meet others or to gather with family and friends. They all are synchronized so that there is always a place in which to dine at all times during the day and week. Dining places are an excellent catalyst for social interaction, and when they are located within the heart of a small community, become important and convenient support for the community. The photographs of the interiors of the restaurants at Serenbe (Figures 10.2a–e) show the rich and friendly atmosphere.

- The Blue Eyed Daisy Bakeshop is located in the center of Selborne Hamlet, and is a casual neighborhood eatery serving breakfast, pastries, sandwiches, salads, soups, and specials for each dinner.

- The Hil Restaurant is also located in Selborne Hamlet and features a seasonal and classic American menu, including a variety of appetizers, gourmet pizzas, entrees, farm-fresh vegetables, and desserts. There is a small full bar in the restaurant as well.
- The Farmhouse at Serenbe is located in the Inn at Serenbe, and was originally part of the bed and breakfast. It features an à la carte menu of southern delicacies and fresh produce from Serenbe Farms.
- The grounds of the Inn and Pavilion are located adjacent to the Inn at Serenbe in either open spaces or the open pavilion. The facility is used for wedding receptions, birthdays, cooking classes, and other community gatherings.
- The general store at the apex of Grange Hamlet hosts wine tastings, and provides a small dining area for ice cream and other delicacies.

The activities that are organized on an annual basis are amazing at Serenbe. From Easter events, and the May Day celebration to the Fourth of July parade, Halloween, Thanksgiving, and Christmas, community members come together and celebrate with one another. Food is another important magnet for community residents to meet. By 2015 there were three restaurants, a small grocery store, and the Serenbe Farms (Figures 10.2a–e). According to Laurence Aurbach, a visitor to Serenbe in 2011:

> Even though the town center portion of Serenbe is only a few blocks long, it is already better in design quality than many New Urbanism developments. Every house backs onto a natural area, which is a big selling point. The trail system is

Figure 10.2 Community farm-to-table: a) Serenbe Farms b) Outdoor picnic table in Selborne courtyard c) Farmhouse Inn d) The Hil Restaurant e) Blue Eyed Daisy

Source: Photographs by Phillip Tabb

terrific. I'd call it the most mixed-use and walkable cluster development. Or the most upscale and sophisticated ecovillage.[3]

Communications networks

With some 7 miles of trails, Serenbe offers multiple paths to connect and engage: the Holiday Bazaar and the Hill Country trail race add to the richness of an active life. Serenbe posts a community calendar and it is amazing the number of activities that occur on a weekly basis. Figure 10.3a shows a local boy riding on his unicycle, which underscores that there are many ways in which to move throughout Serenbe. As already outlined, other modes include walking, biking, horseback riding, and electric carts. Other local residents prepare for the Hill Country Trail Race, which occurs annually in the autumn. There are both 15k and 5k races held throughout the omega centers and roads, woods, pastures, and the waterfall (Figure 10.3b).

Another form of communication in place at Serenbe is the community Facebook page called *Serenbe Neighbors*, a closed group of 338 members (as of 2015). Everyday posts include messages, requests, news, events, photographs, and even warnings (Figure 10.3c). The resident police frequently leave messages about traffic, road conditions, and other matters relating to resident safety. Being able to instantly connect to an entire neighborhood with the touch of a single post is supportive.

Children's places

Too often one can drive by an elementary school or a park or playground and see it empty and lifeless. While adventure playgrounds are an improvement and display a greater repeat appeal to children, they too are often left abandoned. Why is this? Especially in low-density locations, these places are not accessible on foot, or not safely accessible because of automobile traffic. Children are not safe to be left alone to go there. At Serenbe there is a dispersed play concept integrated throughout the community, from farming to ball fields, and small parks to the stables or a treehouse. Rather than focusing on one concentrated play area, there are a number of diverse types of children's play places woven throughout the community, which are applicable to all age groups.

Figure 10.3 Networks: a) Fourth of July parade b) Hill Country trail race
Source: Photographs courtesy of Serenbe Development Corporation
c) *Serenbe Neighbors* webpage
Source: Photograph by Phillip Tabb

Throughout the community are places specifically designed for children, with organized activities occurring throughout the year. There are many shared places for both children and adults. Unlike many urban and suburban environments, where it may not be safe for children to be out on their own, Serenbe fosters places that are both safe and accessible. Because the automobile is limited to use on the omega roads and, in some instances back drives, the inner portions of the hamlets and the interstitial spaces are safe and completely free of automobiles. For many times of the day, the omega road is very safe for children, and it is common to see them walking, riding bikes, skateboarding and on Segways. The speed limit in Serenbe is 15 miles per hour. Children become aware of the paths in Serenbe, as they lead to residential and community areas alike. It is amazing to see how the children adapt, interact, and become familiar with the network connections of the place.

Children's places in Serenbe vary from an organized recreation field, where there is soccer, tennis, basketball, and an outdoor run for dogs, to the treehouses in the forest near Selborne Hamlet, where there is general play as well as the summer Serenbe Playhouse (Figure 10.4a). At the top of Grange Hamlet there is a small green with a built-in trampoline that children seem to enjoy. For the younger children, Serenbe has nearly 100 animals, many of which are housed nearby. When a new piglet, goat, or rabbit is born, news travels fast through the community and children are drawn to the newborn creatures.

There are two fishing lakes at Serenbe: one next to the animal area in the northwestern part of Serenbe, and the other occupying the center of Grange Hamlet (Figure 10.4b). At the edge of the Crossroads cluster, a small play area is tucked into the woods for the smaller children in residence there. The children enjoy using the trails, especially in Selborne Hamlet and Crossroads, where there is a larger concentration of residents at the moment. The Blue Eyed Daisy is a welcome destination and watering hole for kids; there is a bathroom near the back door, which is available for their convenience. Serenbe Playhouse performs for the children at the treehouse, and there are other activities in the Selborne courtyard. Serenbe Camp is offered several times during the summer, both to resident children and those from neighboring areas.

Figure 10.4 Children's places: a) Treehouses
Source: Photograph by Phillip Tabb
b) Boating in Grange Lake
Source: Photograph courtesy of Serenbe Development Corporation

The master plan calls for more places that children and adults can use. At the top of Mado Hamlet the community swimming pool is planned. There is a lap pool for adults and older children, a family pool, and a children's pool. Next to the pool is a daycare center coupled with a pediatric practice. Between Mado and Selborne Hamlets the bonfire site and pavilion are located. This is a semi-remote place in the woods for children and adults to gather and spend time together. It has been planned that play places for younger children are located closer or in the settled areas for adult supervision. For older children, the entire community is a potential play area. For example, there are certain locations along the omega roads that are particularly good for skateboarding. It is wonderful to think that the streets are for kids as well as adults and automobiles; and of course, there are many games to be played and invented in the woods in the centers of the hamlets and along the many trails. The images in Figure 10.4 show activities and facilities in Serenbe that support adults, families, and especially children. The responses here are not only for resident children, but for future generations of children who will be able to experience the land, wildlife, and human-made places.

Children are inherently and intuitively curious naturalists. Farm animals, both domesticated and wild, are an integral part of the Serenbe landscape (Figures 10.5a–d). "Einswine," the free-range pig, wanders around Serenbe without hindrance (some residents say that he loves to hang out with the cows, apparently he thinks he actually is a cow; Figure 10.5e). Children and adults can fish in the pond by the animal village and Grange Lake. Walk deeper into the interstitial space toward Cedar Creek, and more wild animals can be seen, such as squirrel, deer, beaver, armadillo, geese, and tortoise. Children become exposed to animal behavior, ecology, conservation, biology, and the nature of animal–human interaction.

Figure 10.5 Serenbe animal village: a) Llama b) Horses c) Animal village d) Goat enclosure
e) "Einswine" the free-range pig
Source: Photographs by Phillip Tabb

Figure 10.6 Elementary schools: a) Existing Grange Montessori school b) Proposed model of
　　　　　Mado Montessori
Source: Photographs by Phillip Tabb

Another important children's place is the school, and whether or not it is within
walking distance. In Florida, for example, walking distance is mandated to be within
two miles between home and school. According to Safe Routes To Schools (SRTS)
and the National Center for Safe Routes to School, 48 percent of children aged 5 to
14 usually walked or bicycled to school in 1969; while this figure was only 13 percent in 2009.[4] At Serenbe the Children's House Montessori school is within 1 mile of
walking. It is a private, non-profit, non-secular entity, and a collaborative agreement
and partnership has been established between the school and Serenbe. The existing
Montessori school is located in the omega center of Grange Hamlet, with its attendant playground going down the hill. The school serves students from approximately
three years of age to sixth grade (age 11) (Figures 10.6a and 10.6b). In future phases,
another school is planned for Mado Hamlet as a campus of buildings differentiating
incompatible age groups of students. Its location is next to the community pool and
proposed pediatric medical center.

Sacred moments

The sacred is a term used to identify a variety of conditions usually considered sanctified, transcendent, and extraordinary in certain ways. For Serenbe, sacred experiences
are venerated in various places and at differing times, and it is not necessarily important that they be overtly stated or obviously expressed. Rather, sacred design moments
are integrated into the fabric of the secular place, contributing to a process of revelation. They are to be discovered and experienced through a self-reflective consciousness, enhanced by the ensouling qualities of the place. There is, in Edward Casey's
terms, "a refractory survival of the hidden presence of the sacred in certain spatial
oppositions"[5] – ordinary versus special places, or urban versus rural. There was an
intention from the very beginning to integrate the sacred in significant and ordinary
ways. As mentioned previously, sacred or intelligible geometry was an informing part
of the master plan, with instinctual, symbolic, and natural emplacement of the urban
design elements. Strategic ceremonies were an integral part of the Serenbe's development and manifestation process.

Figure 10.7 Sacredness of the land: a) Pasture scene b) Monarch butterfly in Selborne Hamlet
Source: Photographs by Phillip Tabb

The sacred finds expression in Serenbe in several ways. First is the reverence toward the land, and the ways in which residents can participate with nature to foster transcendent experiences. Located within the Piedmont (meaning foothills) eco-region, which is part of the Appalachian Mountain Range, Serenbe is characterized by rolling, hilly pine and hardwood forests and meadows. The range runs down-elevation to the southwest, hence the orientation of Selborne Hamlet.

The natural features are all-important, especially in contrast to generic urban areas found throughout metropolitan Atlanta, where residential areas do not have easy access to continuous natural environments (Figures 10.7a and 10.7b). The omega shapes help enable greater access to nature, both inside and outside the forms. The interstitial space found between the hamlets offers many opportunities for discovering nature. Hidden throughout Serenbe are other, yet to be discovered, places of wonder and numinous qualities.

Second is the presence and function of the omega form and constellation of hamlets. The *omega* (Ω) or horseshoe shape is rare as a settlement pattern but has been used before, such as Pueblo Bonito in northern New Mexico, many sea cove towns found around the world, and curving English linear villages. For Serenbe the omega shape came from a twin-phenomenal response to given landforms, more specifically the natural contours of the curvilinear valleys, and to the objective of creating place-oriented development configurations. The unique qualities and interesting properties or shape grammars include the linear, nucleated, and transected characteristics, along with the power of circularity. The omega geometry is singularly strong but, because it lies on the land, is a more integrated element of the topography and landscape, and becomes an important spatial and functional organization for the urbanized areas of the hamlets. As a double-loaded organization of building sites, it allows access to the center and perimeter for direct contact with nature. From a designer's point of view, geometry is an interesting immaterial aspect of the place, as the everyday sacred is experienced in the patterns of daily life that it organizes.

The apex of the omega form provides the most intense of the urban functions and includes attached buildings where the serpentine road becomes an outdoor room or place. It is typically in this space that both spontaneous and organized community activities occur. The centers of the omegas offer varying natural experiences, from the contemplative stream in Selborne Hamlet, to the more active lake in Grange Hamlet (Figures 10.8a–c).

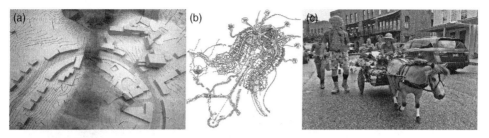

Figure 10.8 Special qualities of the omega form: a) Omega model
Source: Photograph courtesy of Mack Scogin and Merrill Elam Architects
b) Plan of Selborne omega form c) Fourth of July Parade at omega apex
Source: Photograph by Phillip Tabb

Third is the creation of the 88-feet diameter (27-meter) labyrinth, a replica of the Chartres labyrinth that was constructed in the woods over a weekend by family and friends of Serenbe. Made with stones from the site and all over the world, forming the edges and gravel on the paths, the Serenbe labyrinth is modest in its materiality, but its presence is powerful. Each of 40 participants was to bring a rock and story, and place it within the labyrinth. The center was formed by sixfold rosette geometry containing five large marble slabs.

At a normal pace, walking the labyrinth takes about 15 minutes to get to the center. The participant meanders through each of the four quadrants several times before finally reaching the short path into the center. There are 11 concentric rings split into four quadrants. Many who have experienced the labyrinth found it to be quieting, reflective, and renewing. Adjacent to the labyrinth is a small refectory structure over-looking the adjacent pastoral pond that was designed by one of Serenbe's founders, Ryan Gainey, for spiritual restoration. Next to the labyrinth is a low walled-in lawn that is used for weddings. So this particular area of Serenbe is used for contemplative and sacred moments.

Fourth is the integration of Serenbe Farms into the fabric of the community. For Serenbe, the 25-acre (10-hectare) farm provides not only certified organic food, but also another opportunity to interact with the land and each other. The farm produces more than 300 varieties of vegetables, herbs, flowers, and fruit (Figures 10.10a and 10.10b). Interaction occurs both at the farm, where residents can participate in farming activities, and during the Serenbe farmer's and artist's market held every Saturday during the summer months. According to Professor John Ikerd, "we can begin reclaiming the sacred in food and farming by acknowledging, up front and without compromise, the spiritual nature of sustainability."[6] So the sacred is a cycle or thread that forms connections from the sun, land, and harvesting, to preparing, cooking, eating, and finally as absorption of nutrients into our bodies.

Other numinous moments

On axis with the center of Selborne Hamlet to the south is the bonfire site, designated for secluded youth gatherings with contemplative focus (Figure 10.11a). It is located in

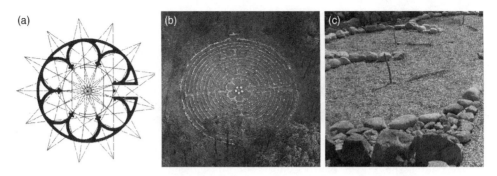

Figure 10.9 The labyrinth: a) Center geometry b) Aerial view of labyrinth
Source: Photograph courtesy of Serenbe Development Corporation
c) Center construction
Source: Photograph by Phillip Tabb

Figure 10.10 Serenbe Farms: a) The Farm
Source: Photograph by Phillip Tabb
b) Farmer's and artist's market
Source: Photograph courtesy of Serenbe Development Corporation

the heart of the interstitial space and therefore quite remote, but still accessible from each of the hamlets. A small creek flows south down the center of Selborne Hamlet, and when it reaches the end it turns west deeper into the woods. A path parallels this creek, then another departs from the main path, leading right to the creek. Presented before the creek is a two-person bench that looks over an intimate waterfall. Inscribed in a concrete slab placed in front of the bench is the following Biblical prose (Figure 10.11b):

> Be still and know that I am God.
> Be still and know that I am.
> Be still and know.
> Be still.
> Be ...[7]

Both the small waterfall and this message contribute to a serene and contemplative state of mind, and can lead to a numinous "thin space" experience, as time seems to slow down and stop. The intimate space, sounds of the creek, and the sequential

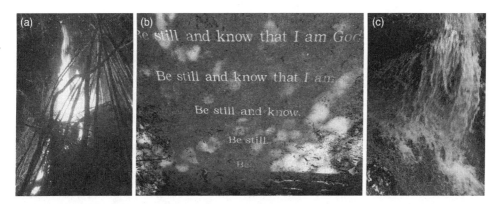

Figure 10.11 Numinous moments: a) Winter Solstice bonfire
Source: Photograph courtesy of Yiming Guan
b) Biblical saying in rock c) Mado waterfall
Source: Photographs by Phillip Tabb

message help facilitate this experience. Treasures such as these occur in special places that the land has to offer.

Further down this path and along the same creek is a rock outcrop and larger waterfall framed by two great sentinel trees: a large southern pine and a deciduous beech (Figure 10.11c). This is a place of vigor and aliveness. It stimulates the senses, as there seems to be an energy created by the force of the waterfall and the opposites of the two trees, who act as guardians of the place. Even further down this creek is its confluence, with the larger Cedar Creek and a very wild and magical landscape through which it passes. It has been said that the mythical Greek god of the wild, Pan, has been there. It is common to find a variety of wild-life dwelling there, as the meadows along Cedar Creek are serene and beautiful. At Serenbe, the philosophy is that a community is a living part of its natural surroundings, not something to be built at nature's expense. It exemplifies a core belief in biophilia: the theory that there is an instinctive bond between humans and other living systems. This approach values nature as well as children, adults and elders. According to Edward Wilson, biophilia is the urge to affiliate and connect with other lifeforms.[8] The experience in this regard is vital, deeply invigorating, and a remembrance that we are a part of nature, not separate from it. At Serenbe the principles of biophilic theory are put into practice, and serenity is a special-focus quality of its expression.

In Selborne Hamlet a space is available to community members for a variety of events. Every Sunday morning the Serenbe Fellowship meets in the Serenbe Community Center for prayer services, lectures and community gatherings. After a period of silent prayer and meditation they engage in dialogue, discussion, lectures, and spiritual sharing. The gathering welcomes people of all faiths. It is important to the community that such events not be connected to one religious practice; rather, that they appeal to the larger and diverse community membership.

Soulfulness is another quality present at Serenbe in ways that elicit excitations full of emotion and passion, with expressions of profound feeling. It is less a transcendent experience; rather, a deepening into a more inner heartfelt presence. In his book *Places of the Soul*, Christopher Day states that "soul can incarnate progressively into a building as it progressively gains substance from wish, through idea, planning, constructional design, building an occupation."[9] Certain qualities influence the soulfulness of a place, that include time, maturity, complexity, materiality, familiarity, and possessing an inner beauty or anima. For Serenbe, this translates from the personal touches that residents give to their homes, to the timeworn paths through hamlet woods. The natural materials found everywhere in the community also contribute to its soulfulness.

Serenbe's sacred moments are punctuations in the secular landscape, helping to provide greater depth of experience, discovery, sense of community, and meaning to patterns of everyday life. In 2004 the west leg of Selborne Hamlet went into construction, and after approximately 20 houses were built, the Blue Eyed Daisy was constructed. This marked the beginning of community-oriented amenities, and provided a context for residents to meet outside of their private homes. Several other sacred moments include the treehouses near Selborne Hamlet, yoga on the grounds at Serenbe, inside the farmhouse for morning breakfast, the summer Serenbe Playhouse performances held in the Selborne live–work courtyard, Serenbe Farm providing organic produce for residents and local restaurants, and interfaith members gathering in the Blue Eyed Daisy after a Sunday meeting.

The serene is expressed in many of these sacred moments as either inspiring awe of the natural beauty of the place, or through the unity experience of community. Having the ability either to go into nature and having an individual experience of solitude, or to connect with community members in the multitude of venues, are amenities rarely afforded in other urban environments. This coupling of the natural and urban areas, and the visibility of cultural and commercial activity, are both sustainable and heartfelt.[10] The numinous is present, but most likely experienced in the woods. The further into the woods, the more the quiet and solitude, and it becomes more unfamiliar. Both the mysterious and trepidation present themselves. The senses become activated as the slightest flicker of light and shadow can be seen. These are moments when walking in the woods, that time seems to stand still, and an inexpressible quality is omnipresent. As Marie Nygren reflected:

> Numinous to me is being in the presence of grace … being in the presence of divine energy. I use all of Serenbe as a teacher and as a sacred space for me. Every aspect of Serenbe is sacred space.[11]

Notes

1 Nationwide Wildlife Removal, "Animal Wildlife Control Info". Available online at www.aaanimalcontrol.com/professional-trapper/wildlife/GA-Atlanta-Wildlife.htm (accessed July 2015).
2 The term "thin place" comes from the pre-Christian culture in Western Europe – particularly Ireland – and refers to a place where the veil between this world and the "other world" or the "eternal world" is thin. Definition taken from "What Are Thin Places?", *Thin Places*. Available online at www.thinplace.net/2008/02/what-are-thin-places.html (accessed November 2015).
3 Aurbach, Laurence, "TNDs With Agriculture, New Neighbors," *Ped Shed*. Available online at http://pedshed.net/?p=47 (accessed November 2015).
4 The National Center for Safe Routes to School, *How Children Get to School: School Travel Patterns 1969 to 2009*, 2011. Available online at http://saferoutesinfo.org/sites/default/files/resources/NHTS_school_travel_report_2011_0.pdf (accessed December 2015).

5 Casey, Edward, *The Fate of Place: A Philosophical History*, University of California Press, Berkeley, CA, 1998, p. 299.
6 Ikerd, John E., "Reclaiming the Sacred in Food and Farming," *Biodynamics*, fall 2012. Available online at http://farmerstoyou.com/organicfoodblog/wp-content/uploads/2012/12/Biodynamics_Fall_2012_John_Ikerd.pdf (accessed November 2015).
7 The Bible, Psalm 46, Verse 10.
8 Wilson, Edward O., *Biophilia: The Human Bond with Other Species*, Harvard University Press, Cambridge, MA, 1984.
9 Day, Christopher, *Places of Soul: Architecture and Environmental Design as a Healing Art*, Aquarian Press, Wellingborough, 1990, p. 106.
10 Casement, Ann and Tacey, David (eds), *The Idea of the Numinous*, Routledge, London, 2006.
11 Interview with Marie Nygren by Texas A&M University student Jocelyn Zuringa, Serenbe Community, November 2015.

11 Serene urbanism analysis

Science sometimes improves hypotheses and sometimes disproves them. But proof would be another matter and perhaps never occurs except in the realms of totally abstract tautology.[1]

The best reason to live here is the life here.[2]

Certain green principles are coded within the term "architecture," which can be useful for understanding the placemaking process. An etymological exploration of the Greek roots of the term "architecture" provided a definition revealing something more noetic, completely different than the modern heroic notions of architecture, and containing more explicit place principles of design. The root terms, *archê, technê*, and *-ure* function as noun, verb, and suffix, and provide insights and keys to its operational meaning.[3] The ancient view suggested a hierarchical approach to the term, and gives an invigorated redefinition where the word itself became a sentence. So embodied into the very word of *architecture* is this threefold essence of speech also found within the simplest sentence. The accumulative meaning derived by combining concepts of these terms becomes "Architecture": the weaving into manifestation of the First Principles.[4] These same principles were used in determining the placemaking factors at Serenbe.

Placemaking factors

The environmental factors influencing placemaking at Serenbe include the topics discussed in previous chapters. A placemaking factor represents certain characteristics associated with urbanism, serenity, sustainability, biophilia, and the numinous. Together with the placemaking principles and patterns, these combine to present a broader landscape for place creation (as indicated in the place pattern matrix in Table 11.1). They include an indication of the presence of serenity (Se), urbanism (Ur), sustainability (Su), biophilia (Bi), and the numinous (Nu). These factors are further discussed here with the objective of articulating specific patterns associated with each of them.

Serene characteristics

Serenity is found at Serenbe largely due to its rural location, quality of the forested land, water features and surrounding Chattahoochee Hills environment, and the overall configuration and compactness of the development design, allowing for easy access

Figure 11.1 Serene characteristics: a) Students on bridge b) Wishing fountain
Source: Photograph by Phillip Tabb
c) Child with piglet
Source: Photograph courtesy of Serenbe Development Corporation

to each hamlet through nature. Many quiet places are found within the interstitial territory between hamlets, and can be accessed daily. The ten factors contributing to the serene include safety, authenticity, coherence, human-scale, harmony and balance, connections to nature, enhanced perception, experience of presence, transformative healing and the existence of grace and beauty.[5]

Figure 11.1a shows students on a bridge observing the pond below, water fountain in the center of the live-work courtyard (Figure 11.1b) and a serene moment of a child with a piglet (Figure 11.1c). These characteristics are as follows:

1. safe, quiet, peaceful, and tranquil environment;
2. strong connections to nature and natural systems;
3. authentic and honest in expression;
4. human-scaled architectural and urban elements;
5. coherent, identifiable and understood;
6. natural materiality, indigenous materials;
7. elemental qualities of fire, water, earth, and air;
8. harmonious, proportioned, and balanced;
9. presence of beauty;
10. spirit of place and genius loci.

Urban characteristics

As discussed previously, Serenbe is not located within an urban center; rather, it is at the edge of a metropolitan region in an area zoned at one dwelling unit per acre, which is considered low density. However, the constellation configuration, Thorburn transect, and omega hamlet forms with its density gradient and mixes of use all contribute to the creation of more urban-like spaces, along with the community activities that coexist with this level of urbanism. There are ten urbanism factors: robust commerce and economic activity, employment opportunities, access to amenities, proximity to a diversity of goods and services, places of spontaneous social interactions, cultural and institutional facilities, entertainment opportunities, context for urban sustainability, greater land preservation, infrastructure efficiency, and place identity.[6]

These consist of:

1. agglomeration and interaction;
2. growth by multiplication instead of gross addition;
3. between-place transportation connections;
4. in-place networks and transportation modes;
5. settlement configuration and internal order;
6. compaction and density of built form;
7. integrated agriculture ("farm-to-table");
8. interspersion and clustering of mixes of use;
9. provision of public indoor and outdoor places;
10. provisions of cultural programs, events, and facilities.

At Serenbe the urban characteristics separate it from other suburban single-use developments. The density is nowhere like larger cities, but does manifest a certain agglomeration, attached buildings, and mixes of use. The restaurants and shops provide meeting places for residents and visitors, and the greens, plazas, and other outdoor spaces accommodate a variety of activities year-round. The hamlets focus on the arts, agriculture, health and wellness, and education, providing many cultural opportunities and contexts for interaction and community formation. Figure 11.2a shows the street density, and Figure 11.2b a community outdoor party.

Sustainability characteristics

In 2008 Serenbe received the Inaugural Sustainability Award from the Urban Land Institute of Atlanta. Therefore, this analysis of sustainability factors is based in part on the measures cited for that award. These ten characteristics are found at the development, urban design, and building scales. The ten factors were configuration, density of built form, mixes of use, integrated agriculture, innovative water waste systems, circulation networks, pedestrian places, use of on-site resources, regional architecture, and EarthCraft building standards.

Figure 11.2 Urban characteristics: a) Attached buildings at Selborne omega apex b) Crossroads
      street party
Source: Photographs by Phillip Tabb

Figure 11.3 Sustainability characteristics: a) Grange Net-Zero houses b) Rainwater harvesting
c) Net-Zero dwelling
Source: Photographs by Phillip Tabb

Figures 11.3a and 11.3b show several green design approaches employed in Grange Hamlet, with Net-Zero residences and rainwater harvesting at the center:

1. land preservation and defined urban territories;
2. integration of alternative transportation modes;
3. climate-oriented architecture and bioclimatic urban design;
4. use of on-site resources, solar electricity, and geothermal;
5. on-site water collection and daylight stormwater management;
6. innovative constructed wetlands waste system;
7. natural landscaping, organic agriculture, and edible landscapes;
8. community energy production;
9. recycling, reuse, and repurposing;
10. energy standards in construction and energy-efficient appliances.

At Serenbe the sustainable strategies first began at the planning scale, with high land preservation percentages, relative compactness of urban forms and the density gradient, mixes of uses supporting sustainability, and the organic farm. At the architectural scale, sustainability grew incrementally, with initially southern vernacular housing forms, EarthCraft green construction standards, and the introduction of renewable energy sources, mainly natural ventilation, natural lighting, geothermal heating and cooling, and in some instances the introduction of photovoltaic electricity.

Biophilic characteristics

The biophilic patterns respond to direct connections to nature and natural processes, drawing from influential perspectives including health conditions, socio-cultural norms, expectations, frequency and duration of experiences, and processes, and speed-scale user perception.

Figure 11.4 shows biophilic patterns, including an intense engagement with nature, framed views into the omega woods, water features, and the stone and wood building materials appropriate to rural and more natural settings:[7]

Figure 11.4 Biophilic characteristics: house and bridge over Swan Ridge Ravine
Source: Photograph by Phillip Tabb

1. physical and visual connections to nature;
2. natural thermal and airflow variability;
3. presence of water;
4. dynamic and diffuse light;
5. connection to natural systems;
6. sensory connections to nature;
7. preferred views;
8. places of refuge and protection;
9. biomorphic patterns;
10. natural materiality.

Biophilic patterns at Serenbe occur in fairly obvious ways. There are constant views to nature and paths that directly connect to the forests, meadows, and ponds. Breezes are captured and directed into the hamlets, and by individual dwellings naturally. The two ponds, streams, waterfalls, and human-made water features are seen throughout Serenbe. Natural light changes with the seasons, and filters through the large Georgia pine trees. There are many natural sounds from birds, horses, and cows to the gentle falling of leaves in autumn. Each omega creates an urban place of refuge with a profound sense of place. Architectural materials are largely natural or rural in character, from lapped siding or board and batten to shake shingles, corrugated metal roofs, and CorTen steel street furniture. Patterns such as these are readily found throughout Serenbe, such as the residence adjacent to the Grange ravine and the forest that it spans. Everyday passage from the residential cluster to the commercial functions provides an encounter with nature.

Numinous characteristics

The numinous encompasses many intangible characteristics that contribute to place-making in unusual ways. The numinous describes a power or spiritually elevated state that accompanies the experience of a charged place, and with it are both the presence of something utterly mysterious and an overwhelming feeling of awe, as well as a sense of fascination, and an amplified presence and awareness. For Serenbe the numinous is found in its extremes: the serene natural places and the vital urban places. At Serenbe they occur in both natural and in community-urban ways throughout the year. Characteristics include:[8]

1. the mysterious, fascination;
2. enlivening and stimulating;
3. creature consciousness;
4. amplified presence;
5. time standing still;
6. presence of the "wholly other";
7. transformation;
8. the ineffable;
9. epiphany, revelation;
10. the sublime, numinous in nature.

At Serenbe the numinous can be experienced in certain places throughout the community. Natural numinous experiences occur in the woods, along the streambeds, and in very special places formed by the topography, geometry of trees, or waterfalls along the streams. Urban experiences occur more culturally through events, celebrations, and art performances. Figures 11.5a–c illustrate the elemental patterns of fire and water, as their constant movements are captivating and mesmerizing.

Placemaking characteristics were evaluated using the method with a matrix of Likert values assigned to the various qualities for the Serene, Urban, Sustainable and Numinous. Spiderweb diagrams (also known as radar charts, star plots or cobweb charts), originally developed by Georg Van Mayr in 1887, are two-dimensional

Figure 11.5 Numinous characteristics: a) Serenbe bonfire
Source: Photograph courtesy of Serenbe Development Corporation
b) Waterfall c) Wild butterfly
Source: Photographs by Phillip Tabb

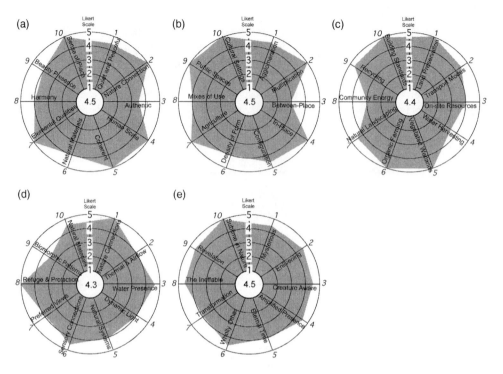

Figure 11.6 Spiderweb diagrams: a) Serene characteristics b) Urban characteristics c) Sustainable
characteristics d) Biophilic characteristics e) Numinous characteristics
The analysis of these five factors was conducted by Texas A&M University students in the fall of 2015, and material was obtained through interviews with local
residents, site observations and photography. Note that the overall Likert scale
scores are fairly similar with the five factors averaging around 4.4.
Source: courtesy of Phillip Tabb

graphic methods for organizing multivariate quantitative variables in radial and
concentric systems of values. Starting at the top of the diagram is characteristic number 1, with the rest of the factors following in a clockwise direction and
the starlike shapes indicating variable values. Spiderweb diagrams were created
illustrating the varying impacts of these characteristics within Selborne Hamlet
(Figures 11.6a–e). It can be observed from the diagrams that for the most part,
each characteristic scored fairly high (between 4.0 and 5.0), and that typically there
were one or two characteristics for each that scored lower (than 4.0). For example, for Urban Characteristics, between-place connections scored lower; and for
Sustainability, community energy systems scored lower. The biophilic and numinous characteristics were relatively consistent. By integrating these five categories
of place characteristics, a more complete picture of the qualities and functions of
serene urbanism can be evaluated (Table 11.1).[9] Table 11.1 shows which of the
characteristics of the five place factors are strong or weaker contributors to placemaking at Selborne Hamlet.

Table 11.1 Matrix of Selborne Hamlet place factors

Place factor	Qualities	Likert rating	Factors with highest rating	Factors with lowest rating
Serene (Se)	Serene is safe, peaceful, authentic, elemental, beautiful with strong connections to nature, coherent with spirit of place	4.5	Connections to nature, human scale, elemental qualities, coherence, and spirit of place	Authentic, sensual materiality, and harmonious
Urbanism (Ur)	Agglomeration, multiplication, in-place and between-place networks, density, mixes of use, outdoor meeting places, cultural events	4.4	Multiplication, internal networks, urban architecture, public gathering places, and cultural settings	External between-place networks, configuration, and density of built form
Sustainability (Su)	Land preservation, bioclimatic design, on-site resources, constructed wetlands, community energy production, high construction standards	4.2	Land preservation, constructed wetlands, integrated agriculture, green construction, and energy efficiency	Rainwater harvesting, automobile use, and community energy production
Biophilia (Bi)	Connections to nature, variability of the elements water and air, preferred views, refuge, protection, biomorphic patterns, and natural materiality	4.4	Connections to nature, presence of water, sensory experiences, and refuge places	Preferred views, and biomorphic patterns, or explicit designs
Numinous (Nu)	Mysterious, fascinating, enlivening, still time, creature-consciousness, transformative and ineffable, amplified presence, and sublime	4.4	Enlivening, creature-consciousness, amplified presence, "wholly other," and numinous experiences	Time stands still, and transformation (all these were difficult to measure)

Note: The place factors and Likert scale ratings were proposed by Texas A&M University students while attending the Study-Away Program there in fall 2015. Each of these factors was analyzed, photograph documented, and accompanied by interviews with local resident experts in these areas.

Place principles and patterns

Place archetypal principles

The First Principles, archetypes, and ectypal patterns form the basis through which Selborne Hamlet is analyzed. Each principle has a presence and certain quality of expression in which both are assessed. Unity is evident in each of the omega hamlet forms, as they are coherent and tend to unify the developed portion of the plan. The Generative Principle is present with the multiplication of hamlets, as well as individual buildings throughout the developed areas. There is an intentional diversity of building types and architectural languages. The Formative Principle is found in the purity of the omega geometry along with the transect of spaces, from rural at the edges to urban at the center. The Corporeal Principle can be clearly experienced as the development is built or in the construction stage. Residents are interested in investing both time and money to live there. The Regenerative Principle can be seen with the iterative development process and the transformative experiences that occur as a result of living there.

Archetypes that are applicable to Selborne Hamlet inform the degree to which the hamlet is whole and unified, its ability to grow and multiply in diverse and site-appropriate ways, its spatial structure and ordering devices, its response to pragmatic and real-world determinants, and finally, the way in which it incrementally evolved over time with ceremonial participation. The ectypal patterns found in Selborne can be clearly identified and described from the overall wholeness, orientation, geometry, scale, and spatial structure attributed to the omega form, to the inclusion of elemental qualities, light, integrated access to nature, and careful design of passage, both to and within the hamlet. The archetypes and ectypes are essentially nonphysical design guides, where typal examples found within Selborne are physical and tangible actualizations with a specific nature and character, as exemplified by the geometry and shape-grammar integral to the omega form.

Place ectypal patterns

The placemaking patterns are ectypal expressions that have guided the design and building of the community. The ectypal patterns used in the analysis of Selborne derive from the earlier works of Michael Brill and his architectural students at State University of New York at Buffalo in 1985,[10] patterns described and illustrated in *Chambers for a Memory Palace*, by Lyndon and Moore,[11] *A Pattern Language* by Christopher Alexander and colleagues,[12] and research and comparative analysis of published place patterns was conducted by MArch, MS and PhD in Architecture students at Texas A&M University. Taken together they are a redux of placemaking patterns forming the basis for the current 20 patterns of this analysis.[13] Following is the complete pattern listing and brief summary of their presence in Selborne for each pattern.

- *Centering* – is a point of attraction and a seed encoding growth of the place, and it can be a special space, square, green, temple, market, street, building, landmark, natural feature, or fountain. It is a physical focal point and usually has an intense activity and meaning. At Serenbe it is the space created by the omega form.

- *Connecting* – is an emergence that connects and progresses from the center of a place to the outer portions of a place, and from the perimeter to the center. It is a transected, spatial organization that relates the innermost urban areas to the outer natural ones. At Serenbe the interconnected roads and network of paths represent it.
- *Bounding* – is the comprehensible edge with an integrating relationship to the center. It has the functions of creating containment within, protection from without, porosity of natural systems flowing through, and meaning through coherence. At Serenbe the omega form, reinforced by forest, roads, and buildings, defines it.
- *Domain* – is the living place between center and boundary, and it embodies a certain hierarchical order, giving meaning, proportion, spatial organization, and the right-placement of internal functions or parts. At Serenbe it is organized by the double-loaded serpentine structure and pattern of paths.
- *Finding direction* – is giving meaning and connections to the terrestrial world of a given place through orientation to its natural features, such as the cardinal directions, the natural contours of the site, or views to special features. At Serenbe it is south-oriented and land-fitted.
- *Descent* – is a direct response to gravity and the grounding of a place into the earth, as well as emergence from the earth. This pattern can express through a well, a building's footings or foundations, basements and connections to the ground, which are symbols of this pattern as they connect to the earth. At Serenbe it can be seen lying on the land, sloping topography.
- *Reaching upward* – is a counteracting force and a symbol of the breakthrough from the lower realms to the world above. The *axis mundi* can be expressed with towers, vertical, ascending rooflines, columns, or shafts of light. At Serenbe it is expressed as a stand of trees and urban buildings.
- *Multiplication* – is the proliferating process by which a space is filled, occupied and expanded, not through constant addition, but through replication. An optimum size is reached, and then repeated. At Serenbe it is found with the overall constellation of hamlets, as well as with individual buildings.
- *Geometric order* – is underlying structure of physical things, and forms significant relationships, proportions, and measures among all the parts, from points to lines, through planes and solids, to multiple forms. At Serenbe it is inherent to the omega shape and other special interstitial places.
- *Spatial and structural order* – is essential in architecture, as it counteracts the forces of gravity, utilizes the strength and properties of materials, and forms strength and integrity in the interconnectedness of parts. At Serenbe it is found within the fabric of the urban place, as well as within the natural areas of the site.
- *Natural order* – is the taming quality of the wild, disordered, and chaotic brought into safe and natural surroundings. This can include agriculture, orchards, landscaping, water features, geological formation, or open spaces. At Serenbe it is found with the forest around omegas, and the natural areas within them.
- *Celestial order* – is a response to the open sky and the changing movements of the sun, moon, planets, and other celestial objects, demarking the changing seasons and times of the day. At Serenbe the heavens, sun, moon, and celestial bodies can be experienced outdoors in various open places.

- *Scale* – is the relationship between the human body and experience of a place relative to the measure, size, proportions, articulations, complexity, detail, and design of the place. At Serenbe human-scale urbanism, buildings, and urban elements are found throughout.
- *Functional order* – is the good and efficient fit between use and form, which includes the performance, operations, technologies, and spatial arrangements integral to a building's occupation. At Serenbe it provides important functions and activities with efficient proximity within the hamlets.
- *Economical order* – is the efficiency, prudence, and saving of time, money, energy, and natural resources with a balance and optimization between first costs, operating costs, and life cycle costs. At Serenbe it provides economic opportunity and affordability.
- *Corporeal materiality* – is the state or quality of material substance in the medium of a building or place. Materiality also expresses through the elemental qualities of water, earth, air, and fire. At Serenbe it is appropriate to everyday materials that are workable and changeable.
- *Elemental materiality* – is the state or quality of material substance in the medium of a building or place. Materiality also expresses through the elemental qualities of water, earth, air, and fire. At Serenbe it can be found with special inclusions of fire, water, earth, air, and ether typically found throughout the natural areas of the site.
- *Passage* – is the neutral, transitional, and preparatory threshold and entrance into a place. It is an experiential pause and between outside and in, or from realms of the mundane to the significant. At Serenbe it occurs with the intelligible progression, entry, and transect of movement into the hamlet or public spaces.
- *Light and illumination* – is the atmosphere, inspiration, and illumination in architecture, and it is in a coexisting dance with shadow to give expression to form. It is a source. At Serenbe it occurs as special urban and natural lighting designed to reduce night pollution.
- *Ceremonial order* – is the consummatory and transformative quality achieved through participation in, engagement with, and celebration of a place. This occurs where there is interaction and ordering between behavior and form. At Serenbe it manifests in everyday numinous experiences, as well as with seasonal and special rituals and ceremonies.

Figure 11.7 illustrates the 20 ectypal place patterns in diagrammatic form. Application of these patterns evolved directly from the five principles to form an ordered and comprehensive list of characteristics. For example, *Bounding* (Pattern 3), describes place-containing forms typically found in Selborne with the surrounding stand of trees, omega road and buildings that echo it, and the containing nature of the omega shape. *Grounding* (Pattern 6) relates to the way that the omega road lays on the land, moving with the changing contours, or with the design of building foundations; and *Nature Within* (Pattern 10) is clearly seen with natural land use found in each of the hamlets' centers. *Passage and Thresholds* (Pattern 18) is seen through the Thorburn transect, where experience between natural and urban environments can transition into the domain of serene urbanism – an essential consequence, given the thesis of this work. *Ceremonial Order* (Pattern 20) was an important pattern, in that it described the interactions between the built place and the ritual and ceremonial

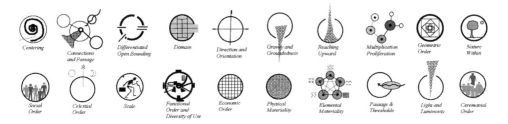

Figure 11.7 The 20 ectypal placemaking patterns

experiences organized by it. It should be noted that both the list of guiding principles and corresponding place patterns within this study do not represent exclusive lists. The combination of all of these 20 patterns contributes to the full potential for place to occur.

Placemaking methodology

The placemaking patterns applied to the Serenbe design and physical construction of Selborne Hamlet formed the basis of the analysis. Selborne was selected because it was the most built out, and therefore contained the principles and ectypal patterns. Visits to the project site broadened the analysis to include a photographic record, field notes, and behavioral maps, resident testimonials, a questionnaire, and data represented in a matrix.[14] The matrix indicates the listing of the patterns, the principles through which the patterns function, numerical ratings for both the presence and quality of expression of each pattern, and finally, a brief description of the physical or typal characteristics of the pattern as specifically found in Selborne Hamlet. The Likert scale[15] was used in this study to determined values by two methods: master plan analysis, and in-situ observations. It is important to realize the presence (quantitative) and quality of expression (qualitative) impacts of each of the patterns, as they constitute the properties and attributes of a charged or sacred place.

1. *Pattern presence* – is a quantitative emphasis on entities, measurements, amounts, and frequency. For Serenbe, it is the identification and description of the existence of the various patterns, detailed geometric analysis, and measure of their magnitude. Raising the question: is a pattern discernable? (a positivist/post-positivist viewpoint).[16]
2. *Quality of expression* – is a qualitative dimension emphasizing relationships, socially constructed reality, and situational constraints. For use in the context of Serenbe, it is the value-laden measure of the placemaking patterns. Raising the question: what is the experience of the pattern, and how is it valorized? (a naturalistic proposition).[17]

Serenbe's hamlets are comparable in form, and therefore an analysis of each of them would produce similar results. Some differences do exist, such as the hamlets' natural centers and nonresidential functions. For example, Selborne's center is forested without an identifiable place-marker, and is oriented to the visual, performing, and culinary arts. In contrast, Grange's center has a large pond that is highly visible and difficult to reach, and is oriented to equestrian and agrarian uses. Therefore, analysis was limited to one hamlet – Selborne – as it was the most built out and analyzed physically. Pattern presence was determined by several site visits to Selborne with direct experience of the hamlet, including photography of examples of the various place patterns. In addition, there was detailed analysis of the physical or formal characteristics indicated on the master plan. Each pattern was identified and evaluated. For example, *Centering* (Pattern 1) was examined within the omega on the master plan, and verifying the presence of the center within the omega hamlet was done while visiting the actual site.

Pattern quality was more difficult, requiring direct experiences of the place which were made into general observations and perceptions, reinforcing the patterns while in-situ. Methods also included discussions with residents and a questionnaire that focused on each of the placemaking patterns. The Likert scale values were then determined through cross-examination of these methods. In this regard, the *Centering* quality was evaluated in the center of the hamlet by sensing and recording its qualities by personal experience and comparing to resident testimonials. For Selborne, the center of the hamlet was the forested area with the small stream running through it. An exact center was not discernable, but the experience of this area had a distinctive sense of place, and was commonly viewed as serene, picturesque, and esthetically pleasing. Therefore, quality of expression was experienced as being high on the Likert scale.

Table 11.2 includes evaluation and comments of the 20 ectypal patterns according to the five archetypal principle sets. Each pattern is assigned a numerical value on the Likert scale (where 1 = lowest to 5 = highest), assessing both the presence (quantitative) and the quality of expression (qualitative) separately. As a guide for identifying values for both pattern presence and quality, the scale denoted: 1–2 = not discernable or poor quality; 3 = pattern present but not remarkable; 4–5 = patterns discernable and quite visible, with strong experiential impact and charged content.

Selborne Hamlet analysis

As previously discussed, the matrix was formed by organizing the 20 place patterns according to the five principles, and determining Likert scale rates for both pattern presence and quality of expression. The values were determined by on-site visits, questionnaires, and master plan analysis. Data from the matrix in Table 11.2 were applied to create diagrams (Figures 11.8a and 11.8b).

Starting at the top of the diagram is *Centering* (Pattern 1) with the rest of the patterns following in a clockwise direction, with the starlike shapes indicating the results of the variable values. In the case of the Selborne analysis, the principle with the highest value for presence (Figure 11.8a) is the Unity Principle; the one with the lowest value for presence is the Corporeal Principle. The Generative, Formative, and Regenerative Principles all received ratings in-between these two. For pattern quality (Figure 11.8b), the highest is the Unity Principle, and the lowest is the Corporeal Principle. Pattern presence received slightly higher values than pattern quality of expression.

The last column in Table 11.2 indicates the place patterns relative to their associated principle, a rating of their presence and quality. It concludes with typal examples of the patterns relative to Selborne Hamlet. Typal explanations include, for example, for *Centering* (Pattern 1), "Omega centers, special natural areas and concentration

Table 11.2 Matrix of Selborne Hamlet place patterns

Pattern (as ectype)	Principle (as archetype)	Presence (quantitative)	Expression (qualitative)	Exemplification (as type)
1. Centering	Unity Principle	4.0	4.5	Omega centers, special natural areas and concentration of commercial zones
2. Connecting		5.0	5.0	Roads, drives, sidewalks, trails, bridle paths, greenways, streams, and visual axis
3. Bounding		5.0	4.25	Hills, natural contours, forested areas, the curved-shaped omega road, and built form
4. Domain		4.5	3.75	Valleys, area contained by omega organization, and hamlets constellation
Average		4.5625	4.375	
5. Finding direction	Generative Principle	4.5	4.0	Omegas oriented to south and to natural centers within "U-shape"
6. Grounding		4.5	4.0	Terraced sites and buildings, agriculture, unique natural features of the land
7. Reaching up		3.0	3.0	Hamlet urban centers, hills surrounding hamlets, trees, Selborne Hotel
8. Multiplying		5.0	4.5	Hamlet replication in naturally formed valleys, housing duplication, fenestrations
Average		4.25	3.875	
9. Geometric order	Formative Principle	5.0	4.5	Strong serpentine geometry (omega), aligned along parallel contours
10. Nature within		5.0	5.0	Nature within and surrounding, 100 farm animals, Serenbe Farms, forest, meadows
11. Social structure		4.25	4.0	Urban spaces/activities, structure of omegas, privacy in interstitial space
12. Celestial order		3.0	3.5	Solar orientation of hamlets and houses, solar technologies, celestial site
Average		4.325	4.25	
13. Scale	Corporeal Principle	4.5	4.5	Residential, with diverse mixes of use and building type, street section, and furniture

(*continued*)

Table 11.2 (cont.)

Pattern (as ectype)	Principle (as archetype)	Presence (quantitative)	Expression (qualitative)	Exemplification (as type)
14. Functional order		4.0	3.5	Omega, transect, and commercial mixed-use, ArtFarm, functional arrangement, density
15. Economic order		4.0	3.5	Smaller variable plot sizes, higher densities, attached housing, the Nest
16. Materiality		4.25	3.5	EarthCraft construction, vernacular and diversity of materials, transect materiality
Average		4.1875	3.75	
17. Elemental	Regenerative Principle	4.25	4.5	Hills, valleys, rock outcrops, red earth, waterfalls, streams, ponds, and bonfire
18. Passage		4.5	4.5	Rural-to-urban transect, many paths leading into the hamlet and urban center
19. Natural light		3.0	3.0	Filtered through the forest, natural daylight, night sky light, and lamps
20. Ceremonial order		5.0	5.0	Sense of community, labyrinth, market, 5k race, theater, rituals and ceremonies
Average		4.3125	4.25	
Total Average		**4.30**	**4.10**	

of commercial zones," and for *Ceremonial Order* (Pattern 20), "sense of community, labyrinth, market, 5k race, rituals, and ceremonies."

Both spiderweb diagrams can be analyzed together and their relative impacts compared. As can be observed from Figures 11.9a–f, all but a few of the place patterns are strongly present within Selborne, and the quality of the expression of these patterns is nearly as high. The analysis revealed that the patterns contributing the most to place-making include: *Connection* (2), *Bounding* (3), *Multiplying* (8), *Geometry* (10), *Nature Within* (11), *Passage* (18), and *Ceremonial Order* (20). Only *Centering* (1) and *Elemental Materiality* (17) scored higher in quality than with presence. Patterns such as *Reaching Upward* (7), *Celestial Order* (12) and *Light/Illumination* (19) were not as expressive in Selborne, probably due to the multiple building scale and horizontal territory of the hamlet, which do not emphasize the vertical or *axis mundi* within the built form of the place. Of course, this is not necessarily the case in denser urban areas with larger or multiple-story buildings, and architecture with more vertically exaggerated spatial designs.

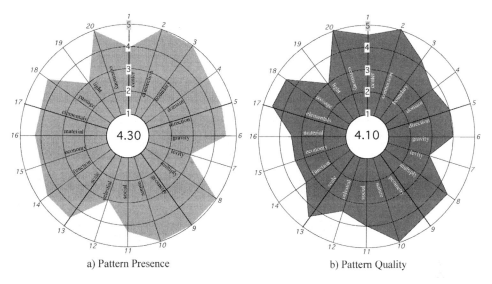

a) Pattern Presence

b) Pattern Quality

Figure 11.8 Placemaking spiderweb diagrams for Selborne Hamlet
Source: Philip Tabb

Figure 11.9 Patterns receiving highest scores: a) Connections b) Bounding
Source: Photograph by Phillip Tabb
c) Multiplication d) Geometric order
Source: Photographs courtesy of Serenbe Development Corporation
e) Nature within f) Ceremony
Source: Photographs by Phillip Tabb

Figures 11.9a–f shows patterns receiving the highest score of 5.0:

- *Connections*, with 7 miles (11 kilometers) of trails and the network of serpentine roads throughout Serenbe;
- *Bounding*, with the stands of trees, topography, and circular omega form;
- *Multiplication*, with the repetition of the hamlets, individual houses, and building elements (porches, dormers, windows, and doors);
- *Geometric order*, with the strong omega serpentine road form, transect, and geometrically significant sites;
- *Nature within*, with the stand of woods and stream in the center; and
- *Ceremonial order*, with the Serenbe Saturday farmer's and artists' market, theatrical productions, weddings, various seasonal parades, Halloween, Easter egg hunt, May Day, interfaith meetings, and 5k race organized around the omega roads.

Figures 11.8a and 11.8b also indicate the ectypal place patterns with the highest presence and quality.

The analysis was intended to identify the placemaking patterns to gain a better understanding of their impact on Serenbe. The analysis indicates a fairly high presence and quality of factors, characteristics, and patterns associated with placemaking. While single patterns are certainly fervent, it is the consummatory effect of all principles and patterns that fully contribute to the nexus of placemaking, and provide a context for secular-sacredness. It is the convenient access to special natural and urban places that brings the sacred into everyday experience. In this regard, according to Mircea Eliade:

> Revelation of a sacred space makes it possible to obtain a fixed point and hence to acquire orientation in the chaos of homogeneity, to "found the world" and to live in a real sense.[18]

Comparative observations

When qualities of the serene, urbanism, sustainability, and placemaking are brought together, there is a powerful confluence that supports a vision and model of a more positive approach to urban planning, especially at the edge. According to Merlyn Driver, it is when the patterns connect that form a developmental and consummatory homology.[19]

In *Place and Placelessness*, Edward Relph suggests that place has several essences, which include place-location, place-landscape, place-time, and place-community.[20] Yi-Fu Tuan in *Space and Place* further explains that city places have fronts and backs, creating processional routes.[21] Edward S. Casey in *The Fate of Place* counters the notion of place essential traits, but rather supports a more phenomenal perspective with place at work, something that is ongoing and dynamic and part of something else.[22] Finally, Belden Lane in *Landscapes of the Sacred* exclaims that "it is the nature of human beings that they cannot get enough of place."[23] These conceptions of place are all present at Serenbe, especially in the varying hamlet forms and constellating scales of application. Serenbe represents the panoply of ongoing development of an experimental community that is designed as a model to counteract the negative effects of suburban sprawl and placelessness. The hamlet-focused design affords an incremental approach to deepening into greater levels of placemaking over time. Serenbe is an in-progress investigation into how to envision, design, and sustain a secular-sacred community today. In other words, it is a reflection that shadows the process of construction along with growing occupation and increasing numbers of residents. It is anticipated that the place patterns will have provided planning guides not only for greater levels of sacredness, but also for a healthier and more livable place.

The placemaking analysis for Selborne indicates a relative consistency and balance among the five principles and 20 patterns. There is a slight difference between the presence and quality, which is in part due to the rural character and emphasis on vernacular architecture that are normally less refined, compared to more urban languages and materials. The patterns with the greatest values seem to support the initial intentions, as Serenbe offers a laboratory in which to test these assumptions and designs, creating a language where community, health and wellness, sustainability, and sacred placemaking converge.

With the sustainability measures, integrated agriculture, and embodied place patterns, it is hoped that a transfer of knowledge might inform future development projects, particularly at the urban edge of metropolitan regions, or in the restructuring of existing suburban areas. Many researchers of placemaking theory may be skeptical of the development of essential traits and formal structures of place, and would posit something more indeterminate and less causal. Instead, this analysis of Serenbe is what Edward Casey might call "place at work," with the dynamic ingredient of "something else."[24] Serenbe suggests that in fact, both coexist: an unchanging archetypal essence, and mutable and evolving phenomenology of place. It is the ceremonial order of Selborne that blends physical characteristics with community participation, and the dynamic behavioral patterns of everyday living – the secular–sacred in place creation. According to Serenbe resident John Graham:

> From the beginning, the founders of Serenbe possessed a vision for a community distinguished by a strong, perpetual commitment to art and culture. These are key to the unique character of Serenbe and its quality of life. The Serenbe Institute's programs in theater, film, and creative time for artists, are important tools for community building, infusing Serenbe with a strong sense of place and personal connectedness.[25]

Conclusions

The forms of new secular-sacred communities, like Serenbe, typically seek to preserve land for future generations and provide diverse kinds of spatial experiences, both urban and rural, that reflect evolving contemporary needs and opportunities for varying sacred experiences. The geometry of Serenbe provides an explicit structure, spatial order, a context for reverence in everyday living, community ceremonial events, and a strong sense of belonging. Socially, while community is expressed by resident gatherings, it also can be experienced in immaterial ways as a felt sense of belonging, or in the dissolving solitude found in omega centers. In this regard, community members share a similar, place-centered style of living, and are part of a larger

Figure 11.10 The Secret Garden as metaphor for placemaking at Serenbe
Source: Photograph by Phillip Tabb

collective of residents. The social environment also creates the place through which a living Serenbe thrives in a biotic community of inclusiveness, interdependence, and participatory interaction. According to founder Marie Nygren, the Serenbe Playhouse production of *The Secret Garden* in 2015 (Figure 11.10) was a metaphor for the spirit of Serenbe – a place contained in magic and healing powers:[26]

> It [Serenbe] was a place of serenity, a place of surrender, a place of peacefulness, a place of beauty, all of those apply so that's how I originally defined Serenbe.[27]

With its sensitivity to sacredness, Serenbe represents a next-generation, small-settlement planning approach in a lineage that began with suburbs and counter-urbanism, and later with sustainable and agricultural urbanism. With population migration from rural areas to larger metropolitan centers, economies, employment, social engagements, educational opportunities, and cultural enrichment falter and are increasingly depleted. The concept of serene urbanism applied to these areas is a beginning to reverse these trends, by presenting the catalytic ingredients of serene nature and vital urbanism.

This serene, urban relationship helps to actualize Serenbe's purpose: being with nature, being in community, being more human, and being with an ineffable higher presence. As Serenbe resident Roy Godwin explained:

> When we, in our interfaith group meet on Easter morning, and we gather after walking the labyrinth to its center, we stand waiting for the sun to rise and listen to birds like an orchestra playing. We listen to the donkeys braying, and listen to the blowing wind through the trees. Standing in anticipation for the first ray of sun that comes over the horizon, there is a *yes* – and there is an appreciation that is provided by Serenbe.[28]

Notes

1 Bateson, Gregory, *Mind and Nature: A Necessary Unity*, E.P. Dutton, New York, 1979, p. 27.
2 Branding slogan from the Serenbe website: http://serenbe.com/ (accessed August 2015).
3 Tabb, Phillip and Deviren, A. Senem, *The Greening of Architecture: A Critical History and Survey of Sustainable Architecture and Urban Design*, Ashgate Publishing, London, 2013.
4 Irwin, Terence, *Aristotle's First Principles*, Clarendon Paperbacks, Oxford,1990.
5 Serene environments can exist in both the natural and urban contexts. While serenity is more commonly associated with beautiful natural landscape, it too can be present in well-designed buildings and urban places.
6 Mondal, Puja, "20 Important Characteristics of Urban Community," *Sociology*, 2015. Available online at www.yourarticlelibrary.com/sociology/20-important-characteristics-of-urban-community-sociology/4873/ (accessed October 2015).
7 Browning, William, Ryan, Catherine and Clancy, Joseph, *14 Patterns of Biophilic Design: Improving Health and Well-being in the Built Environment*, Terrapin Bright Green, LLC, New York, 2014.
8 Casement, Ann and Tacey, David (eds), *The Idea of the Numinous: Contemporary Jungian and Psychoanalytic Perspectives*, Routledge, London, 2006.
9 Research for the Theory of Placemaking class held at Serenbe during the fall of 2015 focused on the five place factors of serenity, urbanism, sustainability, biophilia, and the numinous as filters through which to view Selborne Hamlet. Students conducted research on each topic, interviewed expert residents, and took extensive photographs depicting the qualities of these factors.
10 Brill, Michael, *Using the Place-creation Myth to Develop Design Guidelines for Sacred Space*, self-published, 1985. Patterns included: making location, succession of spaces, differentiated bounding, verticality, celestial order, discriminating views, light from above, and consecration.
11 Lyndon, Donlyn and Moore, Charles, *Chambers for a Memory Palace*, MIT Press, Cambridge, MA, 1994.
12 Alexander, Christopher, Ishikawa, Sara, Silverstein, Murray with Jacobson, Max, Fiksdahl-King, Ingrid, and Shlomo, Angel, *A Pattern Language*, Oxford University Press, New York, 1977.
13 Julie Christina Shafer, "Placemaking Patterns for Serenbe Community," 2012; "Serenbe Place Analysis," Texas A&M University, MArch-directed studies, 2012. Joseph, Melanie, "A Pattern Language for Sacred and Secular Places," MS Architecture dissertation, Texas A&M University, 2006; Rodrigues, Arsenio, "The Sacred in Architecture: A Study of the Presence and Quality of Place-making Patterns in Sacred and Secular Buildings," PhD dissertation, Texas A&M University, 2008.
14 Information was obtained through several analytic and empirical methods, which were synthesized into both quantitative and qualitative evaluation of the ectypal place patterns.
15 Originally developed by psychologist Rensis Likert in 1933. Likert, Rensis, "A Technique for the Measurement of Attitudes," *Archives of Psychology* 140, 1933, pp. 1–55.
16 Groat, Linda and Wang, David, *Architectural Research Methods*, Wiley and Sons, New York, 2002.
17 Denzin, Norman K. and Lincoln, Yvonna S., *Handbook of Qualitative Research* (2nd edn). Sage Publications, Thousand Oaks, CA, 2000.
18 Eliade, Mircea, *The Sacred and The Profane: The Nature of Religion*, Harcourt Brace Publishers, Orlando, FL, 1959, p. 23.
19 Merlyn Driver, "The Pattern that Connects: Gregory Bateson and the Ecology of Mind," *Journal of Wild Culture*, July 4, 2013. Available online at www.wildculture.com/article/pattern-connects-gregory-bateson-and-ecology-mind/1213 (accessed June 19, 2016).
20 Relph, Edward, *Place and Placelessness*, Pion Ltd, London, 1976.
21 Tuan, Yi-Fu, *Space and Place: The Perspective of Experience*, Minnesota University Press, Minneapolis, MN, 1977.
22 Casey, Edward S., *The Fate of Place: A Philosophical History*, University of California Press, Berkeley, CA, 1997.

23 Lane, Belden, *Landscapes of the Sacred, Geography and Narrative in American Spirituality*, Johns Hopkins Press, Baltimore, MD, 1988, p. 7.

24 Casey, *The Fate of Place*.

25 Email communication with Serenbe resident John Graham, concerning his impression of the sacred present in the design, July 15, 2010.

26 *The Secret Garden* was a children's novel first published in 1910 by Frances Hodgson Burnett, and choreographed into a play by the Serenbe Playhouse performed throughout summer of 2015. The Serenbe setting for the play was in a special place in the woods.

27 Personal interview with Marie Nygren by Texas A&M University undergraduate student Mirely Cordova on October 12, 2016 at the Blue Eyed Daisy in Serenbe, Georgia.

28 Interview with Serenbe resident Roy Godwin by Jocelyn Zuniga on October 17, 2015.

Index